WHISPERS

WHISPERS

◇

BELVA PLAIN

Delacorte
Press

Published by
Delacorte Press
Bantam Doubleday Dell Publishing Group, Inc.
1540 Broadway,
New York, New York 10036

ISBN 0-385-29928-1

Manufactured in the United States of America

Published simultaneously in Canada

PART ONE

◇

Spring 1985

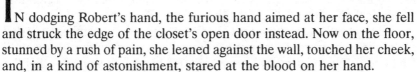

I N dodging Robert's hand, the furious hand aimed at her face, she fell and struck the edge of the closet's open door instead. Now on the floor, stunned by a rush of pain, she leaned against the wall, touched her cheek, and, in a kind of astonishment, stared at the blood on her hand.

Robert's eyes and his mouth had become three dark, round holes in his face.

"Oh, good God!" He knelt beside her. "Let me look. No, let me, Lynn! Thank goodness it's nothing. Just a break in the skin. An accident . . . I'll get a washcloth and ice cubes. Here, let me pull you up."

"Don't touch me, damn you!" Thrusting his hand away, she pulled herself up and sat down on the bed between the suitcases. Her face burned, while her cold fingers felt for the rising lump on her cheekbone. Another lump, thick with outrage and tears, rose in her throat.

Robert bustled between the bedroom and the bathroom. "Damn, where's the ice bucket? In a first-class hotel like this you'd think they'd put—oh, here it is. Now just lie back. I'll fix the pillows. Hold this to your face. Does it hurt much?"

His expressions of anxiety were sickening. She closed her eyes. If she could have closed her ears, she would have done so. His voice, so rich, so beautifully modulated, was trying to soothe her.

"You tripped. I know I raised my hand but you tripped. I'm sorry, but you were so angry, you were almost hysterical, Lynn, and I had to stop you somehow."

She opened her eyes. "I? *I* was so angry? *I* was almost hysterical? Think again and tell the truth if you can."

"Well, I did lose my temper a little. I'll admit that. But can you blame me? Can you? When I depended on you to do the packing and you know how important this convention is, you know this could be my chance for promotion to the New York headquarters, the main chance of a lifetime maybe, and here I am without a dinner jacket."

"I didn't do it on purpose. Now I'll tell you for the third time that Kitty Lombard told me the men won't be wearing tuxedos. I specifically asked about it."

"Kitty Lombard! She steered you wrong on purpose and you're too stupid to know it. How often have I told you that people like nothing better than to see somebody else look like a fool? Especially in the business world. They all want to sabotage you. When will you learn to stop trusting every Tom, Dick, and Harry you come across? Never, I suppose." Striding across the room, in his powerful indignation, Robert looked about ten feet tall. "And by the way, may I remind you again that it's not called a 'tuxedo'? It's a 'dinner jacket.' "

"All right, all right. I'm a hick, a small-town hick, remember? My dad ran a hardware store. I never saw a dinner jacket except in pictures until I met you. But I never saw a man raise his hand to a woman either."

"Oh, let's stop this, Lynn! There's no sense going over it all night. It's almost six, and the dinner's at seven. Your ice is melting. Let me have a look again."

"I'll take care of myself, thanks. Let me alone."

In the bathroom she closed the door. The full-length mirror reflected a small, freckled woman, still girlish at thirty-six, with bangs and a curving cap of smooth sandy hair worn as she had in high school. The face, pleasing yet unremarkable except for a pair of rather lovely light eyes, was disfigured now by the bruise, much larger than she had imagined and already more hideously, brightly blue and green than one would have thought possible. She was horrified.

Robert opened the door. "Jesus! How can you possibly go downstairs looking like that! Unless—" He frowned over his thoughts.

"Unless what, if you please?"

"Well—I don't know. I could say the airline lost the bag with my clothes, and that you have a stomach virus, one of those twenty-four-hour things. Make yourself comfortable, take a hot bath, keep the ice on your face, get in bed, and read. Call room service and have a good dinner. Relax. It'll do you good. A nice quiet dinner without kids."

Lynn stared at him. "Mr. Efficiency. You have it figured out, as always."

Everything was ruined, this happily anticipated weekend away, the new dress, spring-green silk with crystal buttons, the new bottle of perfume, the manicure, all the joy gone. Sordid ruination. And he could stand there, confident, handsome, and secure, ready to cope, to go forward again.

"I hate you," she said.

"Oh, Lynn, cut it out. I am not, I repeat, not going to go over this business ad infinitum. Just pull yourself together. I have to pull myself together for both our sakes, make an appearance and make the best of this opportunity. All the top brass will be here, and I can't afford to be rattled. I have to think clearly. Now I'm going to get dressed. Thank God my other suit is pressed."

"I know. I pressed it."

"Well, you got one thing straight, at least."

"I keep *your* whole life straight every day of *my* life."

"Will you lower your voice? People can hear you in the hall. Do you want to disgrace us both?"

Suddenly, as water is sucked down a drain, her strength rushed out. Her arms, her legs, even her voice refused to work and she dropped facedown onto the wide bed between the open suitcases. Her lips moved silently.

"Peace, peace," they said.

Robert moved about, jingling keys as he dressed. When he was ready to go he came to the bed.

"Well, Lynn? Are you going to stay there like that all rumpled up in your street clothes?"

Her lips moved, but silently, again. "Go away. Just go away," they said.

The door clicked shut. And at that moment the tension broke. All the outrage at injustice, the humiliation of helpless defeat, flowed out in torrential tears, tears that she could never have shed while anyone was watching.

"You were always a proud, spunky little thing," Dad used to say. Oh, such a proud, spunky little thing! she thought as she collapsed into long, heaving, retching sobs.

Much later, as abruptly as the torrent had started, it ceased. She was emptied, calmed, relieved. Cold and stiff from having lain so long uncovered, she got up and, for lack of any other purpose, went to the window. Forty floors below lights moved through the streets; lights dotted the silhouettes of Chicago's towers; light from the silver evening sky sprayed across Lake Michigan. Small, dark, fragmented clouds ran through the silver light and dissolved themselves within it. The whole scene was in motion, while the invisible wind rattled at the window glass.

Behind her the room was too still. Hotel rooms, when you were alone, were as desolate as a house emptied out after death. And Lynn, shuddering, ran to her carry-on bag, took out the photo of her children, and put it on the dresser, saying aloud, "There!" They had created an instant's presence.

And she stood looking, wanting most terribly these two girls whom she had left home in St. Louis only that morning and whom, like any other mother, she had been glad to leave behind for a while. Now, if she possibly could, she would repack her bag and fly back to them. Her beautiful Emily, the replica of Robert, would be at the sophomore dance tonight. Annie would just about now be going back to Aunt Helen's house from a third-grade birthday party. Smart Annie, funny, secretive, sensitive, difficult Annie. Yes, she would fly home to them right now if she could. But Robert had the tickets and the money. She never did have any cash beyond the weekly allowance for the household. And anyway, she thought, remembering, how could I just walk in with this face and without their father?

The silence began to buzz in Lynn's ears. A sensation of fear as of some desperate, unexplainable menace came flooding. The walls closed in.

"I have to get out of here," she said aloud.

Putting on her travel coat, she drew the collar up and wrapped a scarf around her head, drawing it like a peasant's babushka over her cheeks as far as it would go, which was not far enough. Luckily there were only two other people in the elevator during its long descent, a very young couple dressed for some gala event, and so tenderly engrossed with each other that they truly did not give a glance to Lynn's face. In the marble lobby people were either hurrying from cocktails to dinner or else lingering at the vitrines with their displays of glittering splendors, their jewels, leathers, satins, and furs.

Outdoors, cold spring air stung the burning bruise. At a drugstore she stopped to get something for it, a gauze bandage or some ointment, anything.

"I bumped into a door. Isn't that stupid?" she said. Then, shocked at the sight of her swollen eye in the mirror behind the man's head, she added clumsily, "And on top of that, I have this miserable allergy. My eyes—"

The man's own eyes, when he handed her a little package of allergy pills and a soothing ointment, reflected his disbelief and his pity. Overcome with shame at her own naïveté, she rushed away into the anonymity of the street.

Then, walking in the direction of the lake, she remembered vaguely from a previous visit to the city that there would be a green space there with walks and benches. It was really too cold to sit still, but nevertheless she sat down, tightened the coat around her, and gazed out to where the water met the sky. Couples strolled, walking their dogs and talking peaceably. It hurt so much to watch them that she could have wept, if she had not already been wept out.

The day had begun so well. The flight from home was a short one, so there had been time enough for a walk on Michigan Avenue before going back to the room to dress. Robert was a window-shopper. He loved dark, burnished wood in fine libraries, eighteenth-century English paintings of fields and farms, classic sculpture, and antique rugs, all quiet, dignified, expensive things. Often he stopped to admire a beautiful dress, too, like the one they had seen this afternoon, a peach silk ballgown scattered with seed-pearl buds.

"That would be perfect on you," he had observed.

"Shall I wear it to the movies on Saturday night?" she had teased back.

"When I am a chief executive officer, there will be occasions for a dress like that," he had replied, and added then, "It suits you. Airy and delicate and soft, like you."

It had begun so well. . . . Their life together had begun so well. . . .

"Why do they call you 'Midge'?" he had asked her. He had never noticed her before that day. But then, he was the head of the department, while she only sat at a typist's desk. "Why? On the list it says your name is Lynn Riemer."

"I was always called that. Even at home. It's short for 'midget.' I guess it was because my sister's tall."

"You're nowhere near being a midget." He looked her up and down quite seriously. "Five foot two, I'd estimate."

It was his eyes that held her, the brilliant blue, darkening or lightening according to mood, that held every woman in the office, for that matter, and possibly, in a different way, the men too. The men had to have serious respect for authority; authority could praise and promote; authority could also discharge a man to creep home in defeat to his family. But the women's fear of Robert Ferguson was diluted with a tremulous, daring, sexual fervor. This fervor had to be secret. Each would have been embarrassed to admit to another, for fear of seeming ridiculous: Robert Ferguson was totally beyond their reach, and they all knew it, worlds apart from the men with whom they had grown up and whom they dated.

It was not only that with those vivacious eyes and his long, patrician bones he was extraordinarily handsome. It was an aura about him. He was absolutely confident. His diction was perfect, his clothes were perfect, and he demanded perfection of everyone around him. Lateness was not tolerated. Papers put on his desk for his signature had to be flawless. His initials had to be accurate: V.W. Robert Victor William Ferguson. His car must be kept in a quickly accessible place in a parking lot. Yet, for all of this, he was considerate and kind. When he was pleased, he was generous with a compliment. He remembered birthdays, making happy occasions in the office. When anyone was sick, he became earnestly involved. It was known that he volunteered at the men's ward at the hospital.

"He's an enigma," Lynn had once remarked when Robert was being discussed, and he often was discussed.

"I'm going to call you 'Lynn' from now on," he said that day, "and tell everyone here to do the same."

She had no idea why he should have paid enough attention to her to remark upon her name. It was silly. Yet she was sufficiently flustered by the happening to tell her sister Helen that she would not answer to "Midge" anymore.

"Why? What's wrong with it?"

"I have a perfectly good name, and I'm not a midget. Even my boss says it's ridiculous."

Helen had given her a look of amusement that she remembered clearly long afterward. Ever since her marriage and the birth of two babies, Helen had assumed a superior air of motherly protectiveness.

"Your boss? It seems to me you talk about him a good deal."

"I do not."

"Oh, yes, you do. You may not realize it, but you do. 'My boss has a stereo in his office. My boss treated us all to pizza for lunch. My boss got a big raise from the main office—' "

It was true that he was more and more in Lynn's thoughts, that she watched without seeming to do so for his every arrival and departure.

She had begun to have passionate fantasies. So Helen was probably right. . . .

Then one day Robert asked her to go to dinner with him.

"You look as if you were floating on air," Helen said.

"Well, I am. I thought, I still am thinking, Why me?"

"Why not you? You have more life and more energy than any six people put together. Why do you think boys all—"

"You don't understand. This man is different. He's distinguished. His face looks like the ones you see on statues or on those old coins in Dad's collection."

"By the way, how old is he?"

"Twenty-seven."

"And you're twenty. Twenty, going on fourteen. Filled with dreams."

Lynn still kept the dress she had worn that night. Sentimental almost to a fault, she held on to everything, from her wedding dress and her children's christening gowns to the pressed flowers from the bouquet that Robert had sent after that first dinner, a splendid sheaf of white roses tied with pink ribbon.

"Tell me about yourself," he had begun when they sat down with the candlelight between them.

She had responded lightly, "There isn't much to tell."

"There always is, in every life. Start from the beginning. Were you born here in the city?"

"No, in Iowa. In a farming town south of Des Moines. My mother died, and my father still lives there. My sister moved here when she was married, and I guess that's why, after graduation from high school, I came here too. There were no jobs at home anyway. This is my first one, and I hope I'm doing well."

"I'm sure you are."

"I wanted to see the city, to see things, and it's been fun. Having the apartment, going to the concerts—"

He nodded. "A world-class orchestra. As fine as anything in New York."

"I've never been there."

"When I was at the Wharton School, I went often to the theater. It's only a short train ride from Philadelphia."

Her tongue was loosening. The wine might be helping. "I'd like to see the east. I'd like to see Europe, England, France, Rome."

His eyes were shining and smiling at her. "The places that you read about in *Portrait of a Lady* last week?"

She was astonished. "How did you know?"

"Simple. I saw the book on your desk. Don't they call me 'Hawkeye' in the office?"

She laughed and blushed. "How on earth can you know that? Nobody ever says—"

"I've also got sharp ears."

She struck out boldly. "Is that why you invited me tonight? Is that what gave you the idea, that I read Henry James?"

"That had a little to do with it. I was curious. You must admit that the rest of them on the staff don't go much beyond movie magazines, do they?"

"They're my friends. I don't pay attention to things like that," she said loyally. "They're not important."

"Don't think I'm a snob. I don't judge people by their knowledge of what's in books either. But you have to admit that it's pleasant to be with people who like the same things you like. Besides, you're beautiful. That must have had something to do with it, don't you think?"

"Thank you."

"You don't believe you are beautiful, do you? Your eyes say that you're doubtful. I'll tell you. You're a porcelain doll. Your skin is white as milk."

She parried, "Is it good to look like a porcelain doll?"

"I think so. I meant it as a compliment."

This dialogue was certainly different from any she had ever had before, with Bill or anyone else. And she was not sure what she ought to say next.

"Well, go on with your story about yourself. You've only just begun."

"There isn't much more. Dad couldn't afford college, so I went to a very good secretarial school that had courses in English lit. I'd always loved to read, and it's there that I learned what to read. So I read and I cook. That's my second hobby. Maybe it's boasting, but the fact is, I'm a very good cook. And that's all, I guess. Now it's your turn."

"Okay. Born and grew up in Pittsburgh. No brothers or sisters, which made for a bit of lonesomeness. I had a good home, though. My parents were especially loving. They spoiled me a little, I think. In their way they were unusual people. My mother played the piano and taught me to play. I'm not all that good, but I play because it makes me think of her. My father was a learned man and very quiet and kindly, with an old-fashioned sort of dignity. His business took him around the world. Every summer they went to Salzburg for the music festival." He paused. "They were killed in an auto accident the summer I was graduated from college."

She felt a stab of horror. "How awful for you! It's bad enough when someone has a heart attack, as my mother did. But a car accident's so—so unnecessary, so wrong!"

"Yes. Well, life goes on." His face sank into sadness, the mouth and eyes gone still.

At the back of the room, just then the pianist was singing, "A tale told by a stranger, by a new love, on a dark blue evening in a rose-white May."

The poignant words of the forties, so long ago, coming at this moment of Robert's revelations, filled her chest with a longing almost painful, a confusion of sadness and thrilling joy. Tears came to her eyes.

When he saw them, he touched her hand. "Gentle girl . . . But enough of this. Come, we'll be late for the movie."

She went home and lay awake half the night. I want to live with him for the rest of my life, she thought. He is the one. But I'm an idiot. We had an evening together, that's all. He won't seriously want me. How can he? I'm not nearly good enough for him. He won't want me.

He had wanted her, though, wanted her badly. In the office they hid their intense emotion; passing each other, their eyes turned away. Joyously, she kept their secret. She alone came to know the other side of this man whom others found imperious, the part of him that was so very tender. She alone knew about the high tragedy of his parents' deaths, and about his lesser sorrows too.

He confided. "I've been married."

She felt a rush of disappointment, a pang of jealousy.

"We met at college and were married in commencement week. Looking back, I wonder how it ever happened. She was very beautiful and very rich, but spoiled and irresponsible, too, so we were completely unsuited to each other. Querida—her mother was Spanish—was 'artistic.' She did watercolors. I don't mean to disparage her, but she was just a dabbler. She took a job in a small gallery and on her day off was a volunteer docent at the museum. Anything to get out of the house. She hated the house. The place was a mess, no meals, the laundry not even sent out half the time, nothing done. I could never bring anybody home from the office, never solidify the contacts one needs to make it in the business world." He shrugged. "What can I say except that hers was an entirely different way of life from what I was used to? We grated on each other's nerves, and so of course we argued almost daily. She disliked my friends, and I wasn't fond of hers, I can tell you that." He smiled ruefully. "We would have parted even sooner if it hadn't been for the child. Jeremy. He's six now."

"What happened to him?"

"I haven't seen him since he was a year old. But I support him, although he wouldn't be in want if I didn't. Querida went back to live with her parents, so he's growing up in a mansion. She didn't want joint custody, said it was too confusing for a child, and I didn't want to fight her decision."

"Still, how awful for you not to see him! Or for him not to know you."

Robert sighed. "Yes. Yes, it is. But he can't remember me, so for him at his age I suppose it's as if I had died. I hope so much, though, that he'll want to see me when he's old enough to understand." And he sighed again.

"I'm sure he will," Lynn said, in her pity.

"Well, he'll know how to find me. His money goes into the bank every month. So that's the end of my little story."

"It's a sad story."

"Yes, but it could be worse, Lynn. It seems like something that happened a lifetime ago," he said earnestly. "I've never talked about it to anyone before this. It's too private. And I'm a very private person, as you know by now."

Inevitably, the affair of Robert and Lynn had to come to notice. In the second month she took him to Helen's house. Helen's husband, Darwin, was a good-natured man, round featured with an extra chin. Beside him Robert sparkled with his white collar glistening above his dark blue blazer. Darwin looked rumpled, as if he had been napping in his clothes. In a nice way—or perhaps not such a nice way?—Lynn was proud to let Helen see the contrast between the two, proud and a little ashamed of being proud.

The next day Helen said, "Of course you want to know what I thought of your new man. I'm going to tell you right out flat: I didn't like him much."

Lynn screamed into the telephone. "What?"

"I'm always honest with you, Lynn. I know I can be too blunt—but he's not your type. He can be sarcastic, I notice, and I have a hunch he's a snob. He thinks he's better than other people."

Lynn was furious. "Have you anything else nice to say about a man you don't even know? Any more hunches?"

"He has a critical, sharp tongue."

"I've never noticed it."

"I thought it was in poor taste, even cruel of him, to talk about that girl in the office and her long nails. 'Filthy long nails. Can you imagine the bacteria snuggled under them?' It was belittling to name her, and Darwin thought so too."

"Oh, dear! I am so sorry you and Darwin don't approve. Really sorry."

"Don't be angry at me, Lynn. Who wishes you more joy in life than I do? Dad and I. I just don't want you to make a mistake. I see that you're infatuated. It's written all over you."

"I'm not infatuated."

"I feel in my bones that he's not right for you."

"Does it possibly occur to your bones that I might not be right for him? Robert's brilliant. He's head of computer marketing for the whole region. I hear the salesmen talking—" Indignation made Lynn almost breathless. "An international company—"

"Is it that that impresses you? Listen, Lynn. You never know about big corporations. You're on top today and out tomorrow. It's better to be your own boss, even in a small way, instead of at other people's mercy."

Helen's husband had a little plumbing business with five employees.

"Are you accusing me of being ambitious? Me? You think that's what I see in Robert?"

"No, no, I didn't mean that at all. You're one of the least materialistic people. I didn't express myself well. I meant that perhaps you felt—a kind of admiration, hero worship, just because he is so successful and—I only meant, don't get too serious so fast."

"Do you know what I think? I think you're an idiot," Lynn said before she hung up.

But it was not in her nature to hold a grudge very long. Helen was transparent. She was undoubtedly not even aware of it, and would deny it, but her motive was envy, even though she lived happily with Darwin. Pure and simple envy. And Lynn forgave her.

Almost three months passed before they went to bed together; Lynn had to wait for her roommates to go out of town.

On the weekend this finally happened, the two women had scarcely reached the airport before she had a lavish dinner prepared, and he arrived with flowers, record albums, and champagne. In the first moment they stood staring at each other as if this sudden marvelous freedom had transfixed them; in the next moment everything happened, everything moved. The flowers in their green tissue paper were flung onto the table,

Robert's overcoat was flung over a kitchen chair, and Lynn was lifted into his arms.

Quickly, deftly, in the dim light of the wintry day, he removed her clothes, the sweater and the white blouse with the lace collar, the plaid skirt and the underthings. Her heart was speeding. She could hear its beat.

"I never—this is the first time, Robert."

"I'll be very gentle," he murmured.

And he was. Persistent, warm, and gentle, he spoke soft, endearing words while he held her.

"So sweet . . . So beautiful . . . I love you so."

Whatever little fear there had been now dissolved, and she gave herself into total passionate trust.

Much later when they released each other, Lynn began to laugh. "I was just thinking, it's a good thing I hadn't yet turned the oven on when you arrived. We'd be having cinders for dinner."

Over her expert ratatouille and *tarte normande* they talked about themselves.

"Twenty-year-old virgins are becoming very rare these days," said Robert.

"I'm glad I waited." She was still too shy to say: It makes me belong all the more to you. Because, would this last? She trusted, and yet there were no guarantees. Nothing had been said. But I shall die if he leaves me, she thought.

They went back to bed. This time there was no need to be as gentle. She worshiped his strength. For a man so slender he was exceedingly strong. And, surprisingly, she found herself responding with a strength and a desire equal to his. They slept, until long before dawn she felt him return to her and, with willing arms, received him. Sleeping again past dawn, they awoke to see that a heavy snowfall was darkening the world.

"Let's stay indoors the whole day," he whispered. "Indoors, in bed."

All through Saturday and Sunday they knew no surfeit.

"I'm obsessed with you," Robert said. "You are the most erotic woman —I've never known anything like you. And you look so innocent in your sweaters and skirts. A man would never guess."

On Sunday evening Lynn looked at the clock. "Robert, their plane gets in at ten. I'm afraid you have to leave in a hurry."

He groaned. "When can we do this again?"

"I don't know," she said mournfully.

"This is no way to live!" he almost shouted. "I hate a hole-and-corner business, skulking in highway motels. And I don't want 'living together' either. We need to be permanent. Lynn, you're going to marry me."

They set the wedding for June, taking advantage of Robert's vacation to have a honeymoon in Mexico.

"Of course, you'll have to quit your job," he told her. "We can't be in the same office."

"I'll find another one easily."

"Not yet. You'll need time to furnish an apartment. It should be done carefully. Buy things of quality that will last."

Helen generously offered their house for the reception. "You can't very well have it at Dad's, since he's only got three rooms now," she said. "With luck, if the weather's right, we can have the whole thing in our yard. Darwin has plans for a perennial border, and you know his green thumb. It should be beautiful."

To give her fullest credit Helen did not speak one disparaging word from the moment the engagement was announced. She kissed Lynn, admired the ring, which was a handsome one, and wished the couple every happiness.

"Every happiness," she said now as a chill blew in over Lake Michigan, loudly enough, apparently, for the couple with the poodles, who had circled back, to turn and stare. An eccentric woman, huddled there talking to herself, that's what she was. An object to be stared at. Ah, well, there was no stopping memory once it got started back and back. . . .

Robert endeared himself to everyone during that expectant enchanted spring before the wedding. Helen's little boys adored him; he bought small bats, taught them to pitch, took them to ball games, and showed them how to wrestle. While the ice held, they all went skating, and when the days warmed, had picnics in the country.

In Helen's kitchen Lynn cooked superb little dinners, quiches, cassoulets, and soufflés out of Julia Child's new book.

"You put me to shame," Helen said.

After dinner Robert would sit at the old upright piano and play whatever was called out to him: jazz, show tunes, or a Chopin waltz.

At his suggestion the two couples went to hear the St. Louis symphony. Darwin had never gone before and was surprised to find that he liked it.

"Once you acquire the taste, you'll never be without music," Robert told him. "For me it's another kind of food. We've got to get season tickets next year, Lynn."

Naively, kindly, Darwin praised Robert. "It beats me, Lynn, how he *knows* so much. I can just about make it through the daily paper. And he sure knows how to get fun out of life, too, and knows how to fit in with people."

Her father approved. "I like him," he said after Lynn and Robert's weekend visit. "It'll be good to have a new son. And good for him to have a family. Hard on a young fellow to lose his parents like that. What kind of people were they? Do you know anything about them?"

"What is there to find out? They're dead," Lynn answered, feeling impatient.

"That's all he has, the old aunt back in Pittsburgh?"

"And an uncle in Vancouver."

"Practically alone in the world," Dad said with sympathy.

In the hardware store, being introduced as customers came in, most of them from the farms, Robert knew how to meet their jovial simplicity in kind. She saw that they approved of him, as did her father.

"I like him, Midge," Dad kept saying. "You've got yourself a man, not like the kids who used to hang around you. No offense meant. They were all good boys, but wet behind the ears. This one's a man. What I like is, he hasn't let the education or the job go to his head. I'll be glad to dance at your wedding."

A woman remembers every detail of her wedding day. She remembered the long ride, the organ singing, and the faces turned to watch her marching toward the altar.

Her hand had trembled on her father's arm. *Easy now,* he said, feeling the trembling hand. *There's Robert waiting for you. There's nothing to fear.* And then it was Robert who took her hand, while they stood together listening to the gentle, serious admonitions: *Be patient and loving with each other.*

The rest of that day was jollity, music, dancing, kissing, teasing, and ribald, friendly jokes. The office crowd came, of course, and friends from the hometown came. Darwin's and Helen's friends were all there and Robert had invited the friends he had made in St. Louis; he had been away from Pittsburgh too long to expect people he scarcely knew anymore to come to his wedding.

One relative came, Aunt Jean from Pittsburgh, the uncle in Vancouver not being well enough to travel. It was curious, Lynn reflected now, that such a pleasant, rather self-effacing little woman, with graying curls and a conventional print dress, should have been the cause of one out of the two false notes in the wedding.

It was not her fault. It was Robert's. They were at the family table after the ceremony when Aunt Jean remarked, "Someday I'll have to get at my pile of photographs, label them, and bring them when I come to visit you. There are some of Robert that you just must have, Lynn. You'd never believe it, but his hair—"

"For once, Aunt Jean," Robert interrupted, "will you spare us a description of the blond curls I had when I was a year old? Really, nobody cares."

Chastised, she said nothing more, so that Lynn, with a gentle look of reproach in Robert's direction, said gaily, "I care, Aunt Jean. I want to hear anything you can tell me about Robert and all the family, father, mother, grandparents, cousins—"

"It's a small family," Jean said. "We don't have any cousins at all, on either side."

Then Dad, who had heard only this last remark, cried out, "No cousins? Heck, we'll be glad to lend you some. I've got a dozen on my side alone, in Iowa, Missouri, even two in California." And in his friendly way he inquired whether Jean was related to Robert's mother or his father.

"His mother was my sister."

"He got his music from her, didn't he?" Lynn said. "And his father must have been remarkable, from what Robert tells me."

"Indeed."

"It was such a tragedy, the way they died."

"Yes. Yes, it was."

Dad remarked, "It must have been lonesome when Robert was a kid. Christmas with just his parents and you."

"Well, we did our best," said Jean, "and he grew up, and here he is." She gave Robert a fond smile.

"Yes, here we all are, and let's look forward. Reminiscences are for the old," Robert responded, after which he patted his aunt's hand.

He was making amends for having been sharp toward her. But the mild old woman annoyed him. And there seemed to be no reason why she should.

On a day like this, at a moment of lonely desperation, Lynn thought now, you remember these false notes.

There had been dancing on the deck that Darwin had built with his own hands. In the yard his perennial border was rich with pinks and reds;

peonies and phlox, tiger lilies and oriental poppies, fired the blue dusk. Robert was at the railing, looking down at them.

"Isn't it just lovely what Darwin's done with this house?" Lynn asked.

He smiled—she remembered the smile—and said, "It's all right, I guess, but it's really a dump. I'll give you so much better. You'll see."

He meant it well, but just as it had hurt to hear him reprimand his aunt, it hurt to hear him scoff at Darwin's garden, at Helen's little house. Small things to have remembered for so long. . . .

Each night as they traveled through Mexico, when the door closed on their room, Robert said again, "Isn't it wonderful? Not having to scrounge around for a place to go? Here we are, forever and ever."

Yes, it was wonderful, all of it. The sunny days when, in sneakers and broad straw hats, they climbed Mayan ruins in the Yucatán, when they drank tequilas on the beach, or drove through stony mountain villages, or dined most elegantly in Mexico City.

And there were fourteen nights of passion and love. "Happy?" Robert would inquire in the morning.

"Oh, darling! How can you even ask?"

"You know," he told her one day, "your father's a fine old soul. Guess what he said to me when we were leaving for the airport? 'Be good to my girl,' he said."

She laughed. "That's a sweet, old-fashioned thing to say."

"It's all right. I knew what he meant. And I will be good to you."

"We'll be good to each other. We're on top of the world, you and I."

On the very last day they went shopping in Acapulco. Robert saw something in the window of a men's shop, while at the same time Lynn saw something in the window of another shop just down the street.

"You do your errand while I do mine, and I'll meet you down there," he said.

So they separated. Since she was quickly finished, she walked back up the street to meet him. When some minutes had passed and he had not appeared, she went into the men's shop and learned that he had left a while ago. Puzzled, she walked back. By now a rush of tourists just discharged from a cruise ship filled the sidewalks and spilled out into the traffic on the street. It was impossible to see through the jostling mass. She began to feel the start of alarm. But that was absurd, and fighting it down, she reasoned: He has to be here. Perhaps on the other side of the street. Or down that alley, out of the crowd. Right now he's looking for me. Or maybe, not finding what he wanted, he had gone to the next block.

Alarm returned. When an hour had passed, she decided that her search was making no sense. What made sense, she reasoned, was to go back to the hotel where he had probably also gone and where he would be waiting for her.

When her taxi drew up to the entrance, he was indeed waiting. And she laughed with relief.

"Isn't this the silliest thing? I looked all over for you."

"Silly?" he replied very coldly. "I would hardly call it that. Come upstairs. I want to talk to you."

His unexpected anger dismayed her. And wanting to soothe, she replied lightly, "We must have been walking in circles, looking for each other. A couple of idiots, we are."

"Speak for yourself." He slammed the door of their room. "I was about to go to the front desk and have them call the police when you arrived."

"Police! Whatever for? I'm glad you didn't."

"I told you to wait for me in front of that store, and you didn't do it."

Now, resenting his tone, she countered, "I walked up to meet you. What's wrong with that?"

"I should think the result would tell you what's wrong with it. Disorderly habits, and this is the result. Saying one thing and doing something else."

She said angrily, "Don't lecture me, Robert. Don't make such a big deal out of this."

He was staring at her. And at that moment she realized he was furious. Not angry, but furious.

"I don't believe it!" she cried when he seized her. His hands dug into the flesh of her upper arms and ground it against the bones. In his fury he shook her.

"Let go!" she screamed. "You're hurting me! Let go of my arms!"

His hands pressed deeper; the pain was shocking. Then he flung her onto the bed, where she lay sobbing.

"You hurt me. . . . You hurt me."

As quickly as it had come, his anger went. He picked her up and held her.

"I'm sorry. Oh, I'm sorry. I didn't mean to. But I was terrified, Lynn. You could have been kidnapped—yes, in broad daylight—dragged down an alley, whisked into a car, raped, God knows what. This country is full

of thugs." He kissed her tears. "I was beside myself. Don't you understand?"

He kept kissing her cheeks, her forehead, her hands, and when at last
she turned to him, her lips.

"If anything were to happen to you, I wouldn't want to live. I was so
frightened. I love you so."

She put her arms around his neck. "All right. All right, darling. Robert, forget it, it's over. We misunderstood each other. It's nothing. Nothing."

And all was as it had been, as glorious as ever except for the ugly dark
blue blotches on her arms.

Two days later they were home, visiting her father. It was hot, and forget-
ting her raw bruises, she put on a sundress.

"What the dickens are those marks?" Dad asked at once. They were
alone in the house.

"Oh, those? I don't know. I don't remember how I got them."

Dad removed his glasses and came closer. "Identical, symmetrical
bruises on both arms. Somebody did that to you with strong, angry hands.
Who was it, Lynn?"

She did not answer.

"Was it Robert? Tell me, Lynn, or I'll ask him myself."

"No. No. Oh, please! It's nothing. He didn't mean it, it's just that he
was so scared." The story spilled out. "It was my fault, really it was. He
was terrified that something had happened to me. He had told me to wait
on the street, and I wandered around the corner and lost my way. My
sense of direction—"

"Has nothing to do with these marks. Don't you think I was ever upset
with your mother from time to time? You can't be married without getting mad at each other. But I never laid a hand on her. It isn't civilized.
No, damn it, it's not. I want to have a little talk with Robert—nothing
nasty, just a sensible little talk."

"No, Dad. You can't. Don't do this to me. Robert is my husband, and I
love him. We love each other. Don't make a big thing out of this."

"It is a big thing to me."

"It's not, and you can't come between us. You mustn't."

Her father sighed. "It was easier when people married somebody from
the same town. You could have a pretty fair idea of what you were
getting."

"Dad, we can't go back to George Washington."

He sighed again. "I feel," he said, "I don't feel—the same about things."

"Meaning that you don't feel the same about Robert."

Now it was he who did not answer. And that exasperated her. The thing was being carried much too far. She saw a crisis looming, one that might change, might color, all their future. So she made herself speak patiently and quietly.

"Dad, this is foolish. Don't worry about me. You're making a big deal out of something that happened once. All right, it shouldn't have, but it did. I want you to put it completely out of your mind, because I have. Okay?" She put her hand on his shoulder. "Okay? Promise?"

He turned, giving her his familiar, reassuring smile. "Well, well, since you want me to, I'll promise. We'll just leave it at that. Since you want me to, Midge."

It was never mentioned again. But neither Helen nor Dad ever had reason to raise any questions about the marriage of Robert and Lynn. They were to any beholder a successful, beautiful pair.

Emily was born eleven months after the wedding. They had scarcely equipped an apartment before Robert bought a house, a ranch house not far from Helen's but twice the size.

"We'll have more children, so we might as well do it now as later," he said.

They went together to furnish the house. Whatever he liked, he bought, and Lynn had only to admire a chair or a lamp, and before she had even glanced at the price, he bought it. In the beginning she worried that money was flowing out too fast. But she saw Robert was earning bonuses as business expanded. And besides, he kept telling her not to worry. Finances were his concern. She never had cash. She charged things and he paid the bills without complaint.

"I wouldn't like that," Helen said once.

"Why should I mind?" Lynn responded, glancing around the pretty nursery where the pretty baby was waking up from a nap. "I have everything. This most of all." And she picked up her daughter, the daughter who already had Robert's bones and black silk hair and dark blue eyes.

Because Robert had been so aware of names, she had chosen the child's name with subtle care. "Names have colors," she told him. " 'Emily' is blue. When I say it with my eyes closed, I see a very high October sky without a cloud."

Caroline was eighteen months later. "Caroline" was a gold so light that it was almost silver.

And memory, a reel of pictures in reverse, sped on. . . .

"What a fabulous house!" Lynn exclaimed.

The house belonged to her neighbor's parents, who were giving the birthday party for their granddaughter, aged five. The terrace was bordered by a lawn, the lawn extended to a distant meadow, and the meadow attached to a pond, which was barely visible at the foot of the slope.

"What a wonderful day for a party!" she exclaimed again.

And it was a wonderful summer day, a cool one, with everything in bloom and a breeze rustling through the oaks. Under these oaks the tables were set for lunch, the children's table dressed in crepe paper with a balloon tied to every chair. It looked, she thought, like a scene in one of those British films where women, wearing silk or white linen, moved against a background of ivy-covered walls. She, whose daily garb was either shorts or jeans, wore yellow silk, and her girls wore pink sister dresses and white Mary Janes.

"They look almost like twins," one of the women remarked. "Caroline's tall for her age, isn't she?"

"We sometimes think she's three going on ten. She's strong and fast and into everything," Lynn said comfortably.

There was probably nothing more satisfying to a parent than knowing that her children were admired. No book, no symphony, no work of art, she was certain, could rival the joy, the pride, and, she reminded herself, the gratitude that came from these creations, these two bright, sweet, healthy little girls.

Gratitude grew when she thought of two friends who were unable to have a child. And all through the lunch and the pleasant gossip she was aware, deep inside, of thankfulness. Life was good.

After lunch a clown arrived to entertain the children, who sat in a circle on the grass. For a little while the mothers watched him, but since the children were absorbed and fascinated, they went back to their tables in the shade.

"Talk about attention span," someone said. "He's kept them amused for more than half an hour."

It was just about time for the party to break up. Emily came trotting to Lynn with a bag full of favors and a balloon.

"Where's Caroline?" asked Lynn.

"I don't know," said Emily.

"But you were sitting together."

"I know," said Emily.

"Well, where can she be?" asked Lynn, feeling a faint rise of alarm and in the same instant driving it down, because of course there could be no reason for alarm here in this place.

"She must have gone to the bathroom."

So they looked in the downstairs bathroom and all through the house; they searched the bushes where possibly she might be hiding, to tease them. Alarm turned to panic. Kidnappers? But how could anybody have come among all these people without being seen? They searched the fields, treading through the long grass. Then they thought, although no one wanted to voice the thought, that perhaps, being an adventurous little girl, Caroline had gone as far as the pond.

And there she lay facedown, in her ruffled pink dress. Quite near the shore she lay in water so shallow that she could have stood up and waded back.

One of the women there was a Red Cross lifesaver. Laying Caroline on the grass, she went to work while Lynn knelt, staring at her child, not believing . . . no, no it was not possible!

People drew the children away from the sight. Someone had called for an ambulance; someone else had called the doctor in the next house. There was a bustle and hurry and yet it was silent; you could almost hear the hush and a following long, collective sigh.

Men came, two young ones wearing white coats. Lynn staggered to her feet, grasped a white sleeve, and begged, "Tell me! Tell me!"

For answer he put a gentle arm around her shoulders. And so she knew. Hearing the women cry, she knew. And yet, "It isn't possible," she said. "No. I don't believe it. No."

She looked around at all the faces, all of them shocked and pitying. And she screamed, screamed at the fair sky, the waving grass, the summer world. Screamed and screamed. Then people took her home.

She was wild with despair and denial. She *knew*, and yet she would not let herself know. They had to hold her down and sedate her.

When she woke up, she was in her living room. The house was crowded. It seemed as if a thousand voices were speaking; doors were opening and closing; the telephone kept ringing and being answered, only to ring again.

Helen said, "Leave her alone, Robert. She's not even awake."

Robert said, "How can she have been so stupid, so careless? She will never forgive herself for this."

She could not decide whether or not to wake up. In one way the dream was unbearable, so perhaps it would be better to open her eyes and be rid of it; but on the other hand perhaps it was not a dream, in which case it would be better to sink into a sleep so deep that she would know nothing.

Still she heard Robert's sobs, repeating, "She will never forgive herself."

There came another voice, belonging to someone who was holding her wrist: "Quiet, please. I'm taking her pulse," it said sharply, and she recognized Bill White, their family doctor.

"You'd better stop this talk about forgiveness," said Bill White. "First of all it's hogwash. This could have happened just as easily if you had been there, Robert. Secondly, you'd better stop it if you don't want to have a very sick woman here for the rest of her life. Don't you think she will torture herself enough as it is?"

And so she had, and so she did still, here on this bench beside Lake Michigan. The images were imprinted on her brain. Caroline laughing at the clown, Caroline—how many minutes later—dead in the water. Emily's little face puckered in tears and terror. She herself surrounded by kind arms and soft words at the heartbreaking funeral.

"I don't know why my aunt had to come," Robert complained. "Who sent for her, anyway?"

"Helen got her number out of my book. She's your family, she's all you have, and she belongs here."

It was strange that he never wanted Jean. She annoyed him, he said. Well, perhaps. Perhaps her very kindness irritated him. Men were like that sometimes. But Jean had been so helpful during those first awful days, comforting Emily in her warm arms and clearing Caroline's room, which neither Lynn nor Robert could have borne to enter.

Somehow they had endured.

"If a marriage can survive this," people declared, "it can survive anything. Imagine the guilt!"

Yes, imagine it if you can, Lynn thought. But Robert had taken Bill White's words to heart. Through many cruel nights he had held her close. And for a long time they had moved softly about the house, speaking in whispers; she had walked on tiptoes until he had gently called her attention to what she was doing. It was he who had saved her sanity. She must remind herself of that whenever things went wrong. . . .

Yet how could a man as forgiving as he had been, so caring of his family, give way to such dreadful rages? Like this one tonight, like all the other sporadic outbursts through the years? To live with Robert was to dwell in sunlight for months and months; then suddenly a flashing storm would turn everything into darkness. And as quickly as it had come the storm would pass, leaving a memory growing fainter in the distance, along with the hope that this time had been the last.

The children never knew, nor must they ever know. For how could she explain to them the thing that she did not herself understand?

Annie especially, Annie so young and vulnerable, must never know! She had been different and difficult from the start. A red baby, dark, raging, squalling red, she was to some extent like that still, a child of moods who could be childishly sweet or curiously adult; one felt at such times that she was seeing right through one's slightest evasion or excuse. Yet she did rather poorly at school. She was overweight and clumsy at sports, although Robert, who did everything so well, tried hard to teach her. She was a secret disappointment to him, Lynn knew. A child of his, although not yet nine, to show not the smallest indication of doing anything well at all!

The full wealth of his love went to Emily, so like himself, tenacious, confident, competent in everything from mathematics to tennis. Beside all that, at fifteen she was already charming the boys. Life would be easy for Emily.

My children . . . Oh, God, if it weren't for them, Lynn cried to herself, I wouldn't go home at all. I'd get on a plane and fly and fly—anywhere, to Australia and beyond. But that was stupid. Stupid to dwell on the impossible. And if she had packed the suit none of this would have happened. It was her own fault. . . .

It was growing colder. A sharper wind blew in suddenly from the lake. Rushing through the trees, it brought the piercing scent of northern spring. Thrusting her hands more deeply into her pockets, Lynn drew the coat tighter against the chill. Her cheek throbbed.

She was a fool to sit here shivering, waiting to be mugged. But she was too sunken in spirit to move or to care. If only there were another woman to hear her woe tonight! Helen, or Josie, wise, kind Josie, the best friend either Helen or she had ever had. They called themselves the three musketeers.

"We've transferred a new man to be my assistant for marketing," Robert had announced one day more than seven years ago. "Bruce Lehman from Milwaukee. Jewish and very pleasant, but I'm not wildly enthusiastic. He strikes me as kind of a lightweight. No force. It's hard to describe, but I recognize it when I see it in a man. You'd like him, though. He's well read and collects antiques. His wife's a social worker. No children. You'll have to call and ask them over to the house. It's only right."

That was the start of their friendship. If I could only talk to her now, thought Lynn. Yet when the moment came, I probably wouldn't tell the truth. Josie would analyze, and I would shrivel under her clinical analysis.

As for confiding this to Helen, that's impossible. She warned me against Robert once long, long ago, and I will not go whimpering to her or anyone. I will handle this myself, although God knows how.

She stiffened. Her heart pounded. Out of the violet shadows beyond the lamplight a slatternly woman, drunken or drugged, came shuffling toward her and stopped.

"Sitting alone in the dark? And you've got a black eye," she said, peering closer. When she touched Lynn's arm, Lynn, shrinking, looked into an old, sad, brutal face.

"I suppose you ran into a door. A door with fists." The woman laughed and sat down on the bench. "You'll have to think of a better one than that, my dear."

Lynn got up and ran to the avenue, where traffic still streamed. The woman had given her such a fright that, in spite of the cold, she was sweating. There was no choice but to go back to the hotel. When the elevator stopped at her floor, she felt an impulse to turn about and go down again. Yet she could not very well sleep on the street. And maybe Robert was so angry that he would not even be in the room. She put the key in the lock and opened the door.

Fully dressed, he was sitting on the bed with his face in his hands. When he saw her he jumped up, and she saw that he was frantic.

"I looked for you everywhere. It's midnight," he cried. "Long past midnight. In God's name, where were you? I looked for you all through the hotel, up and down the streets, everywhere. I thought—I don't know what I thought." His face was haggard, and his hoarse voice shook.

"What's the difference where I was?"

"I didn't know what you might have done. I was terrified."

"There's no need to be. I'm all right." In one piece, anyway, she thought.

When she took the scarf off and moved into the full glare of lamplight, Robert looked away. He got up and stood at the window, staring out into the darkness. She watched his stooped shoulders and felt shame for him, for herself, and for the entity known as Mr. and Mrs. Robert Ferguson, respectable and respected parents and citizens.

Presently, still with his back turned to her, he spoke. "I have a quick temper. Sometimes I overreact. But I've never really hurt you, have I? Other than a slap now and then? And how often have I done that?"

Often enough. Yet not all that often. But the sting of humiliation far outlasted the momentary physical sting. The bruise of humiliation far outlasted the bruise on the upper arms where fingers had gripped and shaken. And a deep sigh came out of her very heart.

"When did it happen last?" he asked, as if he were pleading. "I don't think you can even remember, it was so long ago."

"Yes, yes I can. It was last Thanksgiving week, when Emily didn't get home till two A.M. and you were in a rage. And I thought, after we talked it over and you were so sorry, that it was to be really the last time, that we were finished with all that."

"I meant it to be. I did," he replied, still in the pleading tone. "But we don't live in a perfect world. Things happen that shouldn't happen."

"But why, Robert? Why?"

"I don't know. I hate myself afterward, every time."

"Won't you go and talk to someone? Get some help. Find out why."

"I don't need it. I'll pull myself up by my own bootstraps." When she was silent before this familiar reply, he continued, "Tell the truth, Lynn. You know I'm a loving, good husband to you all the rest of the time, and a good father too. You know I am." He turned to her then, pleading, "Don't you?"

She was silent.

"I did wrong tonight, even though some of it was an accident. But I told you how awfully important it was. I could only think of what it could mean to us. New York with a fifty-percent raise, maybe. And after that, who knows?" His hands were clenched around the wooden rail of the chair's back as though he would break it. The pleading continued. "It's hard, Lynn, a struggle every day. I don't always tell you, I don't want to burden you, but it's a dog-eat-dog world. That's why that woman steered you wrong about the suit. People do things like that. You can't imagine it because you're so honest, so decent, but believe me, it's true. You have to be alert every minute of your life. There's never a minute that I'm not thinking of us, you and me and the girls. We're one, a tight little unit in an indifferent world. In the last analysis we're the only ones who really care about each other."

At his urging she was slipping inch by inch back into reality, and she knew it. Children, family, house. And the man standing here to whom all these ties connected her. Impulsive thoughts of airplanes flying to the ends of the earth, of floating free and new, were not reality. . . . Home, children, friends, job, school, home, children—

A sudden thought interrupted this litany. "What did you tell Bruce?"

"What I told everybody, that the bag with my dinner jacket was lost."

She heard him making an easy joke of it. *My suit may be on a plane to the Fiji Islands, or more likely, it's still in St. Louis.* He was laughing, making everyone else laugh with him.

"That's not what I meant. What did you say about me?"

"Just said you weren't feeling well. I was vague about it."

"Yes, I daresay you would have to be," she said bitterly.

"Lynn, Lynn, can't we wipe the slate clean? I promise, promise, that I will guard my temper and never, never, so help me, God—" His voice broke.

Exhausted, she sat down on the bed. Let the night be over fast, she prayed. Let morning come, let's get out of this hateful room.

He sat down next to her. "I stopped at a drugstore and got some stuff," he said with a bottle of medicine in hand.

"I don't want it."

"Please let me."

She was too tired to struggle. He had taken a first-aid course and knew how to touch her cheek with care. Softly, softly, his fingers bathed her temples with coolness.

"Doesn't that feel better?"

Unwilling to give him satisfaction, she conceded only, "It's all right."

Relaxed against the pillows, she saw through half-closed eyes that he had unpacked her overnight bag and, meticulous as always, had hung up her robe and nightgown in the closet.

"Your poor, darling, lovely face. I wish you would hit me. Make a fist and let me have it."

"What good would that do?"

"Maybe you'd feel better."

"I don't need to get even. That's not me, Robert."

"I know. I know it isn't." He closed the bottle. "There, that's enough. There won't be any mark, I can tell. That damn door had a mighty sharp edge, though. The management ought to be told. It's so easy to trip there."

It was true. She had tripped. But would she have if his hand had not threatened? It was hard to be accurate in describing an accident. The event flashes past in seconds and the recollection is confused.

She sighed and mourned, "I'm so tired. I don't think I've ever been so tired."

"Turn over and let me undo your dress. I'll rub your back."

Anger still boiled in her chest, a sorrowful, humiliated anger. Yet at the same time, a subtle, physical relief was beginning to wear it down. Robert's persisting hands, slowly, ever so slowly and firmly, were easing the tension in her neck and between her shoulder blades. Her eyes closed. As if hypnotized, she floated.

How intimately he knew her body! It was as if he knew it as well as she knew it, as if he knew it as well as he knew his own, as if they were one body. One . . .

Minutes passed, whether a few or many or even half an hour, she could not have said. But as finally he turned her over, she felt no resistance. Half waking, half dreaming, her willing arms accepted.

When she awoke, he was already dressed.

"I've been up for an hour. It's a bright, beautiful day. I've been watching boats far out on the lake. Would you like to take a walk down there? We can always get a later flight home."

She saw that he was testing her mood.

"Whatever you want. I don't mind either way."

It was not important. She was testing her own mood, which was important. Last night the darkness had been a horror down there near the lake. But those were morbid, useless thoughts now. And something she had read only a short time ago now crossed her mind: A majority of Americans, even in these days, still see nothing so terrible about a husband's occasional blow. Surely this was a curious thing to be remembering now. Perhaps it was a lesson for her. What do you want of life, Lynn? She might as well ask. Perfection? And she admonished herself: Grow up. Be realistic. Look forward, not back.

Besides, you love him. . . .

He sat down on the bed. He smoothed her hair. "I know you must be thinking you look awful, but you don't, take my word for it."

Gingerly, she felt her cheekbone. It did seem as though the swelling had diminished.

"Go put on some makeup. I'll order room service for breakfast. You must be starved."

"I had a sandwich yesterday at lunch."

"A big breakfast, then. Bacon, eggs, the works."

When she came out of the bathroom, he was moving the table on which the breakfast had been laid. "These waiters never do it just right. You'd think they'd know enough to put the table where one can enjoy the view. There, that's better. As soon as we're finished, I want you to go out with me. We've an errand on the avenue."

"What is it?"

"A surprise. You'll see."

In the elevator they met Bruce Lehman.

"I thought you'd have gone home by now," Robert said.

"No, I've got to pick up something first. Remember? How are you feeling, Lynn? We missed you last night." He was carefully not looking straight at her.

Robert answered. "She fell and was too embarrassed to go to the dinner with a lump on her face."

"A bruise can't spoil you, as pretty as you are," Bruce said, now turning his full gaze to her.

Josie liked to say that she had married him because his eyes had a friendly twinkle, and he liked cats. This twinkle was visible even behind his glasses. He reminded Lynn of a photograph in some advertisement of country life, a sturdy type in a windbreaker, tramping a field, accompanied by a pair of little boys or big dogs.

"Mind if we go with you?" asked Robert. "You gave me a very good idea last night."

"Of course not. Come along. I bought a bracelet yesterday for Josie," Bruce explained to Lynn. "I wanted them to engrave her initials on it and it will be ready this morning."

"I was going to surprise Lynn," Robert chided lightly. "Well, no matter. We'll be there in a minute, anyway."

She was disturbed. There was a right time for gifts, a right mood for receiving them. And she remonstrated, "Robert, I don't need anything. Really."

"No one ever *needs* jewelry. But if Bruce can have the pleasure, why can't I have it?"

In the shop, which was itself a small jewel of burnished wood, velvet carpet, and crystal lights, Bruce displayed the narrow gold bangle he had ordered.

"Like it, Lynn? Do you think Josie will?"

"It's lovely. She'll be so happy with it."

"Well, it won't make up for the mastectomy, God knows, but I thought —a little something, I thought—" His voice quavered and he stopped.

Robert had gone to the other side of the shop and now summoned Lynn.

"Come here, I want you to look at this."

Set in a web of woven gold threads was a row of cabochon stones— rubies, sapphires, and emeralds in succession.

"This," Robert said, "is what I call a bracelet."

"Byzantine," the salesman explained. "Handwoven. The originals are in museums."

"Try it on, Lynn."

The price tag was too small to be legible, but she knew enough without asking, and so replied, "It's much too expensive."

"Let me be the judge of that," Robert objected. "If I'm going to buy, I'm not going to buy junk. Either the best or nothing. Try it on."

Obeying, she went to the mirror. Unaccustomed to such magnificence, she felt an awkwardness; she had the air of a young girl.

When Bruce came over, Robert commanded her, "Show Bruce what you're getting."

"It's Robert's idea. I really don't—" she began.

Bruce laid his hand on her arm and quite oddly, she thought, corrected her. "It's beautiful. Take it. You deserve it," and to Robert added, "We have good wives. They deserve our best."

So the purchase was concluded.

"Keep the bracelet in your pocketbook," Robert said. "It's not insured yet, and the suitcase might get lost."

"Like yours," Bruce said.

"You didn't want the bracelet," Robert said when they were flying home, "because you think I was trying to make up for what I did yesterday. But you're wrong. And it's nothing compared with what I'll be giving you someday." He chuckled. "On the other hand, compared with what that cipher bought for Josie—"

"Why do you call Bruce a cipher? He's one of the most intelligent people we know."

"You're right, and I used the wrong word. What I meant was that he'll never set the world on fire. That much I can tell you."

"Maybe he doesn't want to," she retorted with mild indignation.

"He does his work at the office all right and makes a good impression, but in my opinion he lacks brilliance, the kind that keeps a man staying late and coming back on Saturday when everyone else is taking it easy."

"He's had to be home a lot with Josie when she was so awfully sick, you know that. Now that she's so much better, it'll be different."

"Well, they're an odd couple, anyway. She effervesces like a bottle of fizz, while he has the personality of a clam."

"That's not true. He's just not talkative. He listens." And she said quietly, "You've never liked Bruce and Josie, have you?"

"Now, that's not true either." Robert clasped her hand, which lay on the armrest. "Oh, the dickens with everybody except us, anyway. Lynn, I've got a good hunch that there's a big change in the air for us. Things were said last night both to me and about me that make it fairly sure I'll be tapped for the New York post. What have you got to say about that?"

"That I'm not surprised. If anyone deserves it, you do."

"I'll be in charge of marketing the whole works from the Mississippi to the Atlantic."

She was having a private thought, vaguely lonesome: I shall miss Helen and Josie.

"They may be sending one or two others from here, under me, of course. There's a general switching going on all over the map."

"I hope Bruce goes."

"Because of Josie, naturally. You depend too much on her, Lynn."

"I don't depend on her at all. I don't know how you can say that."

"I can say it because I see it." After a minute he mused. "New York. Then, who knows? The international division. Overseas. London. Paris. Up and up to the very top. Company president when I'm fifty. It's possible, Lynn. Just have faith in me."

He was an exceptional man, not to be held back. Everyone knew it, and she, his wife, knew it most of all. Again he clasped her hand, turning upon her his infectious, brilliant smile.

"Love me? With all my faults?"

Love him. Joined to him, no matter what. From the very first day. No matter what. Explain it? As soon explain the force of the rising tide.

"Love me?" he persisted.

"Yes," she said. "Oh, yes."

PART TWO

◇

Spring 1988

2

THE house lay comfortably on a circle of lawn and spread its wings against the dark rise of hills behind it. The architect, who had built it for himself, had brought beams from old New England barns and pine paneling from old houses to recreate the eighteenth century within commuting distance of Manhattan. The windows had twelve lights; and the fanlight at the front door was authentic.

Robert had found the property on his initial visit to New York and had come home filled with nervous enthusiasm. Connecticut was the place! It had charm. It had atmosphere. The schools were good. The neighborhoods were safe. There were wonderful open spaces. Imagine three wooded acres on a narrow, rural road with no one in sight except for the house directly opposite, and that, too, a treasure out of *Architectural Digest*.

Of course, it was expensive. But with his salary and his prospects a mortgage would be no problem. She had only to read the items about his promotion in *The Wall Street Journal* and in *Forbes* magazine to know where he was headed. Besides, a house like this one was an investment, a setting for entertaining—to say nothing of its being an investment in happy living for themselves. Once Lynn had seen the place, and if she liked it, then she must get busy right away and furnish it well. There must be no piecemeal compromises; a first-class decorator must do it all.

She would fall in love with it, he was certain; already he could see her working in the flower beds with her garden gloves and her big straw sunhat on.

So they got out a bottle of champagne and, sitting at the kitchen table, toasted each other and their children and General American Appliance and the future.

Now in late spring, the evening air blew its fragrance through the open windows in the dining room. And lilacs, the source of this fragrance, reared their mauve heads and their healthy leafage above the sills.

"Listen, a mockingbird! I can't imagine when he ever sleeps," Lynn said. "I hear him the last thing when I fall asleep, and in the morning when I wake, he's still singing."

Josie's black eyes, too prominent in her thin, birdlike face, smiled at Lynn.

"You do love this place, don't you?"

"Oh, I do. I know I felt in the beginning that the house was too big, but Robert was right, we really do spread out so comfortably here. And as for its being too expensive, I still have a few doubts, but I leave all that to him."

"My wife is frugal," said Robert.

"A lot of men would like to have that complaint," Josie remarked. She spoke quickly, as was her habit. And again it seemed to Lynn that her remarks to Robert, however neutral, so often had a subtle edge.

Then again it seemed to her that whenever Bruce followed Josie in his so different, deliberate way, it was with an intention to smooth that edge.

"You've done a wonder with the house." His gaze went over Robert's head toward the wide hall in which rivers, trees, and mountains repeated themselves on the scenic wallpaper, and then beyond to the living room where on chairs and rugs and at the windows a mélange of cream, moss-green, and dusty pink evoked the gardens of Monet.

Lynn followed his gaze. The house had indeed been done to a refined perfection. Sometimes, though, when she was left alone in it to contemplate these rooms, she had a feeling that they were frozen in their perfection as if preserved in amber.

"As for us," Bruce was saying, "will you believe that after two years we still have unopened cartons of books in the basement? We left St. Louis in such a hurry, we just threw things together, we never expected to be transferred, it was all so unexpected—" He laughed. "The truth is that we aren't known for our neatness, anyway, neither Josie nor I."

Josie corrected him. "When you have work to do for the company, you're one of the most efficient people I've ever seen."

Robert shook his head. "We were completely settled in a week. I personally can't function with disorder around me. I'm internally compelled toward order. I know that about myself. If a sign says KEEP OFF THE GRASS, I have to obey, while there are other people who have to challenge the sign by walking on the grass." He sighed. "People are crazy."

"I can attest to that," said Josie. "The things I see and hear in my daily work—" She did not finish.

"I wish you'd tell me some of them, Aunt Josie. I keep asking you."

Everyone turned to Emily. There was a fraction of a second's silence, no longer than a collective indrawn breath, as if the four adults had simultaneously been struck by an awareness of the girl's beauty in her yellow dress, with her black silk hair flowing out under a cherry-colored bandeau and the shaft of evening sunshine on her eager face.

"I will, whenever you want. But so much is tragedy, sordid tragedy." And with gentle curiosity Josie asked, "What makes you so interested?"

"You know I'm going to be a doctor, and doctors need to understand people."

There was a fullness in Lynn's throat, a silent cry: How lovely she is! How dear they both were, her girls! And she was thankful for their flourishing; they had taken the move so well and found their places in the new community.

"Emily did incredibly on her PSATs," Robert said. "Oh, I know you don't like me to boast about you, darling, but sometimes I can't help it. So forgive me. I am just so proud of you."

Annie's round face under its halo of pale, kinky hair turned to her father. And Lynn said, "Our girls both work hard. Annie comes home from school, goes right to the piano to practice, and then to her homework. I never have to remind you, do I, Annie?"

The child turned now to her mother. "May I have the rest of the soufflé before it collapses? Look, all the air's going out of it."

Indeed the remaining section of the chocolate fluff was slowly settling into a moist slab at the bottom of the bowl.

"No, you may not," Robert answered as Annie shoved her plate under Lynn's nose. "You're fat enough. You shouldn't have had any in the first place."

Annie's mouth twisted into the square shape of tragedy, an outraged sob came forth, she sprang up, tumbling her chair onto its back, and fled.

"Come back at once and pick up your chair," commanded Robert.

In reply the back door slammed. Everyone took care not to look at anyone else until Emily spoke, reproaching gently, "You embarrassed her, Dad."

"What do you mean? We're not strangers here. Aunt Josie and Uncle Bruce knew her before she was born."

"But you know how she hates being told she's fat."

"She has to face reality. She is fat."

"Poor little kid," Lynn murmured. A little kid who didn't like herself, not her fat, nor the kinky hair that she had inherited from some unknown ancestor. Who could know her secret pain? "Do go after her, Robert. She's probably in the usual place behind the toolshed."

Robert stood up, laid his napkin on the table, and nodded toward the Lehmans. "If you'll excuse me. She's impossible. . . ." he said as he went out, leaving a dull silence behind him.

At the sideboard Lynn poured coffee. Robert had bought the heavy silver coffee service at Tiffany as a "house gift to ourselves." At this moment its formality in the presence of Bruce and Josie made her feel awkward; it would have been natural to bring the percolator in from the kitchen as they had always done. But Robert wanted her to use all these fine new things, "Or else, why have them?" he always said, which, she had to admit, did make some sense. Her hand shook the cup, spilling a few drops. It was an uneasy moment, anyway, in this humming silence.

It was Emily who broke through it. At seventeen she already had social poise. "So you're all going to the Chinese auction for the hospital tonight?"

"I've been racking my brains," Josie reported, "and the best thing I can come up with is to offer three nights of baby-sitting."

"Well, if you need references," Emily said gaily, "tell them to call me. You and Uncle Bruce sat for us often enough, goodness knows."

Lynn had recovered. "I'll give a 'dinner party for eight at your house.' "

"Dad's offering three tennis lessons. He's better than the coach we had last year at school."

"What's this about me?" asked Robert. He came in with his arm around Annie's shoulder and, without waiting for an answer, announced cheerfully, "We've settled the problem, Annie and I. Here it is. One luscious, enormous dessert, as enormous as she wants, once a week, and no sweets, none at all, in between. As a matter of fact, that's a good rule for all of us, no matter what we weigh. Good idea, Lynn?"

"Very good," she said gratefully. As quickly as Robert could blunder into a situation, so quickly could he find the way out.

He continued. "Annie, honey, if you finish your math homework tonight, I'll review it tomorrow and then we'll go ahead to the next assignment so you'll have a leg up on the rest of the class. You will surprise the teacher. How's that?" The child gave a nod. "Ah, come, Annie, smile a little." A small smile crossed the still mottled cheeks. "That's better. You staying with Annie tonight, Emily?"

"Going to the movies, Dad, it's Friday."

"Not with that boy Harris again?"

"Yes, with that boy Harris again."

Robert did not answer. Emily must be the only person in the world who can cause him to falter, Lynn thought.

"Eudora's going to sit tonight," she said. "Emily dear, I think I hear Harris's car."

"You can hear it a mile away. It needs a new muffler," Robert said.

An instant later Emily admitted Harris. He was a tall, limber youth with a neat haircut, well-pressed shirt, and a friendly, white-toothed greeting. It seemed to Lynn that health and cheer came with him. Now he was holding by the collar a large, lumbering dog whose long, ropy hair was the shape and color of wood shavings.

"Hello, Mr. Ferguson, Mrs. Ferguson, Mr. and Mrs. Lehman. I think your Juliet's got something in her ear. She was wriggling around outside trying to rub it on the grass. If somebody'll hold her, I'll try to take a look."

"Not in the living room on the light carpet, please," Robert said.

"No, sir. Is it all right here in the hall?"

"Yes, lay her down."

It was not easy to wrestle with Juliet. Emily held her legs and Robert pressed on her shoulders. Harris probed through the hairy tangle of her ear.

"Be careful. She may snap," Lynn warned.

Harris shook his head. "Not Juliet. She knows I'm trying to help." His fingers searched. "If it's inside the ear—no, I don't see anything, unless it's something internal, but I don't think so—if it is, she'll have to see the vet—sorry, poor girl—am I hurting you? Oops, I think I felt—yes, I did—hey, I've got it, it's a tiny burr stuck in the hair—ouch, that hurts—wait, old lady—I'll need a scissors, Mrs. Ferguson. I'll need to cut some hair."

"She won't miss it," Lynn told him, handing the scissors. "I've never seen such a hairy dog."

"You'd make a fine vet," Bruce said, "or M.D., either one."

Harris, still on his knees, looked up and smiled. "That's what I plan. Emily and I are both in Future Doctors of America."

"Well, you've certainly got a way with animals. Juliet even seems to be thanking you," Bruce said kindly.

"We've always had animals in our house, so I'm used to them," Harris explained, stroking the dog's head. "Just last week we lost one old dog. He was sixteen, almost as old as I am, and I do miss him."

Bruce nodded. "I know what you mean. What kind was he?"

"Just Heinz 57, the all-American dog."

"Juliet is a Bergamasco," Robert said. "I had a hard time finding one, I can tell you."

"I'd never even heard the name until Emily told me what she was."

"Not many people have. It's a very rare breed in this country. Italian."

Lynn laughed. "I don't think she gives a darn about being rare, do you, Juliet?"

The dog yawned, settling back under the boy's stroking hand. Harris spoke to her.

"You feel a lot better now that you're rid of that thing, don't you?"

"Oh, Juliet, we do love you, you funny-looking, messy girl!" Emily exclaimed. "Although I always did want an Irish setter."

"Everybody has an Irish setter," Robert said. He looked at his watch. "Well, shall we go? Leave your car here, Bruce. You can pick it up on your way home. And, Emily, don't be too late."

"That's a nice boy," Bruce remarked as always, when they were in the car.

Lynn agreed. "Yes, he's responsible and thoughtful. I never worry about Emily when he drives. Some of the others—"

"What others?" Robert interrupted. "It seems to me that she's always with him. And I don't like it. I don't like it at all."

"You read too much into it," Lynn said gently. "They're just high school kids."

"Emily is not 'just' anything. She's an exceptional, gifted girl, and I don't want to see her wasting her time. Yes, the boy's nice enough, and his family's probably respectable. The father's a policeman—"

"Is that what you object to?" Josie said bluntly. "That his father's a policeman?"

Lynn cringed. Intimate as she was with her old friend, the secret of Robert's and Josie's dislike for each other remained unacknowledged between them. Neither woman wanted to open this particular Pandora's box.

Bruce gave his wife a mild rebuke. "Of course he doesn't mean that."

It seemed to Lynn that Bruce and she were too often called upon to smooth rough passages. And she said impatiently, "What a waste of words! A pair of seventeen-year-olds."

"Well, I don't know," Bruce said somewhat surprisingly. "Josie and I fell in love when we were in high school."

"That was different," Robert grumbled. "Emily's different. She has a future in the world, and she can't afford to play with it."

"I thought you were still one of those men who think women are better off in the house," Josie told him.

Again Lynn had to cringe. It was a relief that before Robert could reply, the car arrived at the entrance to the country club.

The membership had gotten behind the hospital's gigantic fund drive. Actually, it had been Robert who had brought about the liaison between the club and the hospital's trustees. It was remarkable that after only two years in this community, he had become well enough known for at least ten people to stop and greet him before he had even passed through the lobby.

The auction, in the long room that faced the golf course, was about to begin. Flanking the podium, two tables held sundry donations: glass candlesticks, dollhouse furniture, and an amateurish painting of ducks floating on a pond. On one side there hung a new mink jacket, a contribution from one of the area's best shops.

Robert paused to consider it. "How about this?" he whispered.

Lynn shook her head. "Of course not. You know how I feel about fur."

"Okay, I won't force it on you. On second thought, if you should ever change your mind, I wouldn't buy this one. It looks cheap." He moved on. "How about the dollhouse furniture for Annie?"

"She hasn't got a dollhouse."

"Well, buy her one for her birthday. Let her fix it up herself. Annie needs things to occupy her mind. What's this? Do I recognize a menorah?"

"You do," said Bruce from behind him. "I inherited three from various relatives, and since we hardly need three, I thought I'd contribute one. It's a Czech piece, about a hundred years old, and should bring a very good price."

"I doubt it. There are no Jews in this club."

"But there are some in the neighborhood, and they always give generously," Bruce said, sounding unusually firm.

"That's well known," Lynn offered, worrying that Robert's remark might have sounded too brusque.

Robert moved on again. "Hey, look here. Two Dickenses from 1890. *Bleak House* and *Great Expectations.* These are finds, Lynn." He lowered his voice. "We have to buy something. It wouldn't look right if we didn't. Anyway, I want these."

With the appearance of the auctioneer the audience ceased its rustle and bustle. One by one, with approval and jokes, various offers were made and accepted: Josie to baby-sit, Robert to give tennis lessons, Lynn to give a dinner, and a few dozen more. All went for generous prices. A delighted lady with blue-rinsed hair got the mink jacket, the doll furniture went to the Fergusons, as did the two volumes of Dickens. And Bruce's menorah brought three thousand dollars from an antiques dealer.

Robert said only, "I could use a cup of coffee," as the crowd dispersed into the dining room, where dessert was to be served.

Robert and Lynn saved places for the Lehmans.

"It gets a little sticky," he whispered as they sat down. "We should be mingling with people here, and yet I should be with Bruce too."

"He seems to be doing all right," Lynn observed, for Bruce and Josie were standing in an animated little group. "They make friends easily," she went on.

"Yes, when he makes the effort. He should make it more often for his own good. Well, I'm not going to waste time sitting here waiting for them. There are a dozen people I ought to see, and I want to get the tally besides. We must have made over twenty thousand, at least. I want to get hold of a local editor, too, and make sure that my name is in the write-up and that General American Appliance gets credit."

Robert's fingers drummed on the table. "No. Tomorrow morning will be better for that. A few private words over the telephone away from this crowd will accomplish more."

Josie, Bruce, and another man had detached themselves from their group and now came over to the table. Bruce made introductions.

"This is Tom Lawrence, who bought your dinner offer, Lynn, so I thought you two ought to meet."

Robert said cordially, "Please join us, Mr. Lawrence, you and Mrs. Lawrence."

"Thanks, I will. But there is no Mrs. Lawrence. Not anymore." The

After a moment Robert, laying his book aside, said decidedly, "Josie's too opinionated. I've always said so. It's a wonder to me why he isn't sick of her, except that he's too much of a weakling, a yes-man, to do anything about it."

"Sick of her! Good Lord, he's no yes-man, he adores her! And as to being opinionated, she's not. She's merely honest, that's all. She's outspoken."

"Well, well, if you say so. I guess I'm just a male chauvinist who's uncomfortable with outspoken women."

Lynn laughed. "Our Emily's a pretty outspoken woman, I'd say."

"Ah, that's different." And Robert laughed too. "She's my daughter. She can do anything she wants."

"Except choose her own boyfriends?"

"Lynn, I only want what's best for her. Wouldn't I give my life for her? For all of you?"

"Dear Robert, I know that."

He picked up his book and she went back to hers. Presently Robert laid his down again.

"By the way, did you have the fender fixed where you scraped it?"

"Yes, this morning."

"Did they do a good job?"

"You'd never know there'd been a mark."

"Good. There's no sense riding around in a marked-up car." Then he thought of something else; it was as if he kept a memo book in his head, Lynn often told him.

"Did you send a birthday present to my aunt?"

"Of course I did. A beautiful summer bag."

"That's right, considering all those sweaters she knits for the girls."

There was a hurtful, grudging quality in this comment that Lynn was unable to ignore.

"Robert, I think you treat her very badly."

"Nonsense. I was perfectly nice to her last year at Christmas."

"You were polite, that's all, and it wasn't last year, it was the year before. The reason she didn't come last year was that she felt you didn't want her. You, not I. I actually like her. She's a kind, gentle lady."

"She may be kind and gentle, but she's a garrulous old fool and she gets on my nerves."

"Garrulous! She hardly opens her mouth when you're around."

He did not answer. And Lynn persisted.

man's smile had a touch of mischief, as if he were amused at himself. "You assumed I had a wife, or else why would I be bidding on a dinner party? I can't blame you, but the fact is that although I keep a bachelor's house, I like to entertain." He turned to Lynn. "Bruce told me that you're a fabulous cook and I ought to bid on your dinner. So I did."

"You bid more than it's worth," Lynn said. "I hope you won't be disappointed."

"I'm sure I won't be." Now Lawrence turned to Robert. "And you're the man, I noticed, who got my Dickens. A fair exchange."

"Not really. They're handsome books. I wonder that you parted with them."

"For the same reason that Bruce here parted with his candle holder— menorah, I mean. Both my grandfathers were book collectors, and since I'm not a collector of anything, it seemed to me that I didn't need duplicates. Also," he said somewhat carelessly, "one of my grandfathers helped found this club and the hospital, too, so the cause has extraspecial meaning for me."

"Ah, yes. Lawrence Lawrence. The plaque in St. Wilfred's lobby."

Lynn, watching, knew that Robert was taking the man's measure. He would recognize assurance and alacrity. Now Robert was asking how Bruce and he had become acquainted.

"We met while jogging on the high school track," Lawrence responded. "We seem to keep pretty much the same schedule."

"You must live near the school, then."

"I do now. I gave up a bigger house after my divorce. I used to live out on Halsey Road," he said in the same careless way.

"That's where we are!" Lynn exclaimed. "We bought the Albright house."

"Did you? Beautiful place. I've been at many a great party there."

"You should see it now. We've done so much with it that you might not recognize it," Robert said. "It needed a lot of work."

"Really," said Lawrence. "I never noticed."

He doesn't like Robert, Lynn thought. No, that's absurd. Why shouldn't he? I'm always imagining things.

Suddenly Josie laughed. "Do you know something funny? Look at Lynn and look at Tom. Does anybody see what I see?"

"No, what?" asked Robert.

"Why, look again. They could be brother and sister. The same smooth sandy hair, the short nose, the cleft chin—it's uncanny."

"If so, I'm honored." And Lawrence made a little bow toward Lynn.

"I don't see it at all," Robert said.

The instant's silence contained embarrassment, as if a social blunder had been made. Yet Josie's remark had been quite harmless.

And Lynn said pleasantly, "You must tell me when you want your dinner for eight, Mr. Lawrence."

"Tom's the name. I'll get my list together and call you. Will the week after next be all right?"

"Don't forget we are taking Emily to visit Yale," Robert cautioned.

"I won't forget. The week after next will be fine."

Presently, the room began to empty itself. People looked at their watches and made the usual excuses to depart. The evening had played itself out.

"Who is this fellow Lawrence, anyway?" Robert inquired on the way home.

Bruce explained. "He's a bright guy, and partner in a big New York law firm."

"That doesn't tell me much. There are a lot of bright guys in big New York firms."

"I don't know much more than that, except that he's been divorced a couple of times, he's close to fifty, and looks a lot younger. And I know he comes from what you'd call an important family," Bruce added with what Lynn took to be a touch of humor.

"I'm not happy about having Lynn go over to a strange man's house."

"Oh," Lynn said, "don't be silly. Does he look like a rapist?"

"I don't know. What does a rapist look like?" Robert gave a loud, purposeful sigh. "My wife is still an innocent."

"It's a dinner party for eight. And I'm planning to take Eudora to help. So that should make you feel better. Really, Robert."

"All right, all right, I'll feel better if you want me to."

"People were saying some nice things about you tonight, Robert," Bruce said. "About the hospital, of course, and also the big pledge you got GAA to make to the Juvenile Blindness campaign."

"Yes, yes. You see, you people used to think all that had nothing to do with marketing electronic appliances, but I hope you see now that it does. Anything that connects the name of GAA to a good cause counts. And the contacts one makes in the country club all connect to these causes and their boards. You really ought to join a club, Bruce."

"You know I can't join this one."

"That's disgusting," Lynn said. "It makes me want to stand up and fight."

"You may want to but you'd better not. I keep reminding you," told her, "that reality has to be faced. Bruce is smart enough to a Join a Jewish club, Bruce. There are a couple just over the West line. And the company'll pay. They'll be glad to."

Lynn, looking back from the front seat, could see Bruce's shru

"Josie and I never did go for club life, Jewish or not."

"It's time you began, then." Robert spoke vigorously. "You need on some of these boards, go to the dinners and have your wife go luncheons. You owe it to the firm and to yourself."

"I do what I can," Bruce answered.

"Well, think about what I'm telling you. And you, too, Josie."

Lynn interjected, "Josie works. And anyway, I can't imagine h changing gossip with company wives. You have to be careful of wha say. They judge everything, your opinions, your clothes, everything. of those afternoons can wear one out."

"It's the price you pay for being who you are and where you are. think it a small enough price, too, if it leads to a big job in Eur Robert declared.

A small chilly dread sank in Lynn's chest. She knew the patter promotion: two or three years in each of several European count then possibly the home office in New York again. Or else a spell ir Far East with another return. And no permanence, no roots, no plac plant a maple sapling and see it grow. There were myriads of people would forgo a thousand maples for such opportunities, and that was for them, but she was not one of those people.

Yet Robert was. And he would well deserve his rewards when came. Never, never, she thought as always, must she by the slightest or word hold him back.

As if he were reading her mind, at that very moment Bruce remar "When there's another big job in Europe, and with all that's happer abroad, there's bound to be one soon, you're the man to get it, Rot Everybody knows that."

Later when they were reading in bed, Robert asked, "What are doing tomorrow?"

"I'm taking Josie and a few friends to lunch, remember? It's her bi day."

"Missing the women's tennis tournament?"

"I have to. Josie works all week, so Saturday is the only day we make it."

"Emily's very fond of her. She had a lovely afternoon tea when Jean was visiting in New York last month."

"All right. Leave me alone about Aunt Jean, will you? It's unimportant."

He turned and, in pulling the blanket with him, dropped the book with a loud thump onto the floor.

"Sorry. Damn! I'm restless."

She put her hand on his arm. "Tell me what's really bothering you."

"Well, you may think it's foolish of me, you probably will think so. But I told you, I don't like the idea of your going to cook dinner in another man's house where there's no wife. I wish to hell you had thought of something else to contribute to the auction."

"But cooking is what I do best. It'll be fun. Didn't you watch the bidding? He paid a thousand dollars for my services, I want you to know."

"Bruce shoved him onto you. That's what happened."

"You're surely not going to be annoyed with Bruce. Robert, how silly can you be?"

"I don't like the man's looks. Divorced, and divorced again, and—"

Trying to tease him out of his mood, she said, "Apparently he looks like me, so you should—"

"So yes, he is something like you, and you—"

He turned again, this time toward Lynn, to meet her eyes, so that she could see close up his darkening blue irises, black lashes, white lids, and her own reflection in his pupils. "You grow more lovely with each year. Some women do."

She was pleased. "I do believe you're jealous."

"Of course I am. Isn't it only natural? Especially when I have never once in all our life together—I swear it—I have never been unfaithful to you."

The white lids, like shell halves, closed over the blue. And with a violent motion he buried his head in her shoulder.

"Ah, Lynn, you don't know. You don't know."

That he could want her still with such fierce, sudden spasms of desire, and that she could respond as she had first done when they began together, was a marvel that flashed upon her each and every time, as now. . . .

The wind fluttered the curtains, the bedside clock ticked, and a car door cracked lightly, quickly shut. Robert roused from his doze.

"Emily?"

"She's home. I kept awake to be sure."

"She stays out too late."

"Hush. Go to sleep. Everything's all right."

With all safe, Emily and Annie in their beds, now she could sleep too. Her thoughts trembled on the verge of consciousness, her body was warmed by the body beside which she had been sleeping for thousands of nights. Thousands.

There went the mockingbird again. Trilling, trilling its heart out without a care in the world, she thought, and then abruptly thought no more.

Tom Lawrence asked, "Are you sure I'm not in your way?"

Perched on a barstool in his glossy black-and-white kitchen, he was watching Lynn's preparations.

"No, not at all."

"This is a new experience for me. Usually when I have guests, I have a barbecue outdoors. Steaks, and ice cream for dessert. Fast and easy."

Since this was quite a new experience for Lynn, too, she had to grope for something to say, however banal, to avoid a stiff silence. "It's a pity not to use all these beautiful things more often," she remarked as she filled the cups of a silver epergne with green grapes.

"That's a great idea, putting fruit in that thing. I forgot I had it. You know, when we split up and I moved, my former wife and I agreed to divide all the stuff we owned, stuff from her family and mine, plus things we'd bought together. I didn't pay any attention, just let her do it all. The whole business was a mess. The move. The whole business." Abruptly, he slid from the stool. "Here, let me carry that. Where does it go?"

"It's the centerpiece. Careful, the arms detach."

The dining table stood at the side of a great room with a fireplace at each end. One saw that there was no more to the house than the splendid kitchen and what must be two bedrooms leading off this great room. A quick glance encompassed paintings, bookshelves, a long glass wall with a terrace, and thick foliage, dense as a forest, beyond it.

"What an elegant little house!" she exclaimed.

"Do you think so? Yes, after almost three years I can say I finally feel at home here. When I first moved in, my furniture looked alien. I hardly recognized it."

"I know what you mean. When the van comes and sets your things down in a strange place, they look forlorn, don't they? As if they knew and missed their own home. Then when the empty van drives away—oh, there's something final about it that leaves one just a trifle sad, I think."

And for an instant she was back in the little house in St. Louis—"little," contrasted with the present one—with the friendly neighbors on the familiar, homelike street. Then she said briskly, "But of course one gets over it."

His reply was wholly unexpected. "I imagine that you make yourself 'get over' things pretty quickly, though. You make yourself do what's right."

Astonished, she looked up to meet a scrutiny. Returning it, she saw that except for some superficial features, this man did not resemble her at all; he was keen and worldly wise, which she definitely was not; he would see right through a person if he chose to.

"What makes you say that?" she asked curiously.

He smiled and shrugged. "I don't know. Sometimes I get a sudden insight, that's all. Unimportant. And possibly wrong."

"Maybe you sense that I'm a little nervous about this evening. I'm hoping I haven't bitten off more than I can chew."

He followed her back into the kitchen. "Please don't be nervous. These are all real people tonight, a few old friends driving out from New York and not a phony among them. They'll be stunned when they see this table. I'm sure they're expecting Tom Lawrence's usual paper plates."

Arrayed on the counters were bowls and platters of food that Lynn had already prepared at home: a dark red ham in a champagne sauce, stuffed mushroom caps, plump black olives and silver-pale artichokes tossed into a bed of greens, golden marinated carrots, rosy peaches spiced with cinnamon and cloves. Back and forth from the pantry to the refrigerator she moved. Then to the oven, into which she slid a pan of crisp potato balls, and to the mixer for the topping of whipped cream on a great flat almond tart.

When all was finished and she was satisfied, full confidence returned. "This kitchen's absolutely perfect," she told Tom, who was still there quietly observing her work. "The restaurant-sized oven, the freezer—all of it. I'm really envious."

"Well, you deserve a perfect kitchen, you're that expert. Have you ever thought of going professional?"

"I've thought about it sometimes, I'll admit. I've even thought of a name, 'Delicious Dinners.' But what with a lot of volunteering and the PTA and our big house taking time out of every day, I don't know how—" She paused and finished, "Robert is very fastidious about the house." She paused again to add, "Anyway, I'm not in a hurry," and was immediately conscious of having sounded defensive. "I need a last look at the table," she said abruptly.

"Excuse me." Tom was apologetic. "But the silver—I mean, aren't the forks and spoons upside down, inside out?"

Lynn laughed. "When the silver's embossed on the back, you're supposed to let it show."

"Oh? Now I've learned something," he said. His eyes smiled at her.

They're like Bruce's eyes, she thought. There isn't another thing about him that's like Bruce, but that. Her hands moved, smoothing the fine cloth, rearranging the candlesticks. There aren't that many people whose eyes can smile like that.

"You've suddenly grown thoughtful, Lynn. May I call you that?"

"Of course. Oh, thoughtful? I was remembering," she said lightly, "when Robert bought the etiquette book so I'd learn how to give proper dinners when we moved here. I thought it was silly of him, but I find it's come in handy, after all."

The doorbell rang. "Oh, that's Eudora. She cleans and baby-sits for us. I've asked her to help. I'll let her in."

When Lynn returned, Tom said, "I wish you'd set another place at table, one for yourself, now that you've got help in the kitchen."

"I'm here to work. I'm not a guest," she reminded him. "Thank you, anyway."

"Why shouldn't you be a guest? There'll be all couples tonight except for me. And I really should have a female to escort me, shouldn't I?"

"That wasn't the arrangement."

His smile subsided as again he gave her his quick scrutiny. "I understand. You mean, if you were to be a guest, then your husband would be here too."

She nodded. "Anyway, I couldn't depend upon Eudora in the kitchen. She'll be fine to bring in the plates after I fix them and to clean up with me afterward."

She hurried away into the kitchen. Why was she flustered? Actually, the man had said nothing so startling. And she turned to Eudora, who was waiting for instructions.

"They'll be here in a minute. Turn the oven on low to warm up the hors d'oeuvres. Half an hour for drinks. I'll toss the salad. It goes on the blue plates—no, not those, take the other ones."

"They're having a good time," Eudora said much later. The swinging door opened and closed on genial laughter as she went in and out. "I never did see people clean plates like this."

"Good. Now carry the cake in so they can see it first. Then you can bring it back, and I'll slice it."

"You sure are some cook, Mrs. Ferguson. I'm old enough to be your mother, and I never even heard of the things you fix."

"Well, I'd never seen some of your good Jamaican dishes, either, until I knew you."

Although she had been standing on her feet all day, Lynn suddenly received a charge of energy. What had begun as a lark, an adventure, had become a test, and she had passed it. She had been paid for her skill, and she felt happy. So, when the door opened and Tom said his guests were demanding to see the cook, she was quite ready to go with him.

"Just do let me fix my face first. I'm all flushed from the stove."

"Yes, it's awful to be flushed like a rose," he retorted, pulling her with him.

In a moment she appraised the group: they were sophisticated, successful, bright New Yorkers, the kind who wear their diamonds with their blue jeans when they want to. They marry and divorce with equal ease when they want to. Good natured and accepting, it takes a lot to shock them. Robert would despise their type. All this went through her head.

They were most kind, heaping praise on Lynn. "What a talent. . . . You could work for Le Cirque or La Grenouille. . . . I ruined my diet tonight. . . . Absolutely marvelous."

The evening rose to a peak. Warmed by the food and wine, the group left the table in a high, restless mood. Tom turned on the record player, the men pushed back the scatter rugs, and dancing began.

He held his hands out to Lynn. "Come, join the party."

"It's rock and roll. I'm awful at it," she protested.

"Then it's time you learned," he answered, and pulled her out onto the floor.

At first she felt foolish. If Emily, who danced like a dervish, could see her mother, she'd die laughing. The best Lynn could do was to watch the others' dizzy twists and gyrations and try to imitate them.

Then after a while, the drumming, primitive, blood-pounding beat began to speak to her. Quite unexpectedly, she caught the beat.

"Why, you've got it!" Tom cried. "You've got it!"

This whirling, which should have been exhausting, was instead exhilarating. When Lynn became aware that Eudora was standing at the door to signal her departure, it surprised her to find that it was already almost eleven o'clock. She would have guessed the time to be no later than nine.

Pressing some bills into Eudora's hand, she whispered, "You remembered to leave the crystal?"

"Oh, I hate to leave you with it, Mrs. Ferguson, but I'd hate to be responsible for it too."

"That's all right, Eudora. I'll wash it fast and start right home."

Back in the kitchen with the apron on again, Lynn was rinsing the goblets when Tom, with eyes alight and in a merry mood, came looking for her.

"Hey! What are you doing in here?"

"Eudora was afraid to touch your Baccarat. She knows what it costs."

"Oh, leave it. We're all going to dance outdoors. It's a perfect night."

"I can't. Really. I can't."

"Yes, you can. I insist. For ten minutes. Come on."

The outdoor lanterns gave the effect of moonglow, barely glimmering toward the edge of darkness, where the hemlock grove fenced the little clearing on which the terrace lay. It had rained during the day, and the smell of damp grass was tart.

One of the men complained, "Age is creeping up, Tom, because I'm beat. How about some slow golden oldies for a change?"

"No problem. I've got all the tunes your parents danced to. Now, this is really nice," he said as his arm brought Lynn close. "When you come down to it, the old way is better."

Unlike Robert, he was not much taller than she, so that their faces almost touched. Their feet moved in skillful unison to the swing of the sentimental music.

"You have a sweet mouth," Tom said suddenly, "and sweet eyes."

An uneasy feeling stiffened Lynn, and he felt it at once.

"You didn't like me to say that, did you?"

"I didn't expect it."

"Why not? If a compliment is sincere, it should be spoken and accepted."

"Well, then, thank you."

"You still look uncomfortable. You're thinking I'm just a smooth talker. But you are really someone special, I have to tell you. Refreshing. Different."

She could feel his breath on her neck. The hand on the small of her back pressed her so close to him that she could feel his heartbeat. And the dreamy charm of the night changed into nervous misgiving.

"It's after eleven," she cried. "I have to go right away. Please—"

"So there you are!"

The harsh voice rang as Robert came from around the corner of the house into the light. Just then the music stopped, leaving the dancers stopped, too, arrested in motion, all turned toward the voice.

"I telephoned, I got no answer, I came over and rang the doorbell and still got no answer."

"This is my husband," Lynn said. "Tom Lawrence—but how stupid of me! Of course you know each other. I'm not thinking." And she moistened her lips, to which there had suddenly come a curious, salty taste, like that of blood, as if blood had drained upward from her heart.

"I'm so sorry. We've been out here, and the music's drowned out all the bells. Come in and join us," Tom said cordially. "Your wife made a marvelous dinner. You've got to sample some of the dessert. I hope there's some left, Lynn?"

"Thank you, but cake is hardly what I need. It's going on twelve, and I'm not usually out at this hour rounding up my wife at a dance."

Crazy thoughts went through Lynn's head: He looked sinister and black, a figure in mask and cape from an old melodrama, angry-dark, why can't he smile, I'll die of shame before these people. And in a shrill, gay tone not her own, she cried out, "What an idiot I am, I forgot to wear my watch, all these nice people made me come out of the kitchen and dance with them, I'll just get my bowls and things—"

"Yes, you do that," Robert said. "You do just that. I'll wait in front." He turned about and walked away through the shrubbery.

Tom and the whole company, men and women both, went into the kitchen with Lynn. Rattling and prattling, she let them help gather her possessions, and load her car, while Robert sat stiffly at the wheel of his car, and the hot, awful shame went prickling along her spine.

"You follow me home," he said.

Past quiet houses already at rest in the shadows of new-leaved trees, his car sped like a bullet aimed at the heart of the friendly countryside. She knew that he sped so because he was furious, and knowing it, her own anger grew. What right had he? Who did he think he was?

"Damn!" she cried. That an evening, having begun so nicely, could end in such miserable confusion, with Tom Lawrence's unwelcome attention and Robert's nastiness!

He had already driven his car into the garage and was waiting for her in the driveway when she arrived home. I want the first word, she thought, and I'm going to have it. Nevertheless, she spoke with quiet control.

"You were unbelievably rude, Robert. I almost didn't recognize you."

"Rude, you say? Rude? I went there as any other husband would, looking for his wife."

"You embarrassed me terribly. You know you did."

"I was concerned. Close to midnight, and no word from you."

"If you were so concerned, you could have telephoned."

"I did telephone, I told you. Where's your head? Didn't you listen to me? And then I went over to find you, not in the kitchen doing this ridiculous dinner, and where were you? Dancing, if you please. Dancing."

"I had been dancing for a couple of minutes, and I was just leaving that very second when you came."

"You had been dancing much longer than a couple of minutes. And don't try to deny it because I was there."

Caught in her lie, no, not a lie, a fib, an innocent fib, such an innocent business altogether in which to be embroiled, she lashed out.

"You were standing there behind the trees snooping? It's degrading. I should think you'd be ashamed, Robert. The way you just burst out of the dark, enough to scare the life out of people. Don't you think they all knew you must have been spying? You were horrible. You wouldn't have put on an act like that if any of them could be of use to you in your business. Otherwise, you don't care what you say to people."

"That's not true. But it is true that I don't give a damn about a lot of pseudosophisticated phonies. I recognize the type at a glance. I wouldn't trust one of them any farther than I can throw a grand piano, and that includes Lawrence."

"You're so critical. You're always carping. You don't approve of anybody."

The headlights of her car, which she had forgotten to turn off, blazed up on Robert. And he seemed, as he stood there, as strong as the dark firs behind him.

"Turn those lights off," he snapped, "or you'll have a dead battery." And turning his back, he climbed the steps to the deck at the back of the house.

She turned the lights off. She was too tired to put one foot ahead of the other, too tired to fight this war of words that she knew was far from over. But with a long sigh she followed him to the deck.

"Pseudosophisticated phonies," he repeated.

"What is it, Robert?" she asked. "Tell me what it is that makes you despise people you don't even know. What makes you so angry? Don't you like yourself?" And saying so, she felt the faint sting of her own tears.

"Please," he said, "spare me your pop psychology, Mrs. Freud."

He took out his keys and unlocked the house door. Juliet came bounding, barking fiercely, but, seeing who was there, jumped up on Robert and wagged her tail instead. He thrust her away.

"Not in the mood, Juliet. Down." And abruptly returning to Lynn, he demanded, "I want an apology. There'll be no sleep for either of us tonight until I get one."

How a handsome face can turn so ugly! she thought. In the half-dark his cheeks were faintly blue, and his eyes were sunk in their sockets.

"An apology, Lynn."

"For what? For overstaying my time by an hour? For having a little fun? You could have come in and joined the party. Tom asked you to."

"Oh, of course, if Tom asks."

"What does that sarcastic tone mean, I'd like to know?"

"It means that I don't like the way he was looking at you, that's what."

"The way he looked at me," she scoffed. "I don't know how he did because I wasn't studying his expressions, I assure you. But if," she cried indignantly, "if he or anyone should take it into his head to admire me a little, you'd have no right to object. Not you. You love it when women fawn on you. Don't tell me you don't, because I've seen it a thousand times."

"Now, you listen to me and don't change the subject. But no, on the other hand now that you've brought up the subject, I'll tell you this: I have never encouraged any woman. Never. Nor done anything in any way that I couldn't do right in front of you. I'll swear on the Bible."

"The Bible! All of a sudden the Bible. When were you last in church?"

"Never mind. I believe. I have my moral standards. One mistake, one misstep down a slippery slope, and you can't—"

"What is this? Who's made any missteps? What in heaven's name are you talking about? I can't figure you out."

"Damn it, if you'll stop interrupting me, I'll figure it out for you."

From the roof peak the mockingbird began a passionate crescendo, then a trill and a plaintive diminuendo. The sweetness of it went to Lynn's heart and pierced it.

"Let's stop this," she said, trembling. "I've had enough. There's no sense in it. I'm going inside."

He clutched her sleeve. "No, you're not. You'll hear me first."

She pulled, and hearing the sleeve rip, the fine sleeve of a cherished dress, she was enraged.

"Let go of me this minute, Robert."

"No."

As she wrenched it away, the sleeve tore off at the shoulder. A muffled cry came from his throat. And he raised a menacing hand. His arm shot out, grasping her shoulder, and she spun, fled, and fell headfirst off the deck into the hawthorn hedge. She heard her own terrible scream, heard the dog going wild, heard Robert's outcry, thought, *my face!* and knew not to break the fall with her hands but to protect her eyes instead.

"Oh, God," Robert said.

When he lifted her, she screamed. She was flayed, stripped, skinned on the backs of her hands, her legs, her cheeks . . . She screamed.

"I have to get you up," he said, sounding as if he were speaking through clenched teeth. "If you can't bear it, I'll have to call an ambulance."

"No. No. We'll try. . . . Try loosening one at a time. I'll bear it."

Annie was out on a sleep-over at a friend's house. And Emily must not be home yet, or she would have heard by now and come running. And she gave thanks that they were not seeing this, a happening that must seem both hideous and absurd, with the dog now leaping, now howling, as if it, too, were in pain, shattering the quiet of the night.

Weeping and whimpering she lay and, while Robert brought a flashlight from the car and set to work on her torn arms and legs, tried not to scream. One by one the thorns were parted from her flesh. Only once or twice did she cry out loud.

When finally he raised her and she stood wavering on the grass, they were both sweating and stained with bloody droplets. Wordless, they simply stared at one another. Then she stumbled up the shallow steps, moaning softly.

"I've turned my ankle. I can hardly walk."

"I'll carry you."

He picked her up and bore her as lightly as he would have borne a child. He laid her on the bed and took her clothes off.

"Soap and water first," he said. "Don't be afraid, I'll be very careful. Then antibiotic cream. That'll do until you see a doctor in the morning."

"I'm not going to see any doctor. You don't need a doctor for a sprained ankle or a thorn."

"You had eighteen thorns. I counted."

"All the same, I'm not going," she insisted feebly, and was perfectly aware that this was masochism, that it was her intent to make him feel his guilt, guilt for the wounded hands clasped on her naked, wounded breast, for the ruined yellow dress that lay on the floor like dirty laundry, guilt for the whole horror of this night.

"Well, suit yourself," he said. "If you change your mind and don't want to drive, call a taxi. I can't take you. My desk in the office is piled with work, and work won't wait just because it's Saturday."

When she crept under the blanket, he was still standing looking down at her.

"What do you want?" she whispered. "Anything you want to say?"

He lowered his eyes and took a long breath. "Yes. I was angry. But I didn't throw you into the hedge."

"You pushed me. You were going to hit me, you were inches from my face."

"I was not."

"You were, Robert."

"Are you a crystal gazer or something, who can foretell what a person's going to do?"

"You grabbed my shoulder and shoved me. And I saw your face. It was ugly with rage."

"In the first place, it was too dark for you to see whether my face was ugly or not. This is garbage, Lynn."

All she wanted was to lie in the darkness and rest. "Why don't you let me alone?" she cried. "Haven't you any mercy? At least let me try to sleep if I can."

"I won't bother you, Lynn." He walked to the door. "I hope you can sleep. I doubt that I can. A miserable night. These miserable misunderstandings! Go downstairs, Juliet. Stop pestering."

"Leave the dog here. I want her."

Now darkness filled the room. The little sounds of the night were soft, a rustle in the oak near the window and the tinkle of Juliet's tags. The dog came to the bed, reached up, and licked Lynn's sore hand, as if comfort were intended; as always, then, comfort brought the most grateful tears. And Lynn lay still, letting them flow, feeling them cool and slippery on her cheeks. After a while the dog thumped down on the floor near the bed, the tears stopped, and she closed her eyes.

Still no sleep came. Emily was not home yet. It must be very late, she thought. But it was too painful to turn over in the bed and look at the clock. From downstairs there drifted the pungent smell of pipe tobacco, and she knew that Robert was sitting in the corner of the sofa watching television or reading, or perhaps just sitting. No matter. She didn't want to think of him at all. Not yet.

After a time she heard the small thud of a car door being closed, followed by Emily's feet creeping down the hall to her room. Where had the girl been so late? But she was home and safe.

At last it seemed that blessed sleep might come. It had not yet come when Robert entered the room and got into bed, but she pretended that it had.

In the morning, still feigning sleep, she waited until he had dressed and gone downstairs. Then she got up and limped painfully to the mirror, which confirmed what she had expected to see: a swollen face with small, reddened eyes sunk into bloated cheeks. The whole unsightly face was puffed, and there were dark droplets of dried blood on the long scratch. Merely to look like this was another undeserved punishment.

She was standing there applying useless makeup and trying to decide whether the wearing of dark glasses would help or whether it would be better simply to brave things out, when Robert came in.

"I hope you feel better," he said anxiously.

"I'm fine. I'm just fine. Can't you see?"

"I see only that you're hurt. And that hurts me, even though right now you may not think it does. But I am just so sorry, Lynn. So sorry it happened. I can't tell you."

"It didn't just happen: I'm not going to accept that stuff anymore. Somebody made it happen, and I'm not the somebody."

"I understand how you feel." Robert was patient now, and contrite. "I realize how it must appear to you. I was angry—we can talk about that some other time—I scared you with my anger, which was wrong of me, and so you ran and then—"

She interrupted. "And then I don't want to hear any more."

"All right. Come down and eat your breakfast. Let's keep things normal in front of the girls. Annie's just been brought home. I've told them about your accident, so they're prepared."

"My accident. Ah, yes," Lynn mocked, wiping off the eye makeup, which made her look like a sick owl. She would just honestly let the girls see she had been crying. They'd see the injuries anyway.

Emily had set the table in the breakfast room. Coffee bubbled in the percolator and bread was in the toaster. Evidently, she had gone outside and picked a spray of lilacs for the green bowl. Emily was a take-charge person.

"You're up early for someone who went to bed late," Lynn said pleasantly.

"A bunch of us are driving to the lake," said Emily, carefully not looking at Lynn's face, "where Amy's folks keep the boat. What's wrong with your foot? You've hurt that too?"

"It's nothing much. I just can't get a shoe on, so I'll stay home today."

Annie was staring at Lynn. "You look awful," she said. "You've been crying too."

Emily admonished her, "Mind your business, silly."

Robert spoke. "Your mother hurt herself. Don't you cry when you're hurt?"

No one answered. The silence was unhappy, restless with the awareness that it would have to end, and the fear that it would end badly.

"It was twenty minutes after twelve when you walked in last night," Robert said, addressing Emily. "Did you know that?" he asked, addressing Lynn, who nodded.

"I forgot to look at the time. A bunch of us were studying at Sally's," Emily explained.

"That won't do," Robert said. "You're damaging your reputation, if nothing more, coming home at that hour."

"We'll talk about it this morning, Emily," Lynn said.

"No." Robert looked at his watch. "I have to run. Emily, you are not to leave the house tonight. *I* want to talk to you. You and I are going to have a very serious talk, straight from the shoulder, one that you won't forget in a hurry. When I'm through, you'll know what's expected of you."

The emphasis on the "I" was directed at Lynn; she understood that clearly, having been told often enough that she wasn't firm, didn't consider appearances, and the girls would never learn from her.

"Oh, what an awful mood," Emily said when Robert had left.

Annie got up. "I promised Dad I'd practice this morning, and since he's in a bad mood, I guess I'd better do it," she said in a tone of resignation.

"That's not why you should," Lynn said gently. "You should do it because—well, because you should do it," she finished with a smile.

When Annie was in the living room drumming out a minuet, Lynn said to Emily, "Sit down while I have my second cup. You shouldn't stay out so late. You know that without my telling you. Were you really at Sally's all that time?"

"I was. Believe it or not, we were studying for finals, Mom."

Robert's blue eyes looked candidly back at her from Emily's face.

"I believe you." And thoughtfully, as if she had weighed whether or not to ask the question, she ventured it. "Was Harris there?"

"Yes. He brought me home."

"After twelve, your father said."

"He was sitting in the dark when I came in. Then he came to the hall and stood there just glaring at me. He didn't say a word, and neither did I."

"That was wrong of you."

"I'm sorry, Mom. But he needn't have looked so ferocious. I know I should have phoned, but I forgot to look at the time. That's not a crime."

"I suppose Sally's mother wasn't there, as usual?"

"Well, she's divorced, she goes on dates." Again the clear eyes met Lynn's. "So, no, she wasn't there."

"Wrong. All wrong," Lynn said. "And Harris—he's a fine boy, I see that, and it's not that we don't trust you, but—"

"But what, Mom?"

"Your father is very, very angry. You must try to do the right thing, you understand, or you'll be grounded. You really will, Emily, and there'll be nothing I can do about it."

There was a silence except for the balanced cadence of Annie's minuet.

Emily reached across the table and touched Lynn's hand. "Mom?" And now the clear, the honest, the lustrous eyes were troubled. "Mom? What's wrong with Dad? I wish he were like other people's fathers. He gets so mad. It's weird."

On guard now, Lynn answered as if she were making light of the complaint.

"Why? Because he's going to give you a scolding that you deserve?"

"No. It has nothing at all to do with that."

"What, then?"

"Oh, things. Just things. He gets so mad sometimes."

"Everybody gets cranky now and then. He works very hard. Sometimes he's terribly tired and as you say, it's only sometimes."

Emily shook her head. "That's not what I mean."

Lynn feared, although she did not want to think specifically of what it was that she feared. So she spoke with a touch of impatience.

"You'll have to give me an example, since I have no idea what you're talking about."

Still Emily hesitated, with a wary, doubtful glance at Lynn. Finally she said, "Remember when I met Aunt Jean in the city and she took me to tea? Something happened that I didn't tell you about."

"Yes?"

"Don't be scared, it's nothing awful. What happened is, we were talking and you know how she likes to tell about old times, when the neighbor's house burned down and what a cute little boy Dad was, and then suddenly she let something slip about Dad's first marriage—Mom, how is it we never knew he was married before?"

So that's all it was. Nothing, or comparatively nothing. . . .

Carefully, Lynn explained, "I don't really understand why it had to be such a secret, but it's your father's life and he wants it that way. That must have been a terribly hard time for him and he simply doesn't want to be reminded of it. People often do that; they just bury their bad memories."

"The second Aunt Jean said it she looked horrified, she was so scared that I felt sorry for her. She kept saying how sorry *she* was, and begged me to promise not to tell, to forget that I'd heard it. And of course I promised." Emily turned away for a moment and then, turning back to Lynn, admitted with shame that she had broken the promise. "I held back as long as I could, but last week I told Dad."

"Oh, that was wrong, Emily."

"I know, and I feel bad about it. You asked about Dad being so angry at me, though, and—"

"And?" Lynn prodded.

"He was absolutely furious. I've never seen him like that. Mad, Mom! I couldn't believe it. He glared at me. 'That's no business of yours,' he told me, 'and I don't want the subject to be mentioned ever again. Is that clear?' It stunned me."

"I hope he won't take it out on poor Aunt Jean."

"I made him promise not to let her know I had told on her. So I guess it will be all right. I hope so."

Now Lynn wondered whether Jean had said anything more, anything about Robert's boy, for instance. There must be more pain in that loss than he had ever admitted; it was natural, then, that he would want to forget the boy's existence. And, worrying, she asked, "Is that all Jean said?"

"Two or three words, and clapped her hand over her mouth. I told you." Emily frowned in thought, and shook her head in doubt.

"Don't you ever feel strange about it? If I were you—I mean, you might be passing each other on the street, and not know."

"Hardly likely. This is a big country. Besides, why should we know each other, in the circumstances? It's far better that we don't. Most times a divorce is a closed chapter—understandably."

"But aren't you even the least bit curious? I know I would be."

"You don't know. One doesn't know how to act in a situation, or how to feel, until it happens."

No, I never would have wanted to connect in any way with Robert's glamor girl, Lynn thought, as always with a slight bitterness, but this morning with an extra bitterness. She remembered when she had first known Robert, raw little girl that she had been, an innocent so unsure of herself, how she had flinched at the thought of Robert making love to her predecessor, so rich, so beautiful and careless, that she could afford to toss such a man away.

It was strange to be having these thoughts at the kitchen table this morning, on this particular morning.

Nervously, Emily played with a spoon. "All the same," she said, "Dad can be very odd."

"He's not, Emily. I don't want you to say that or think it."

And suddenly the girl began to cry. "Oh, Mom, why am I afraid to say what I really want to say?"

Again fear, hot as fire, struck Lynn's heart.

"Emily darling, what is it?"

"Something happened to you last night."

"Yes, yes, of course it did. I fell in the dark, fell into the hedge." She laughed. "It was a mess, falling into the hedge. Clumsy."

"No," Emily said. The word seemed to choke in her throat. "No. Dad did it. I know it."

"What? What?" Lynn's hands clenched together in her lap so that her rings dug into the flesh. "That's ridiculous. However did you get such an idea? Emily, that's ridiculous," she repeated in a high, unnatural tone.

"One time before we moved here, once when you came home from Chicago, I remember, I heard Aunt Helen say something to Uncle Darwin about how awful you looked. She said she thought maybe—"

"Emily, I'm surprised. Really, I am. I'm sure you didn't hear right. But even if you did, I can't help what Aunt Helen may have dreamed up."

"You wouldn't have cried so last night if it were only the pain. It's got to be more than that."

"Only the pain! All those thorns? Well, maybe I'm a coward and a crybaby. Maybe I am, that's all."

Emily must not lose faith in her father. It's damaging forever. A woman remembers her father all her life. My own dearest memories are of my dad. He taught me how to stand up for my rights and how to forgive; when he had to scold he was gentle. . . .

Lynn quieted her hands, resting them on the tabletop, and made a firm appeal.

"Trust me, Emily. Have I ever lied to you?"

But disbelief remained in the girl's quivering lips. Two lines formed on her smooth forehead.

"He was so ferocious this morning."

"Darling, you keep using that nasty word. He was in a hurry to get to the office, I told you. He was distressed." She spoke rapidly. "Your father's such a good man! Need I tell you that, for heaven's sake? And you're so like him, a hard worker, determined to succeed, and you always do succeed. That's why you've been so close, you two. You've had such a special relationship. It hurts me to think you might lose it."

"Don't you think it hurts me too? But you have to admit Dad can be very strange."

"Strange? After all the caring, the loving attention he's given you all your life?"

"You don't convince me, Mom."

"I wish I could."

"I feel something. It's stuck inside my head. But I can understand why you're talking to me this way."

The kettle whistled, and Emily got up to turn it off. She moved with elegance, even in jeans and sneakers; her slender waist, rounding into the swell of her hips, was womanly, while her skin was as unflawed as a baby's. Suddenly it seemed to Lynn that she was being condescended to, as if the young girl, out of a superior wisdom, were consoling or patronizing the older woman. Her very stance as she turned her back to stack the dishwasher, the very flip of her ponytail, gave rise in her mother to resentment. And she said somewhat sharply, "I trust you'll keep these unbecoming thoughts to yourself. And keep them especially away from Annie. That's an order, Emily."

Emily spun around. "Do you really think I would hurt Annie any more than she's already hurt? Annie's a wreck. I don't think you realize it."

This stubborn persistence was too much like Robert's. Lynn was under attack. Arrows were flying. It was too much. Yet she replied with formal dignity. "You exaggerate. I'm well aware that Annie is going through a difficult stage. But Annie will be just fine."

"Not if Dad keeps picking on her about being fat," Emily said, and added a moment later, "I wish things seemed as simple as they used to seem."

Her forced smile was sad, and it affected Lynn, changing the earlier flash of resentment into pity.

"You're growing up," she said wistfully.

"I'm already grown, Mom."

Across the hall Annie was still pounding at the minuet. Suddenly, as if two hands had come down in full angry force, the melody broke off into a cacophony of shrill chords, as if the piano were making violent protest.

The two women frowned, and Emily said, "She hates the piano. She only does it because he makes her."

"It's for her own good. She'll be glad someday."

They gave each other a searching look that lasted until Emily broke the tension.

"I'm sorry I said anything this morning. Maybe this is only a mood that will wear away." From outside came the light tap of a horn. "That's Harris. I'm off." The girl leaned down and kissed her mother's cheek. "Don't worry about me. I won't make any trouble. Forget what I said. Maybe I don't know what I'm talking about. But take care of yourself, Mom. Just take care of yourself."

The kitchen was very still after Emily went out. Then the screen door slammed on the porch. The dog rose, shook itself, and followed Annie outside. In the silence a plaintive repetition sounded in Lynn's ears. *Dad can be very strange. Take care of yourself, Mom.* And as if in a trance she sat with her fingers clasped around the coffee cup, which had long grown cold.

She tried to concentrate on errands to be done, the house to be tidied and clothes to take to the cleaners, all the small ways in which living continues even when the worst things have happened, for if the pipes break on the day of the funeral, one still has to call the plumber. And yet she did not rise to do any of these things.

The doorbell brought her out of her lethargy. Expecting the delivery of some packages, she put her sunglasses back on; they were light and concealed very little, but the United Parcel man would probably not even look at her, and if he did look, wouldn't care. Barefooted, in her housecoat, she opened the door into the glare of revealing sunlight and faced Tom Lawrence.

"You forgot this," he said, holding out her purse, "so I thought I'd—" His eyes flickered over her and away.

"Oh, how stupid of me. How nice of you." Absurd words came out of her mouth. "I look a mess, I fell, sprained my ankle, and can't get a shoe on."

He was looking at the tubbed geraniums on the top step. That was decent of him. He had seen, and was embarrassed for her.

"Oh. A sorry end to a wonderful evening. Ankles turn so easily. It takes a few days to get back to normal. I hope you'll feel better."

She closed the door. Mortified, she thought, I wish I could dig a hole and crawl into it. What can he be thinking! I never want to see him again. Never.

After a while, with main effort, she recovered. Alone in the house, she could admonish herself out loud.

"What are you doing, not dressed at eleven o'clock? Get moving, Lynn."

So, slowly and painfully, she limped through the house doing small, unimportant chores, raised or lowered shades according to need, wrote a check at the desk, and threw out faded flowers, allowing these ordinary acts to soothe her spirit as best they could.

Presently she went into the kitchen. For her it had always been the heart of the house, her special place. Here she could concentrate a troubled mind on a difficult new recipe, here feel the good weight of copper-bottom pots in her hands, and here feel quietness.

A lamb stew simmered, filling the room with the smell of rosemary, and an apple pie had cooled on the counter when, late in the afternoon, she heard Robert's car enter the driveway.

Robert's mouth was as expressive as his eyes; she could always tell by it what was to come next. Now she saw with relief that his lips were upturned into a half smile.

"Everybody home?"

"The girls will be home in a minute. Emily went to the lake, and Annie's at a friend's house."

"And how are you? You're still limping. Wouldn't it feel better with a tight bandage?"

"It's all right as it is."

"Well, if you're sure." He hesitated. "If that's Emily"—for there came the sound of wheels on gravel—"I want to talk to her. To both of them. In the den."

"Can't it wait until after dinner? I have everything ready."

"I'd rather not wait," he answered, walking away.

She thought, He will take out his guilt over me in anger at them.

"Your father wants to see you both in the den," she told the girls when they came in. As they both grimaced, she admonished them. "Don't make faces. Listen to what he has to say."

Never let them sense any differences between their parents about discipline. That's a cardinal rule for their own good. Rule number one.

Now again her heart was beating so rapidly that she felt only a need to flee, yet she followed them to the den, where Robert stood behind his desk.

He began at once. "We need more order in this house. It's too slipshod. People come and go as they please without having even the decency to say where they're going or when they're coming back. They have no sense of time. Coming home at all hours as they please. You'd think this was a boardinghouse."

The poor children. What had they done that was so bad? This was absurd. And she thought again: It is his conscience. He has to turn the tables to put himself in the right.

"I want to know whenever and wherever you go to another house, Annie. I want to know with whom you are associating."

The child stared. "The other fathers aren't like you. You think this is the army, and you're the general."

It was an oddly sophisticated observation to come from the mouth of an eleven-year-old.

"I won't have your impudence, Annie."

Robert never raised his voice when he was angry. Yet there was more authority in his controlled anger than in another man's shouts; memory carried Lynn suddenly back to the office in St. Louis and the dreaded summons from Ferguson to be "reamed out"; she had never received that summons herself, but plenty of others had and never forgot it afterward.

"You'd better get hold of yourself, Annie. You're no baby anymore, and you're too fresh. Your schoolwork isn't good enough, and you're too fat. I've told you a hundred times, you ought to be ashamed of the way you look."

Gooseflesh rose on Lynn's cold arms, and she stood there hugging them. It was unbearable to be here, weakened as she was today, but still she stayed as if her presence, silent as she was, was some protection for her children, although she was certainly not protecting them against these words, and there was no need to guard them from anything else. Never, never had Robert, nor would he ever, raise a hand to his girls.

Her mind, straying, came back to the present. He had been saying something about Harris, calling him a "character." That nice boy. She could not hear Emily's murmured answer, but she plainly heard Robert's response.

"And I don't want to see him every time I walk into my home. I'm sick of looking at him. If I wanted a boy, I'd adopt one."

Annie, whose face had turned a wounded red, ran bawling to the door and flung it open so violently that it crashed against the wall.

"I hate everybody! I hate you, Dad!" she screamed. "I wish you would die."

With her head high, tears on her cheeks and looking straight ahead, Emily walked out.

In Robert's face Lynn saw the reflection of her own horror. But he was the first to lower his eyes.

"They needed what they got," he said. "They're not suffering."

"You think not?"

"They'll get over it. Call them back down to eat a proper dinner in the dining room."

"No, Robert. I'm going to bring their supper upstairs and leave them in peace. But yours is ready for you."

"You eat if you can. I have no appetite."

She went upstairs with plates for Emily and Annie, which they both refused. Sick at heart, she went back to the kitchen and put the good dinner away. Even the clink of the dishes was loud enough to make her wince. When it grew dark, she went outside and sat down on the steps with Juliet, who was the sole untroubled creature in that house. Long after the sky grew dark, she sat there, close to the gentle animal, as if to absorb some comfort from its gentleness. I am lost, she said to herself. An image came to her of someone fallen off a ship, alone on a raft in an empty sea.

And that was the end of Saturday.

On Sunday the house was still in mourning. In their rooms the girls were doing homework, or so they said when she knocked. Perhaps, poor children, they were just sitting in gloom, not doing much of anything. In the den Robert was bent over papers at the desk, with his open briefcase on the floor beside him. No one spoke. The separation was complete. And Lynn had a desolate need to talk, to be consoled. She thought of the people who loved her, and had loved her: her parents, both gone now, who would have forfeited their lives for her just as she would do for Emily and Annie; of Helen, who—and here she had to smile a bit rue-fully—would give a little scolding along with comfort; and then of Josie.

But to none of these would she or could she speak. Her father would have raged at Robert. And Helen would think, even if she might not say, "You remember, I never liked him, Lynn." And Josie would analyze. Her eyes would search and probe.

No. None of these. And she thought as always: Marriage is a magic circle that no outsider must enter, or the circle will never close again. Whatever is wrong must be solved within the circle.

She walked through the house and the yard doing useless make-work, as she had done the day before. In the living room she studied Robert's photo, but today the rather austere face told her nothing except that it was handsome and intelligent. In the yard the two new garden benches that he had ordered from a catalog stood near the fence. He was always finding ways to brighten the house, to make living more pleasant. He had hung thatched-roof birdhouses in secluded places, and one was already occupied by a family of wrens. He had bought a book of North American birds and was studying it with Annie, or trying to anyway, for the child's attention span was short. But he tried. So why, why was he—how, how could he—

The telephone rang in the kitchen, and she ran inside to answer it.

"Bruce went fishing yesterday," Josie reported, "and brought home enough for a regiment. He wants to do them on the outdoor grill. How about all of you coming over for lunch?"

Lynn lied quickly. "The girls are studying for exams, and Robert is working at his desk. I don't dare disturb him."

"Well, but they do need to eat," Josie said sensibly. "Let them come, eat, and run."

She was always sensible, Josie was. And at that moment this reasonableness of hers had its effect on Lynn, so that she said almost without thinking, "But I'll come by myself, if that's all right with you."

"Of course," said Josie.

Driving down Halsey Road through the estate section, and then through the town past the sportswear boutiques, the red-brick colonial movie, and the saddlery shop, all at Sunday-morning rest, she began to regret her hasty offer. Since she had no intention of confiding in Josie, she would have to make small talk, or at least Josie's version of small talk, which would involve the front page of *The New York Times*. Yet she did not go back, but drove through the little town and out to where the great estates had long ago been broken up, where new tract houses stood across from the pseudo-Elizabethan tract houses that had been put there in the twenties.

It was one of these that the Lehmans had bought, a little house with mock-oak beams and leaded glass windows. It was a rather cramped little house.

"He can afford better," Robert had remarked with some disdain.

And Lynn had answered innocently, "Josie told me they couldn't afford anything better because of her medical expenses."

Robert had exclaimed, "What? Well, that's undignified, to say the least, going all over the neighborhood telling people about one's business."

"She's not going all over the neighborhood. We're friends."

"Friends or not, the woman talks too much. I hope you don't learn bad habits from her." And then he had said, "Bruce is cheap. He thinks small. I saw that from the beginning."

But Bruce wasn't "cheap." Josie's sickness had cost a small fortune, and as Josie herself had said, who knew what was yet to come? It was she who hadn't let him spend more. He would have given the stars to her if he could.

He was in the backyard when she drove up, sanding a chest of drawers, concentrating with his glasses shoved up into his curly brown hair.

He summoned Lynn. "Come, look at my find. What a job! I picked it up at an antiques barn way past Litchfield last week. Must have twenty coats of paint on it. I have a hunch there's curly maple at the bottom. Well, we'll see."

His enthusiasm was appealing to her. His full lips were always slightly upturned, even in repose; she had the impression that he could sometimes hardly contain a secret inner happiness. A cleft in his chin gave sweetness to a face that, with its high cheekbones and jutting nose, might best be described as "rugged." A "man's man," you could say; but then she thought, a "man's man" is all the more a woman's man too.

"You've really been having a great time with your antiques since you moved east," she said.

When she moved from the shade into the glare he saw her face. For an instant his eyes widened before he bent back over his work and replied, as though he had seen nothing.

"Well, of course, New England's the place. You can't compare it with Missouri for early Americana. You'd think that the old villages had been combed through so long now that there'd be nothing left, but you'd be surprised. I even found a comb-back Windsor. It needs a lot of work, but I've got weekends, and with daylight saving I can squeeze in another hour when I get back from the city. Where's Robert? Still working, I think Josie said?"

"Yes, as usual, he's at his desk with a pile of papers," she replied, sounding casual.

"I admire his energy. To say nothing of his headful of ideas. There's no stopping him." Smiling, Bruce turned back to the sander. "As for me, I'm driving my wife crazy with this stuff. She doesn't care about antiques."

"She cares about you, and that's what matters," Lynn told him, and went inside conscious of having blurted out something too serious for the time and place.

Josie was on the sun porch with the paper and a cup of tea. She looks thin, Lynn thought, thinner since I last saw her a week ago. Still, her bright expression of welcome and her strong voice were the same as always. The body had betrayed the spirit. And this thought, coming upon her own agitation, almost brought tears to Lynn.

"Why, whatever's happened to you?" Josie cried, letting the paper slide to the floor. "Your face! Your legs!"

"Nothing much. I slipped and fell. Clumsy."

"Is that why you've been crying?"

"That, and a silly mood. Forget it."

"It would be sillier to forget it. You came for a reason."

Lynn tucked her long cotton skirt over her spotted legs. "I fell into the hawthorn hedge in the dark."

"So it hurts. But what about the mood?"

"Oh, it's just been a bad day. The house is in turmoil, perhaps because they got upset over me. And we just don't seem to know sometimes how to handle the girls. Although it will straighten out, I'm sure. When you called, I suppose at that moment I needed a shoulder to cry on, but now that I'm here, I know I shouldn't have come."

Josie regarded her from head to foot. "Yes, you should have come. Let me get you a cup of tea, and then you can tell me what's on your mind. Or not tell me, as you please." She went quickly to the door and turning, added, "I hope you will tell me."

"We don't seem to know how to handle the girls," Lynn repeated. "But you know our problems already. I needn't tell you that Robert doesn't approve of Emily's boyfriend. And Annie won't try to lose weight, she stuffs herself, and Robert can't stand that."

She stopped, thinking again, I shouldn't have come here to dump all this on her. She looks so tired, I'm tired myself, and nothing will come of all these prattling half-truths, anyway.

"I do know all that," Josie said. "But I don't think you're telling me the whole story," she added, somewhat sternly.

Like my sister, Lynn thought, she can be stern and soft at the same time, which is curious. I never could be.

"They're good girls—"

"I know that too."

"Maybe I'm making a mountain out of a molehill. These are hard times in which to rear children. I'm sure lots of families have problems worse than ours. Yes, I am making too much of it," Lynn finished, apologizing.

"I don't think you are."

There was a silence in which Lynn struggled first with words that were reluctant to be said, and finally with words that struggled equally hard to be released.

"Yesterday Robert was furious because Emily came home too late."

"Do you think she did?"

"Yes, only I wouldn't have been so angry about it. And Annie, you know she wants to have her hair straightened and Robert says that's ridiculous, and there is always something going on between Robert and Annie, although he does try hard. Yesterday she screamed at him. She was hysterical, almost. She hates everybody. She hates him." And Lynn, ceasing, gave Josie an imploring look.

"Tell me, is it only Robert who is having this trouble with the girls? Just Robert?"

"Well, yes. It's hard for a man to come home from a trying day and have to cope with children, when what he needs most is rest. Especially a man with Robert's responsibilities."

"We all have our responsibilities," Josie said dryly.

For a moment neither woman said more. It was as if they had reached an impasse. Lynn shifted uncomfortably in the chair. When Josie spoke again, she was careful to look away from Lynn and down at her own fingernails, saying with unusual softness, "Isn't there anything more?"

Lynn drew back in alarm. "Why, no. What should there be?"

"I only asked," said Josie.

And suddenly Lynn began to cry. Muffled broken phrases came through her tears.

"It wasn't just the children this time. It was because of me—at Tom Lawrence's house—it was too late, and Robert came—and I was dancing —Robert was angry, really so awfully—of course I knew I shouldn't have been dancing, but—"

"Now, wait. Let me get this straight. You were dancing with Tom, and Robert—"

"He was furious," sobbed Lynn, wiping her eyes.

"What the hell was wrong with dancing? You weren't in bed with the man. What do you mean, you shouldn't have been? I've never heard anything so ridiculous," Josie said hotly. She paused, frowned as if considering the situation, and then spoke more quietly. "And so you went home and had an argument near the thorn hedge and—"

Lynn put up her hand as if to stop traffic. "No, no, it wasn't—" she began. For a red warning had flashed in her head. Robert is Bruce's superior in the firm. It won't do, no matter how much I care about Bruce and Josie, for me to undermine Robert at his work. I've said too much already. Stupid. Stupid.

It was just then that Bruce came into the room.

"I'm taking time out. You don't mind, Boss?" he began, and stopped abruptly. "Am I interrupting anything? You two look so sober."

Lynn blinked away the moisture that had gathered again in her eyes. "I was spilling out some minor troubles, that's all."

Josie corrected her. "They are not minor, Lynn."

"I'll leave you both," Bruce said promptly.

But Lynn wanted him. It would have been inappropriate and subject to misinterpretation for her to tell him: Your presence helps me. You are so genuine. So she said only, "Please stay."

"You've told me, and since I would tell Bruce anyway after you left, he might as well hear it from me now." And as Lynn sat like a patient, listening miserably while a pair of doctors discussed her case, Josie repeated the brief, disjointed story.

Bruce had sat down in an easy chair. His legs rested on an ottoman, while his arms were folded comfortably behind his head. This informal posture, and his deliberate, considering manner of speech, were reassuring.

"So you had a row over the girls. Does it happen often?"

"Oh, no, not at all. Annie and Robert—"

Bruce put his hand up. "I don't think you should be talking to me about Robert," he said gently.

Lynn felt the rebuke. She ought to have remembered Bruce's sense of ethics. And she stood up, saying quickly, "I've really got to run home and see about lunch. We can talk another time."

"Wait," said Bruce. "Josie, do you agree with me that Lynn needs advice? You're much too close to her to give it, but don't you think somebody should?"

"Definitely."

"What's the name of that fellow you knew who went into counseling, Josie? You had such a high opinion of him, and he settled in Connecticut, I think."

"Ira Miller," Josie said promptly. "You'd like him, Lynn. I can get you the address from my alumni bulletin. I'll just run upstairs."

"I'm not sure I want to do this," Lynn told Bruce when they were alone.

"You have lovely girls," he said quietly. "Your little Annie is my special person. You know that. And if they're a problem or making trouble, you need to find out why, don't you?"

He was trying not to look at her face or her dreadful legs when he repeated the question. "Don't you?"

"I suppose so."

"You know so, Lynn."

"Yes." They were right. She had to talk to somebody. There was a volcano in her head, ready to erupt in outrage and grief. Relief must come. It must. And it was true that to a stranger she would be able to say what she could not say to these old friends: My husband did this to me.

"I called him for you," Josie reported. "I took the liberty of making an appointment for you tomorrow afternoon. He couldn't have been nicer. Here's the address."

As they walked Lynn to her car, Bruce said, "I hear your dinner was a big success."

"Goodness, how did you hear that?"

"Tom Lawrence. I met him yesterday morning jogging."

"Oh, dear, I suppose he told you how awful I looked when he came to the house to return my purse? I was still in my housecoat, and—"

"The only thing he told me was that you should do something with your talent, and I agree."

"It'll be about half an hour's drive tomorrow," Josie said. She smiled encouragement. "And that's even allowing time for getting lost."

"Good luck," Bruce called as Lynn drove away.

Robert, finding the reminder on Lynn's writing desk, demanded, "Dr. Miller, three o'clock. What kind of doctor is this?"

These were the first words he had spoken to her that Sunday, and she gave him a short answer. "What are you doing at my desk?"

"I was looking in your address book for a periodontist that somebody asked about."

"I don't look at things on your desk."

"I never said you shouldn't. I have no secrets." He strode to the large flattop on the other side of the room. "Come on. Look. Open any drawer you want."

"I don't want to open any drawer, Robert. All right, I'll tell you. Dr. Miller is a therapist. That's what we've come to."

"That's not necessary, Lynn." He spoke quietly. "You don't need it."

"But I do. And you need to go too. Will you?"

"Definitely not. We had a disagreement. What's so extraordinary? People have disagreements all the time and get over them. No doubt this is some bright idea of Josie's."

"It is not," she answered truthfully.

"Bruce's, then."

Hating to lie, she did not answer.

"I'm not spending money on this stuff, Lynn. I work too hard for it. Paying some stranger to listen to your troubles." His voice rose now, not in anger but in plaint. "I've never prevented you from buying anything you wanted, have I? Just look around at this house." His arm swept out over the leather chairs, the tawny rug, and the golden light on the lawn beyond the windows.

"Furniture isn't everything, or rings either," she responded, twisting the diamond on her finger.

"I should think you'd be ashamed to go and spill out your personal affairs. You're overreacting, you're over emotional. A man and wife have a nasty argument, and you behave as if the end of the world had come. No, I don't want you to go. Listen to me, Lynn—"

But she had already left the room.

In midafternoon the turnpike was an almost vacant path through a pastel landscape, pink cherry bloom, white apple bloom, and damp green leafage. The station wagon rolled along so easily that Lynn, turning off at the exit, found herself an hour too early for her appointment.

She drew up before a square house on a quiet street of developer's houses, all alike, except that this one possessed a wing with a separate entrance. A dirt bike propped against the wall of the garage and a glimpse of a jungle gym in the backyard were encouraging; the man would be experienced, and his words would not all come out of books.

Thinking it absurd to sit in the car for an hour, she rang the bell. A nondescript woman in a purple printed dress, who might have been either the doctor's wife or his mother, opened the door. No, the doctor was not in yet, but Lynn might come inside and wait.

The wait felt very, very long. Now that she had taken this great step, now that she was actually here, an anxious haste overcame her. Let me get this over with, it pleaded. As the minutes went by so slowly, so slowly, a faint fear began to crawl up from the pit of her stomach, to quicken her heart and lump itself in her throat. And she tried to stamp the fear out with reassurance: It is like waiting for your turn at the dentist's, that's all it is.

But this office was too small. There was no willing stranger to talk with or even to observe.

Her heart was racing now. She crossed the little room, took a couple of magazines, and was unable to read. Nothing made sense, neither the summer fashions nor the economic development of Eastern Europe. Nothing. She got up to examine the pictures on the wall, skillful portraits and pictures of places where the subjects of the portraits had been. Here they were posed on beaches, in ski clothes, and smiling under the iron arches of the Eiffel Tower. When she had seen all these, she sat down again with her heart still racing.

What was she to say to this unknown man? How to start? Perhaps he might ask why she had come to him. How, then, would she explain? Opening sentences formed and reformed silently on her lips. Well, on Saturday night there was a terrible scene. Cruel, bitter words were spoken, words that I had not dreamed could be said in our home, where we loved—love each other. But on the other hand, don't all children sometimes say that they hate their parents? So that it means nothing, really? Really? But Emily said that Robert . . . that Robert . . .

A husky middle-aged man appeared at the inner door. They matched, he and the woman in the purple print, so she must be his wife, Lynn thought absurdly, and was at the same instant aware that she was not thinking straight.

"Will you come in, please, Mrs. Ferguson?"

When she stood up, the walls whirled, and she had to grasp the back of the chair.

"I'm suddenly not feeling well, Doctor." The words came brokenly. "Maybe it's the flu or something. I don't know. I'm dizzy. It just came over me. If you'll excuse me, I'll come again. I'll pay for this visit. I'm sorry," she stammered.

The man's eyes, magnified by thick glasses, regarded her gravely. And

she was suddenly reminded of her bruises, the unsightly marks on which
scabs had not yet formed.

"I had—you can see—I had a little accident. I fell. We have a thorn
hedge, so pretty, but those thorns, like needles—"

"Oh? An accident?" He paused. "Well, you mustn't drive while you're
dizzy, you know. Please come in and rest in a comfortable chair until you
feel better."

Feeling forced to obey, she took her seat in a large leather chair, laid
her head back, and closed her eyes. She could hear papers rustling on the
desk, the opening and closing of a drawer, and the pounding of her blood
in her ears.

After a while a pleasant voice caused her to open her eyes.

"You don't have to talk if you don't want to."

"It does seem foolish to sit here and say nothing. Really, really, I think
I should go," she repeated, as if she were begging permission.

"If you like, of course. But I don't think you're coming down with the
flu."

"The dizziness is gone at least, so perhaps not."

"I am curious to know why you came here at all. Can you tell me that
much?"

"It's strange. I imagined you would ask me that."

"And did you imagine what your answer would be?"

"Josie—Josie Lehman said I should ask advice." She wiped her sweating palms on a handkerchief. "We don't, I mean, sometimes my husband
and I don't seem to handle the children, I mean we don't always agree.
We have a teenage daughter and a girl of eleven, she's very sensitive, too
fat, and my husband wants her to lose weight, and of course he's right,
and you see—well, this weekend there were, there were misunderstandings, a quarrel, you see, and Annie, she's the younger one, told Robert
she hated him, and I didn't quite know what to do."

And Emily said: Dad did it to you.

I can't, I can't say that.

Lynn's eyes filmed. Fiercely she wiped the damned humiliating tears
away. She had vowed not to cry.

"I'm sorry," she murmured.

"That's all right. Why not cry if you need to?"

"So. So that's what it is, you see. Maybe I'm exaggerating. Now that I
hear myself, I think I probably am. It's one of my faults. I get too emotional."

There were a few moments of silence until the pleasant voice addressed her again.

"You haven't told me anything about your husband."

"Oh, Robert, Robert is an unusual man. You don't often meet anyone like him, a Renaissance man, you might say. People do say. He has so many talents, everyone admires him, his scholarship and energy, he does so much good in the community and takes so much time with the children, their education, so much time—"

I hate you.

Dad did it to you.

"Yes?" said the voice, encouraging.

"I don't know what else to say. I—"

"You've told me what your husband does for the children and for the community, but not what he does for you."

"Well, he's very generous, very thoughtful and—" She stopped. It was impossible; she was not able to say it; she should not have come here.

"Is that all? Tell me, for instance, whether you are often angry at each other."

"Well, sometimes Robert gets angry, of course. I mean, people do, don't they? And often it's my fault—"

Nausea rose into her throat, and she was cold. On a blazing summer afternoon she felt gooseflesh on her arms. And she stood abruptly in a kind of panic, wanting only to flee.

"No, I can't say any more today. No, no, I'm not dizzy now, truly I'm not. I can drive. It's just a headache, a touch of fever. I am coming down with something after all. I *know* I am. But I'll come back," she said. "I surely will. I know I should."

Asking no more, the doctor stood and opened the door.

"I'll give you an appointment, Mrs. Ferguson. I'm going away for three weeks. When I come back, if you want to keep the appointment, I will be glad to talk to you. And in the meantime it would be a good idea to keep a daily record of everything you all do together. Write it down, the happy hours as well as the other kind. Then we'll talk. If you wish," he repeated. "Will you do that?"

"Yes, yes, I will. And thank you, thank you so much," she said.

Safely alone in the car, safely away from the measuring eyes behind the thick glasses, she felt at first a deep relief. But very gradually, as the distance between herself and those eyes increased, and the distance between herself and home diminished, she began to feel instead the heat of a cowardly shame, as if she had been caught in some dishonorable act, a harmful lie, a demeaning theft, or as if she had been found wandering demented through the streets in her underwear. Why, why, had she not told the whole truth? The man had known there was something else. He had seen right through her.

The after-work traffic was heavy, so it was past the dinner hour when she reached home to find Robert's car already in the garage. Ready for a confrontation, she steadied herself and walked into the house. Well, I did it, she would say, and I'll face right up to him. Yes, I'll say, I'm going again, and there's nothing you can do about it.

They were all still at table. Robert got up and pulled out Lynn's chair, Annie smiled, and Emily said, "I put your chicken casserole into the microwave and made a salad, Mom. I hope you weren't saving the casserole for anything. I didn't know."

"Saving it for all of you, dear. And thank you, Emily. You're as helpful as my right hand."

"Annie set the table," Emily said pointedly.

"If I had two right hands, then you'd be the other one, Annie."

The atmosphere was tranquil. One could always sense something as palpable as wind or temperature in a room where any strong emotions, healthy or otherwise, had stirred the air. Here, now, a breeze rippled the white silk curtains, Juliet dozed under the table, and three calm faces turned to Lynn. Can they all have forgotten? she asked herself incredulously. It was true that Robert's black moods could quickly, with the flip of a coin, turn golden. Also it was true that, when in his own golden mood, he knew how to charm a person whom he had just hurt and angered. Besides, the girls had the wonderful, forgetful resilience of youth. For that at least, she should be thankful. Still, it was astonishing to see them all sitting there like that.

Annie inquired, "Where were you so late, Mommy?"

"Oh, I had the usual errands and didn't look at my watch."

Unconsciously, Lynn glanced toward Robert, whose glance, above the rim of his cup, met hers. He put the cup down, and she looked away.

"Aren't you going to tell Mom now?" asked Emily, addressing Robert.

At once alarmed, Lynn gave a little cry. "Tell Mom what? Has something happened?"

"Something very nice, I think," Emily said.

Robert, reaching into his jacket pocket, drew out a long envelope and, with a satisfied air, handed it to Lynn.

"Plane tickets," he told her.

"Kennedy to San Juan and transfer to St.—" she read. "Robert! What on earth?"

"Ten days in the Caribbean. We leave Saturday morning. That gives you a few days to get ready and to feel better. He wore a proud smile. "Now, what do you say to that?"

What I want to say, she thought, is: How dare you! What do you think I am? Instead, and only because the girls were present, she replied, "The girls can't miss school, Robert. I don't know what can be in your mind."

"They aren't going to miss school. This vacation is for you and me."

It was a cheap—no, an expensive—bribe. She could feel the heat in her cheeks. And still for the girls' sake, she said evenly, "It makes no sense. Who'll be in charge here? I'm not walking away and leaving a household to fend for itself."

"Of course not. That's all been taken care of. I've spent the whole day making arrangements. Eudora will sleep in while we're gone. The girls use the school bus, and if there's need to go anyplace, Eudora'll take them in her car or Bruce and Josie will, on the weekends. I talked to Bruce," Robert explained. "They'll be glad to take the girls to the town pool, and Bruce will drive Annie to her tennis lesson. I don't want her to miss it, and he doesn't mind."

Annie, who returned Bruce's love tenfold, now interjected a plea. "You know I like going with Uncle Bruce, Mommy. Please say yes, Mommy."

"So you see, it's all arranged. No problems. Nothing to do but pack a few clothes," Robert said positively.

Feeling trapped, Lynn pushed away from the table, saying only, "We'll talk about it later. I don't like having things sprung on me like this. Now, you have homework, girls. Leave the kitchen; I'll clean up by myself."

When she went upstairs, Robert followed. Once in their room, she turned on him.

"You think you can bribe me, don't you? It's unspeakable."

"Please. There's no bribe intended, only a cure. A cure for what ails us."

"It'll take more than ten days in the island paradise," she said sarcastically. "A whole lot more, to do that."

At the window she stood with her back to him. The view of trees and hill, always so restful to her soul, was melancholy now as the hill hid the lowering sun and shadowed the garden.

"The girls want us to go. You heard them."

Of course they do, she thought. It will be an adventure for them to lord it over the house with their parents away. Why not? And she thought, too, now with a twinge of unease, Emily will stay out too late with Harris.

Robert persisted. "I'm not worried about them, you know. Bruce and Josie are as dependable as you and I are."

Yes, she thought, when they can be useful, you will use the Lehmans, even though you don't like them. Still she said nothing, only, for some unconscious reason, turned up her palms, on which tiny dark-red scabs like polka dots had begun to form.

"I don't want to go," she said abruptly.

"You saw that man today," he said.

"I did," she retorted, "and what of it?"

"I didn't believe you would. I'm completely shocked. I didn't think you really meant to."

"I meant to, Robert."

"And what did he—"

"Oh, no!" she cried. "You don't ask a question like that. Don't you know any better? Unless you will consent to go with me."

"If it will satisfy you," he said, seizing her words. "I don't believe we need anything except to get away together. But if it will satisfy you, I will do anything," he finished humbly.

And she stood there still staring at her hands.

"We're tired, both of us." He, whose speech was always so deliberate, now rushed and stumbled. "This last year or two has been hectic, there's been no rest, you and I have scarcely had an hour alone together. The new house for you, new office and work for me. New faces for me, new schools, friends, all these hard adjustments—"

In the face of his distress she felt triumphant, and yet something in her had to pity that distress.

"Listen. I know my temper's hot, but I don't lose it often, you have to admit. And I'm always sorry as hell afterward. Not that that does much good, I know. But I'm not a bad sort, Lynn, and I love you."

From below came the sound of Annie's plodding minuet. Emily came bounding upstairs to answer her ringing phone. As if he had read Lynn's mind—as he almost always could—Robert said softly, "They need us, Lynn. Our children need us both. We can't punish them. Let's put this crazy business behind us. Please."

"Oh," she said with a heavy sigh.

He paced the room while again his words rushed.

"I was jealous, I was furious that night. The sight of you dancing with that man when I had been worried about you made me frantic. You looked so intimate together. I realize now how stupid it was of me. You're an innocent woman, you could never—" And he stopped while his eyes went bright with the start of tears. "Then you said there was something wrong with me."

"I was very, very angry, Robert, and I still am."

"All right. Angry or not, will you go? For the family's sake, will you go?" He laid the thick envelope on the dresser. "I was lucky to get these tickets. They're all booked up for honeymooners this time of year, but there was a cancellation. So you see, it was meant to be. Oh, Lynn, forgive me."

He was still standing there, with the tears still brilliant on his lashes, when without replying, she turned away.

Down the long road beside the marshes the plane sped, raised itself mightily into the bright air, and circled southward.

"Well, here we are," said Robert.

Lynn said nothing. Nothing was required. Resentment was still sore in her, burning like ill-digested food. Because of her wish to be finished with a hideous anger, to conceal from her children whatever could be concealed, she had been led and inveigled, tricked, into sitting where she now sat.

"You'll be glad you've gone," he said soothingly.

She turned the full force of her scorn upon him. "Glad? That'll be the day."

Robert, with a look of appeal, pursed his lips to caution: Shh. They were sitting three abreast. An old man, so hugely fat that his bulk hung over his seat into Robert's space, sat by the window. The aisle seat was Lynn's.

"Miserably cramped," Robert murmured. "First class was taken up, dammit."

Ignoring him, she took a book out of her carry-on and settled back. It had always been her way to "make the best" of things, and whether she liked to admit it to herself or not, there was, even in these circumstances, a certain anticipation of pleasure in the sight of palms and blue water. Having spent most of her life in the Midwest, she still found these a marvelous novelty; she had visited the lovely, lazy Caribbean islands only twice before. There's no point, she argued now, in wearing a hair shirt. I shall swim, I've brought three great books, and luckily for me, I'm thin enough so that I can afford to eat; I hope the food will be good. And I don't have to talk to Robert.

He mumbled again, "I'm going to try for first class going home. I can't tolerate this. It's worse than the subway."

When she did not comment, he made no further effort, and little more was said between them all the rest of the way.

From the balcony on the first morning, she looked out upon water and sky. There was no one in sight except for the beachboys, who were setting up a row of yellow umbrellas, and far out a little bobbing boat with a Roman-striped sail. I suppose, she thought idly, if one were to head straight east from here, one would land someplace in northern Africa.

"Why, you're up early," Robert said brightly. "You beat me this morning. Wonderful, isn't it?"

"Yes. I'm going for a walk on the beach."

"If you'll wait a minute, I'll go with you."

"Thank you, but I want to walk by myself."

"All right," he said agreeably.

The sun had not been up long, and the air was still cool. She walked easily on the firm sand at the water's edge, left the hotel's property behind, and continued along what seemed to be an unending stretch of beach edged by pine grove, beach grape, and clustered greenery nameless to her. Occasionally, she passed what must be the winter homes of American or British millionaires, low, gracious houses steeped in the shade of banyan and flamboyant trees.

Rounding an abrupt curve, she faced a grassy hill that blocked her path, steep as a ladder, with water on three sides. It would be a struggle to the top, but not daunted, she began the climb. Once there and breathless, she sat down to look about and gaze and was struck with the kind of wonder that fills the soul in some ancient, high cathedral.

No, not so. For here was a far greater splendor. Such blue! Almost green at the shore where the green hill was reflected, this water shaded into purest turquoise; then three quarters of the way to the horizon lay a broad band of cobalt so even as to have been drawn with a ruler. On the farthest outer edge the horizon was a thin, penciled line, above which there spread another blue, the calm, eternal blue of a sky without cloud.

The wind rushed and the tide in soporific rhythm splashed on the rocks below. Before her lay an immense dazzle, the mysterious power of brilliant light; so it had been for untold eons and would be for untold eons more, she thought, until the sun should burn itself out and the earth freeze. The thought was hardly original, but that made it no less awesome.

Lying back on the rough sweet grass, she looked up at the shimmering sky. All the transient things, the injustice, the hurt, the unfairness, what were they in the end that we should waste our lives on them? My God, how short life was!

Now came a flock of seabirds, racing from nowhere, turning and turning in their descent to skim the water and soar again upward. They were so joyous—could birds be joyous?—and she laughed at herself for thinking so and at her own pleasure in watching them. And her first thoughts returned with a thrill of sorrow, repeating: How short life is. And we walk with blinders on.

For half an hour or maybe longer, she lay while the hilltop breeze cooled the sun's burning. Stretching, she felt how young and healthy her body was. Even her foot was beginning to ease, and the heat seemed to soothe her wounds. She felt a surge of strength, as if she had absorbed the power of the light, as if she possessed the power to do anything, to bear anything, to solve anything.

Then she lectured aloud. After all, Lynn, he didn't want, he didn't try, to hurt you. He's beside himself now with regret and guilt. This can go on forever, this rage of yours, if you allow it to. But it will corrode you if you do. Listen, he could have been eaten up with rage at you because of our tragedy, our Caroline. . . .

And she reflected, I shouldn't have stayed late at that damn-fool dinner. That's what began it all. I should not have let myself be lured into staying. What if I had been waiting at home for Robert and then found him having a careless good time with a pretty woman?

She remembered Tom Lawrence's cheek so close to her own, almost touching, his mischievous, clever eyes, bright like his hair and his fresh skin, and the cheerful effects of this brightness. *You have such sweet eyes, a sweet mouth, Lynn.* Flattery, all flattery, possibly with the hope that it might lead to something, and possibly not that at all. How was she to know? I know so little, she thought. Married at twenty and sheltered ever since, when and where could I have learned about the world?

No, she said then to herself, and sat up. Naïveté like that is inexcusable. I should have known better. I should at least have been smart enough to foresee consequences. My husband has a temper, that shouldn't be news to me. . . .

Our children need us, he'd said. It's true, she thought now, he is never too tired or busy to do something for them. Waiting in Washington between planes, he hails a taxi to the National Gallery of Art. *We can show them a good many pictures in ninety minutes,* he says, imbuing us all with his energy. He gets out of the hammock where he has been resting and runs into the house to fetch the encyclopedia because he wants to make sure he has given his daughter the best answer to her question. He sits up all night with Annie when she has her tonsils out.

He could also be harsh with them, and too demanding. Yes, yes, I know. But they were quite fine the last two days before we came here. Regardless of everything, they do love him. People say things they don't really mean.

Our children need us. They need us both.

There's nothing that can't be worked out by applying some simple common sense.

Back in the room, a note lay on a table next to a book. The note said, *Gone to breakfast. I'll be in the dining room or else on the beach.* The book was opened to a poem, a poem that Lynn did not need to read because she almost knew it by heart. Nevertheless, she read it again.

> *"O fierce and shy, Your glance so piercing-true*
> *Shot fire to the struck heart that was as tinder—*
> *The fire of your still loveliness, the tender*
> *High fortitude of the spirit shining through.*
> *And the world was young. O—"*

She laid the book down and shivered. He had given these poems to her when they were first married, and they had often read them together; sometimes he had read aloud in his grave, expressive voice; they had been so madly in love.

> *"The high fortitude of the spirit shining through.*
> *And the world was young—"*

"Oh, Robert," she said.

She found him reading on the beach. At her approach he looked up, questioning.

"I've come to bury the hatchet," she told him shyly.

Two poor tears sprang into the corners of his eyes, and he took her hand into his and held it. It seemed to her that a stream of common blood was running through their joined hands. She felt the pride and relief of calm forgiveness.

"You read the poem?" When she nodded, he cried anxiously, "Lynn, Lynn, you're everything in the world to me. Without you I'm nothing. You do know that, don't you? Are we all right again? Are we?"

"Let's not talk about it anymore. It's over."

"We can have our bad times, but at least they don't last. Right, darling?" He jumped up. "Well, as you say, enough. What shall we do first, now? Jog or swim?"

"Let's walk. There's something I want to show you, where I've been."

So they retraced her path between the incoming tide and the silver twisted branches of the sea grape, past the fine houses in their gardens, Robert speculating on the price of each.

"Hey! How far is this thing you want to show me? Aren't you tired yet? This is your second trip."

"No, I'm a walker, and it's worth ten trips. You'll see."

"You're as young as you ever were."

It was true. Her body in the scarlet swimsuit was as taut and limber as it had been when she was twenty. And rejoicing in this health, in the breezy morning and the decent peace she had made, she strode, ignoring her slight limp, up the hill.

They stood quite still at the top.

"I see what you mean," Robert whispered.

This time, though, there was a sign of life in view: a white yacht moving sedately on a line with the horizon.

"Look at that grand thing," he said. "Wouldn't you love to own it? We could go off to the South Seas, all around the world."

"No," she responded seriously, "even if we could afford it, which we likely never will, I wouldn't want it."

He shook his head as if she were beyond understanding.

"What do you want? Don't you ever want anything?"

Still very seriously, she told him, "Only peace and love, that's all. Peace and love."

"You have them. You shall have them." He dropped down on the grass. "Sit here. Let's stay a minute." When she complied, he turned serious too. "I know I'm not always easy to live with. I'm not home enough. I'm a workaholic. And you're very patient, I know that too. At the office and on the commuter train I hear stories that can make one's hair stand on end, about women having nervous breakdowns, drinking alone during the day, or else having an affair with a hairdresser." He laughed. "Imagine you having an affair! I think you'd flee in terror if a man were to lay a hand on you. And when I hear all this, don't think I fail to appreciate what you are, the time and effort you put in with the children, your solid health, your good cheer, everything. I should do more. I should take more upon myself."

"You do plenty. More than many fathers do. Much more," she said sincerely.

"No, I should do better. You don't play piano, so you can't help Annie with it. I was thinking she should switch to popular music. It will help her socially when she's a few years older." He sighed. "And I worry about Emily and that boy. I know you don't like to hear it, but—"

"Not now, Robert. It's too beautiful here to think of worries, even though I don't agree that Harris is a worry. Shall we go back?"

Half walking, half sliding, they descended the hill and trudged along the shoreline, their feet slapping through the wet sand.

For a time neither spoke, until Robert said, "Oh, I just want to say one thing more and then—you're right that this is no place or time for problems—but is Emily just being an average teenager, growing away as she's supposed to grow, or is there something else? Lately when we're together I've had the feeling that she's annoyed with me." And when Lynn did not reply at once, he said, sounding wistful, "I wish you'd be truthful if there's anything you know."

She hesitated. "She feels that you weren't always open with her and shut her out."

"Shut her out? From what?"

"Oh, things. Little things. For instance, she said—when she mentioned Querida a while ago you were furious. You shouted at her. You wouldn't tell her anything."

He protested. "Of course I wouldn't. Why does she need to know? That brilliant aunt of mine! It's a wonder she didn't let slip about the boy too. There'd be a hundred questions about that, wouldn't there? Well, my conscience is clear. I've done right by him, but he's no part of my life. The bank informs me that he lives in Europe. I don't even know in what country. I don't support him anymore. He's an adult. It's a complete separation. There's nothing unusual about that these days, with families dispersed over the globe." Stopping his agitated walk, he stood still, looking out over the water. "Why are we talking about this foolishness, anyway?"

"You asked about Emily."

"Yes. Yes, I did. Well," he said, looking down at her with a troubled expression, "is there anything else?"

I've gone partway, and I might as well go all the way, she told herself. And fixing her eyes upon Robert, she said quietly, "She thinks you did that to me the other night."

He took a deep breath, and she saw how her words had struck him.

"And what did you say? Did you—explain? Did you—"

She answered steadily, still with her eyes fixed on his. "I told her that was arrant nonsense. That I was astonished she could ever have such a thought."

Robert bowed his head. They were two people in pain. How odd, Lynn thought, to stand here in this streaming sunlight, with all this animated life around us, children on floats, people splashing into the waves, calling and laughing, while we have a dialogue so tragic, so profound. No one seeing them here could possibly guess. She pitied the man who stood there with bowed head, and she touched his arm.

"Enough, Robert. I've had no breakfast, and I'm starved. Is there a place on the terrace where I might get a cup of coffee and a roll?"

His response was a grateful, a humble, smile. "Of course. I've explored the whole place and all its hidden corners. There's a hidden corner with umbrella tables in the shade near the pool. Let's go. And after that, a swim. And after that," he said, recovering, "there's a fishing trip scheduled for this afternoon, a short one to an out island in a catamaran. Or we might sign up tomorrow for an all-day trip with snorkeling and a picnic lunch on one of the farther islands. Or would you like a water-ski lesson? I looked over the schedule this morning."

She had to smile. It was so like Robert to organize, to account for every minute.

"Swim first, then take the others as they come. Remember, you said we needed to relax."

"Right. Right you are."

Later in the afternoon they came back laughing at themselves after their first lesson on water skis, and took seats in the shade near the pool. Little groups of young couples were chatting at surrounding tables.

"Honeymooners, most of them," Robert observed. "You could be a bride yourself. You don't look any different from them."

"Brides are older these days."

"You're turning just faintly brown," he remarked.

"In spite of sunblock and a shady hat? I'll go home looking like a lobster. Ah, well, since that's the case, I might as well be fat too. I'll have ice cream."

She was aware as she ate that he was watching her, as if he were enjoying her enjoyment. She finished the ice cream with a feeling of satisfaction, thinking, How physical we are! The taste buds are satisfied, the stomach is filled, the air is fresh, not too hot and not too cool, and somehow all our troubles vanish—for a while, anyway.

A lizard, green as a gem, slid along a wall. Blackbirds stalked among the tables picking up fallen crumbs. A tiny yellow bird alighted on the table, paused on the edge, and then, on its frail, twiggy legs, hopped to the ice cream dish where lay a small, melted puddle. Totally still, Lynn sat watching the little beak thrust and thrust again; with the other part of her vision she was still aware of Robert watching her with the same affectionate concentration that she was giving to the bird.

"It's adorable," she said. "That little brain can't be any bigger than half a pea."

"It's you who are adorable," he told her.

An elderly couple sitting at the next table overheard him, for the man, catching Robert's eye, smiled and nodded.

"We were watching you two on water skis," he said with a heavy German accent.

"Oh, we were both awful," Robert answered. "It was our first time."

"So you were very brave, then. My wife and I"—he raised gray eyebrows in an expression of mock sorrow—"we are too old to learn new things."

And so a conversation began. Introductions were made, and brief biographical sketches drawn. The Hummels were from Stuttgart; he was a banker, semiretired, but only semi; they did a good deal of traveling, mostly in Eastern Europe of late, where so many astonishing changes were occurring. This trip, their first to the Caribbean, was purely for pleasure, to celebrate their fiftieth wedding anniversary. Later, at home, there would be a party with family and friends, but first they wanted this time alone.

"And is today the day?" asked Robert.

"Today is the day," Herr Hummel acknowledged, and his wife, a portly woman with beautiful upswept white hair and no devices behind which to hide her age, nodded and smiled.

"It's so lovely here," she said. "Usually we go to the Riviera for sun, but it is nothing like this. All these strange, wonderful flowers—" And she waved toward a clump of shrubbery that bore in clusters what looked like red beads, each the size of a pinhead. "What do you call those?"

"Ixora," Robert answered.

"Ah, you study flowers," said Mrs. Hummel.

"Not really." Robert laughed. "I just happened to pass some on my way to breakfast this morning and saw a marker with the name."

"He remembers everything," said Lynn.

"So you have," Mr. Hummel remarked, "a memory like—what is the word? Like a camera, you know."

"A photographic memory," Lynn said. "Yes, he has."

"Perhaps," said Mr. Hummel, "you will tell me if I go too far, intrude on your time, but perhaps you will have a drink of champagne with us tonight? It is tomorrow we leave. Perhaps you will have dinner with us, a table for four?"

"Why, that would be very nice," Robert answered cordially.

When they were alone, Lynn was curious. "Why did you say yes to dinner with them?"

"Well, he's a banker with connections in the new republics. It never hurts to pick up information and connections wherever you can. Besides, they're nice people, and you can see they're feeling a little bit lonesome."

She was amused. Even away on vacation his mind was with General American Appliance.

"It's dress up tonight," he said. "I read it on the bulletin in the lobby. Dancing and entertainment."

"Limbo and calypso, I'm sure. Funny, I keep loving calypso no matter how often I hear it."

"That dress is perfect, well worth the money."

White silk was even whiter and pearls more luminous against sun-tinged skin. She was pleased with herself.

"Where's the bracelet?" Robert asked.

"Which one?" she replied, knowing which one he meant because he always asked about it.

"The cabochons. The good one."

"It's much too valuable to take traveling," she told him.

It was indeed a special piece, always remarked upon whenever she wore it, and yet she wore it only when he reminded her to. It made her remember the sinking despair of that bleak windy night on the bench overlooking Lake Michigan. It wasn't healthy to relive a night like that one.

The Hummels had reserved a table near the dining-room balcony overlooking the sea. Champagne was already in a cooler. They were beaming, he in a summer dinner jacket and she in light blue chiffon, rather too fancy. A pair of solid burghers, Lynn thought, and felt kindly disposed to them. Fifty years married!

"It is so nice to be with young people for our little celebration," said Mrs. Hummel. "You must tell us more about yourselves. You have babies at home?"

"Not babies," Lynn answered. "Not babies. A daughter of seventeen and an eleven-year-old."

"My goodness, we have grandchildren older. A boy twenty-seven. He works in Franz's bank," she added proudly.

The conversation now divided, Mrs. Hummel describing to Lynn every member of her large family, while the men, led by Robert, pursued a different direction. With half an ear Lynn, who was hardly interested in the Hummel grandchildren, was able to hear some of the men's talk.

"I'm starting a course in Hungarian," Robert said. "I don't know where I'll get the time, but I'll have to make the time."

"A man of your type makes the time. I know your type."

"Thank you, but it's a difficult language. An Ugric language, related to Finnish, I'm told. I decided to start with it because, by comparison, Hungary is already somewhat prosperous. My firm deals in home appliances, as you know, and as the country gets richer, the demand will grow."

"Have you been in Hungary yet?"

"No, I want to prepare a team for Russia, Poland, and the whole area before I talk to the top brass—the president, that is. I've got to get a better handle on the languages, though. It makes an impression if you can show your contacts that you're at least making the effort to learn their language."

"You're right. It's true that not everybody speaks English. People seem to think that everybody does."

"—often think boys are easier to bring up," Mrs. Hummel was saying. "I suppose your husband would love to have a boy."

"I guess he would, but two are enough, and he adores our girls."

"Actually, I'm in marketing, but one needs to broaden one's scope. I have to know what they're doing in product development if I'm to do a competent job in marketing, don't I?"

"Ya, ya. Technology changes by the hour. You give me your card, I'll give me mine, and if I can be of any help, who knows, we may work some good things out together. No?"

"I'd be delighted. Now I think we're neglecting your great occasion. I'm going to order another bottle, and we're going to drink to the next fifty years."

"Your husband is a very ambitious, very intelligent young man, Mrs. Ferguson," Mr. Hummel told Lynn.

"It's heartwarming," Mrs. Hummel said, "to see a couple still young and beautiful together. All these discontented couples, I never understand, so many of them. Franz and I are seventy-three. I'm seven months older, but we never tell anybody." All four laughed, and Lynn said politely, "Neither one of you looks his age."

"Really?" Mrs. Hummel was gratified. "If it's so, it's because we have been so happy with each other. My mother always told me—there is a *sprichwort*—a saying, about not going to sleep angry."

"Never let the sun go down on your anger," Lynn said. "My mother told me that too."

"Ah, yes. And it works, it really does."

"Interesting types," Robert said when they got up to dance.

"Rather out of fashion these days in this world."

"Well, if they are, it's too bad about this world."

They were in the open courtyard. When the music paused, one heard the swish of the waves, hushed now at low tide. Into the perfumed night the music blended. "Smoke Gets in Your Eyes" and "Always and Always" they played.

It might be corny, Lynn said to herself, and yet the music is as lovely as the day it was written before I was born. And it still appeals to a longing that doesn't die, no matter what the style or the generation and whether people admit it or not.

"Do I dance as well as Tom Lawrence does?" Robert whispered.

She drew back and reproached him. "For someone who can be so tactful when he wants to be, I'm surprised at you."

"I'm sorry. It was meant to be funny, and it wasn't at all. I'm sorry." He kissed her ear and held her more closely. "Forgive me."

Passing the Hummels, who were dancing stiffly apart, the two couples smiled at each other.

"Never let the sun go down on your anger," Robert murmured. "We're going to remember that."

Yes. Yes. A whole fresh start. The champagne is going to my head. Such a lovely feeling. And above Robert's shoulder the sky was suddenly filled with blinking stars.

"Are there more stars here? Is that possible, Robert? Or am I drunk?"

"You may be drunk, but it does seem as if there are more because there's no pollution, and the sky is clear. Anyway, the constellations are different here. We're close to the equator."

"You know so much," she whispered.

And she looked around at the men moving to the music in slow circles. Not one could compare with Robert, so distinguished, so admired, so full of knowledge, with such marvelous eyes, now gazing into hers with that long, long look. *"I can't help falling in love with you."* Their bodies moved to the nostalgia and the yearning, were led by it, slowly, closer and closer; as one body, they were barely moving, swaying together in one spot.

"I can't help falling in love with you," he sang into her ear. And she thought: I was so angry that I wished he would die. Oh, God, oh, God, and overcome with tears, she reached up to his mouth, and there on the dance floor, kissed him over and over.

"Oh, my dear, my dearest."

"Let's get out of here," he whispered. "Say good-night to those people and get out of here. Quick, I can't wait."

In the room he slammed and fastened the door, crying, "Hurry, hurry!"

"I am. Don't tear my dress."

"I'll buy you another one."

He seized her and carried her to the wide, cool bed. Palms rattled at the window and the sea wind blew all through the first time and the second, and then all night, long after they had fallen asleep.

They swam and went deep-sea fishing, then played tennis, took long runs on the beach, and lay resting in the shade. Others went to the free-port shops and returned with the usual bags of liquor and perfume, but Lynn and Robert went no farther than a sailboat could carry them. After the Hummels departed, they were always, by tacit agreement only, together.

In the mornings when the first tree frogs began to peep, they made love again.

"No work, no errands, no telephone, no clock, no kids," he whispered.

It was delicious, unhurried luxury. It was like being remade, like being married all over again. Robert had been right. This was what they had needed.

Part Three

◇

Summer 1988– Spring 1989

3

NO one was home when they arrived except Juliet, who gave them a tongue-licking welcome and then turned over to have her belly scratched.

"Where is everybody?" Lynn wondered.

"Maybe there's a note on the bulletin board in the kitchen."

She opened the kitchen door, stood a second in total bewilderment, and gasped.

"Oh, my God! What have you done?"

Robert came in grinning. "Like it? Like it?"

"How on earth did you ever do this?"

"It was easy. Just paid an arm and a leg for their guarantee to finish it in ten days, that's all."

A glistening new kitchen had been installed with a restaurant-sized stove, a double-sized refrigerator-freezer, a trash compactor, and a center island above which hung the best new European cookware. Closets and glass-fronted cabinets had been expertly reorganized and consolidated; a library of cookbooks stood in vivid jackets on the shelves, and African violets in lavender bloom flourished on the broad new windowsills.

"I think I'm going to faint," Lynn said.

"Well, don't do that. You're supposed to produce good meals here, not faint."

"It's perfect. It's gorgeous, you're a magician, you're Santa Claus, you're an angel."

"A talented worker deserves a good workroom. I've done some thinking, and I truly realize what this means to you, so if you want to do some
sort of baking or catering on a small scale, if it will make you happy, why,
now you've got the place to do it in. And if not, well, you've got a
handsome kitchen, that's all."

"You couldn't, you absolutely couldn't, have given me anything more
wonderful."

She was hugging him when the front door opened to a chorus, "Welcome home!" and the girls, with Josie and Bruce and Harris, came in
with arms full.

"Chinese takeout," Emily said. "We didn't expect you to make dinner
in this palace the minute you got home."

"I came over every day to watch the miracle take shape," Josie said.

"Girls, I hope you didn't make any trouble for Uncle Bruce and Aunt
Josie," Robert said.

"We had a fine time," Bruce assured him. "We ate out, we ate at our
house, and last Sunday Harris took us to the woods and made a meal
from scratch. He started a fire without matches."

"Without matches," Lynn repeated, turning to Harris, who was actually blushing.

"Well, I was an Eagle Scout. You have to know how to survive in the
wilderness."

"The Connecticut wilderness?" asked Robert.

Josie corrected him. "It's the same thing whether you're here or in the
wilderness of Timbuktu."

Bruce laughed. "Timbuktu is not a wilderness, Josie."

"Harris," said Emily, "tell them about you-know-what at school."

"No, they're your parents, you tell them," Harris answered quietly.

"We both got an A in the advanced chemistry finals. The only ones in
the class."

Harris corrected her. "You got an A, and I got an A-minus."

Robert put his arm about his daughter's shoulder. "I'm so proud of
you, Emily."

Bruce spoke to Harris, who was standing a little apart. "You must be
coming close to a college decision. Have you any special place in mind?"

"Wherever I can get the best scholarship," the boy replied seriously.
"They're kind of scarce these days."

"Well, summer vacation's almost upon you, so just relax awhile and
leave those worries for September," Lynn said cheerfully. "And you
know what we're going to do? Next Sunday I'm going to inaugurate this

kitchen. I'm going to make a big supper. All of you come. Annie, bring a friend or two, and, Bruce, if your cousin should be in town by then, bring him along. We'll eat on the deck."

"It's been raining all week," Annie said, pouting.

"Well, all the better. That means we're due for a long spell of sunshine," Lynn told her.

A long spell, a lasting spell of sunshine in many ways, she assured herself.

It was as she had predicted, the proverbial day in June, cool and blue. All the previous afternoon and all morning she had been working and humming to herself in the new kitchen, and the result was a summer banquet, "fit for the gods," as Robert put it.

On the big round table in the kitchen's bay window stood a lobster ragout fragrant with herbs, crisp green peppers stuffed with tomatoes and goat cheese, warm French bread, a salad of raw vegetables in an icy bed of lettuce, a pear tart glazed with apricot jam, and a chocolate torte garnished with fresh raspberries and *crème anglaise*. In a pair of antique crystal carafes, bought by Robert, were red wine and white, while for Annie and her friend Lynn had set out a bowl of ginger-ale punch in which there floated a few balls of vanilla ice cream.

"If you'd like me to grill a couple of hamburgers outside for the little girls, I'd be glad to, Mrs. Ferguson," Harris offered.

She looked at him and laughed. "You're just too polite to tell me that those kids won't like the lobster ragout, and you're right. I should have thought of that myself."

Harris laughed back. What a nice boy, she thought, handing him a plate of raw hamburgers.

Bruce had brought his cousin, who was visiting from the Midwest. He was a quiet man, much like Bruce himself, who taught physics at a high school in Kansas City. Harris and Emily immediately got talking to him about physics and premeds. Annie and her friend were full of giggles over some private joke. It gladdened Lynn to see Annie having an intimate friend.

Bruce's cousin admired the view. "You have a beautiful place here," he told Robert, who sat across from him.

"It needs a lot of work yet. I'm thinking of putting a split-rail fence along the boundaries. And of course, we should have a pool. I want a naturalistic pool, not one of those ordinary rectangular affairs, but something free form with woodsy landscaping. It'll be a big job."

"I'm perfectly content with the pool at the club," Lynn reminded Robert.

"My wife is easily satisfied," Robert said.

"You always say that," Josie remarked.

And Robert remarked, "Well, it's true."

"There's nothing wrong with the pool at the club," Lynn insisted, out of a certain consideration for the feelings of the schoolteacher, whose income, one could be sure, did not provide either for a private pool or a country club membership, adding, "especially when the company pays for the club. Otherwise, I wouldn't even want that."

"Let's all help carry things back to the kitchen," Bruce suggested. "Having stuffed ourselves like this, we need the exercise."

Robert sprang up. "After that, how about badminton, or croquet? I've just set up a game on the side lawn, so take your choice."

When the table had been cleared, Lynn sat down to rest.

"Do you know the best thing about vacations, Josie? That they stay with you. Here I am, happy to be home, and yet a part of me is still down on the island. I can still feel that soft, damp air."

"I'm glad," said Josie.

"I can't thank you and Bruce enough for taking care of the girls."

"Don't be silly. We love them, and they were wonderful."

Juliet, having been unlawfully fed with hamburger scraps, came sniffing to Josie now in hopes of more.

"Yes, yes, you're a good dog," she said almost absently, while her hand played in the thick ruff of hair around the dog's neck. "A good dog," she repeated, and then suddenly she raised her hand to confront Lynn with what Lynn knew she had been meaning to say all the time. "So. You have an appointment with my friend, I think."

"I'm not going to keep it. I must call him."

"I think you should keep it," Josie said.

"Things change, Josie. Being away together, you get a different perspective. Robert's right. When we moved, we all had too many adjustments to make. It's been especially hard for the girls, unsettling, bad for the nerves, even though on the surface they handled it well. It's foolish to take every blow-up too seriously, as if the end had come. In this last week alone since we've been home, why—I can't tell you how good it's been. Robert's even been so nice to Harris. I convinced him that he shouldn't worry, that they're just kids having their first crush, and he finally agreed that I'm right, that Harris is a very fine person. And Robert's gotten the girls interested in the hospital fund drive, so they're selling tickets to everybody they know. They'll be calling you next, I'm sure."

"It's nice to hear all that, but I still think you ought to go, Lynn."

"I wouldn't know what to say to the man. I'd feel like a fool," Lynn said firmly. "No. I'm canceling the appointment. To tell the truth, I forgot about it or I would have done it already."

So she closed the subject. She regretted the day she had run to Josie and complained. She was a big girl, for heaven's sake, and would solve her own problems. She already had solved them.

June was a crowded month, a month of rituals. Annie had a birthday party complete with pink crepe-paper, pink icing, and a new pink dress. Friends had weddings and proud commencements. It was a time of graceful ceremonies, set about with flowers. And through these festive days Lynn moved with a fresh sense of well-being.

On a hot Saturday, the last in the month, Robert went to the city for a morning's work. Lynn, knowing that he would never alter his habits, agreed to meet him later in the afternoon at the club's pool. Arriving early, she found a chair in the shade and, glad of the privacy afforded by Annie's and Emily's occupation elsewhere, settled down to read until Robert should arrive. She was somewhat irritated, therefore, when she saw a man approach carrying a folding chair, and more than irritated when he turned out to be Tom Lawrence.

Lawrence was dressed for golf, wearing a light straw hat, which he now tipped to her, replaced, and removed again, this confusion giving her the impression that he was as discomfited as she was.

"In this heat you've got to be crazy to go out on the fairway," he complained. "I need to cool off in the shade. Do you mind?"

"Not at all."

He sat down, and she returned to her book with a finality intended to discourage any further conversation. For a few moments he waited, saying nothing, and then spoke.

"Actually, I was on my way out, when I caught a glimpse of you. I wanted to talk to you. I wanted to apologize."

She raised her eyes from the book and looked at him. The happy thought came to her that this time, unlike the last, she could face him confidently; she was wearing the scarlet swimsuit that had been so successful on the Caribbean beach; her body was unblemished and her face unmarked by having wept.

"What for?" she asked.

"I was to blame for making you late that night and making your husband furious."

"He wasn't furious," she said, resenting the man's intrusion.

"Oh, come." The tone was gentle. "He was furious. Everyone saw it."

"I can't help what everyone saw," she said coldly. "And it was none of their business, anyway." To her shame angry tears began to form, as they always did whenever her emotions, grieving or joyous, were stirred. Damn tears. She blinked them back, but not before he had seen.

He shook his head. "It's a pity for you to be unhappy."

She turned upon him then. "How can you talk to me this way? What do you know about me? I'm not unhappy. Not."

"You were miserable when I saw you the next morning. And I do know something about you. I know that your husband lays a heavy hand on you, and I don't mean just psychologically either."

She was appalled. She was totally shocked. She had a positively Victorian impulse to say something like "How dare you?" and then flounce off in seething indignation. But of course, that would be ridiculous. There were people sitting all around the pool who would notice. All this rushed through her head, and she said only, "I have never heard anyone talk so outrageously in all my life. You're making a fool of yourself too. You don't know what you're saying."

"But I do know. I used to do divorce work, and I've seen the signs too often to be mistaken."

Her heart was pounding. She pulled herself up into a haughty posture and said, making each word sharply distinct, "My husband happens to be a useful, respected citizen with a good name. He's a senior officer with one of the world's largest corporations, General American Appliance. Perhaps," she added sarcastically, "you have possibly heard of it?"

"Yes, I've been a stockholder for years. As a matter of fact, the president, Pete Monacco, is a friend of mine. He married my cousin. A sort of third cousin, I believe."

"Well, good for you. With connections like that you should know better than to cast aspersions on a man who does what Robert does, in this community alone. The hospital, AIDS, the new town library—" She was almost sputtering. "You ought to be ashamed of yourself!"

Lawrence was undaunted. "The one has nothing to do with the other. A man can be a distinguished citizen and still be violent toward his wife."

His voice and face were kind. He sat there, easily, cradling the straw hat on his knee. He might have been talking about something as trivial as the heat. But his words were blunt and hard as a hammer.

"You don't know how good Robert is, how totally devoted to his family. You don't understand."

For answer Tom simply shook his head. And this stubborn refusal to retract his words made her anger boil afresh.

"What's the matter with me? What kind of a fool am I? Why am I even *talking* like this to a stranger? Allowing you to say such things to me. It's degrading to us both. And I'll tell you something: If you're still around, we'll invite you to our fiftieth anniversary and dare you to come. Dare you."

He stood up. "I admire you for your defense, Lynn. I know your kind of woman. You have a vision of romance. 'Till death do us part,' no matter what. It's the 'no matter what' that's wrong. Otherwise I'm all in favor of fiftieth anniversaries, I assure you."

She got up and walked toward the pool. Only a dive into the water would silence this man.

"Romantic visions of everlasting love. That's what you're living by."

"Yes," she said over her shoulder, "yes, I believe in that. I live by it."

"Take care you don't die by it, Lynn."

Those were the last words she heard before the water splashed over her.

"You seem disturbed about something," Robert said, when, not long afterward, he joined her.

"This sickening heat is enough to disturb anybody."

Later he remarked, "I thought I saw Tom Lawrence leaving the club when I drove in."

"Yes, he was here."

"Did you talk to him?"

"A few words. Not much more than hello and good-bye."

Still later, at dinner, he said, "The company president is flying in on Monday to give a talk. He's some impressive guy. Powerful. It's easy to see how he got where he is. Funny how things change, though," he mused. "A generation ago nobody with an Italian name would have headed a company like ours."

"What's wrong with an Italian name?"

"It just didn't use to happen, that's all. Now it happens every day."

What made her say what she next said, Lynn could not have explained. "Tom Lawrence is related to him."

"How do you know that?"

"He told me so today."

"You must have had quite a talk with him, then," Robert said after a moment.

"Not at all. I told you that we said a few words. And he happened to mention Mr. Monacco."

Robert looked amused. "I don't mind that you talked to him, Lynn, since that's what you're thinking of. So he told you he's related to Monacco? That's odd. I had the impression that Lawrence was old American stock."

"It's his second cousin who's married to Monacco."

"Oh." Robert looked reflective. "I wish I had a connection like that, distant or not. Business is contacts, it's channels. I've got a head full of ideas, but how to get to the right ears with them? One department overlaps another—" With a small, self-deprecating frown he paused. "Too bad. I would have done differently if I had known about Lawrence. But I'll make up for it. We're certain to run into him again at the club."

Lynn was aghast. "You surely aren't going to ask for an introduction to Mr. Monacco, are you?"

"No, no, no. That's not the way things are done. You get acquainted with somebody, invite him to dinner, get talking, and after a while—after a while, who knows what can happen?"

What can happen, she repeated to herself, is too awful to think about.

Still she could not help but think about it. The unmitigated gall of that man! Who was he to play detective-psychologist, and to pry into the innermost heart of a stranger's life? She could only dread the next time she would have to see Tom Lawrence.

Indeed, she was so agitated for a week or more that she kept waking up in the middle of the night to relive the scene at the pool's edge. She felt actually ill. Her stomach churned. And suddenly, one morning as the kitchen warmed with the pungent smells of coffee and bacon, she had to run from the room.

"I can't stand the smell of food," she complained when she came back. "Even the sight of it makes me sick."

"That certainly doesn't sound like you." Robert looked at her thoughtfully. "I don't suppose you could possibly be—"

She stared at him. "Oh, no. What are you saying?"

"We had some pretty good times down on the island."

She was barely able to absorb the possibility. Why, Emily was already seventeen!

"Would it be awful if I were? Would you mind awfully?"

"Do I look as if I would mind?" He chuckled.

"Maybe I am a little late," she admitted. "But since I often am, it hasn't occurred to me that it could be anything."

"Don't look so terrified. We always wanted three, and would have had them if we hadn't lost Caroline." Robert kissed her cheek. "It may be nothing, but see a doctor tomorrow, anyway. Or this afternoon, if you can."

She went to the doctor, received an affirmative answer, and came home in a state of shock despite what Robert had said. Her head was full of troublesome possibilities. How would Annie take the news? And she'd heard that at Emily's stage of life, a mother's pregnancy could be a painful embarrassment.

But Robert held her close. "Darling, darling. I'm delighted." Back and forth, he strutted, across the bedroom. He laughed. "Maybe it will be a boy. Not that it wouldn't be wonderful either way, but it would be fun to have a boy for a change. This is absolutely the best news, Lynn. You'll have to postpone your business venture for a while, but I guess there couldn't be a better reason. And don't you worry about the girls. Annie will have a live toy, and Emily's a real woman. She'll be a help, you'll see. Let's go downstairs and tell them."

"Oh, let it wait, Robert, this is much too soon."

"Why wait? Come on," he insisted.

His delight overflowed and was contagious.

"Well, Annie, you've been wanting us to let Juliet have puppies, so will this do instead?" He swung the heavy child off the floor and hugged her. "Room for one more, hey, girls? Always room for one more and plenty of love left over."

"Wait till I tell people in school," said Annie. "I'll bet I'm the only one of my friends who'll be having a new baby."

"Not yet, dear," Lynn warned. "It's not till the end of February. I'll let you know when you can talk about it. And, Emily, are you sure you don't feel 'funny'?"

She was moved when, unknowingly, Emily repeated Robert's words about Caroline, the little sister whom she could barely remember. "There would have been three of us if Caroline hadn't died."

The little white coffin, the overwhelming scent of white roses, enough to make you faint, hushed words meant to comfort, and arms supporting her.

Now again it was as if all of them, husband and children, were rallying to support her. She felt a sudden strong sense of unity among them, and a surge of excitement, a physical vibration, went through her body. On all their faces she seemed to see a look of curiosity, of respect and tenderness. And it came to her that, in this roundabout way, she might possibly be making up to Robert, in part, for the child who through her fault had been lost.

"Let's drive over to tell Josie and Bruce," she said suddenly.

"No, no. This is private talk between women. You run to see Josie, since I see you're bursting to tell. Just don't stay too long."

Bruce was in the backyard putting the finishing touches on the chest of drawers.

"That's beautiful," Lynn said.

"I was right. It's curly maple." He shoved his glasses up into his hair and looked at her quizzically. "Josie didn't expect you, did she? She's got a late meeting at the office."

"No. I was passing nearby and remembered something. Not important. That's a beautiful piece," she repeated. "What are you going to do with it?"

"Darned if I know. Maybe keep it and give it to Emily someday when she gets married. She likes old things. Feel the wood." He guided her hand over the top of the chest. "I've been working two months on this. Feels like satin, doesn't it?"

She smiled. "Like satin."

He was so steady, so relaxed, working there near the shed in the cool of the late afternoon. She wondered what it would be like to live with a man who moved and spoke without haste. He never seemed to be *going* anywhere, but rather to be already *there,* and content to be there. She imagined that he must be a considerate lover.

"You look preoccupied," he said while his hand moved up and down with the waxing cloth.

"I am, somewhat."

"Nothing bad, I hope."

"Not at all." A smile, quite involuntary, spread across her face and quickly receded as she told herself: It is utterly selfish of me to bring this news with such pleasure when they have—at least I know Bruce has—always wanted children so badly.

He had seen the quick flash of her smile. "What is it? Tell me."

"I'm going to have—I'm pregnant."

His wide mouth opened and shut. He laid the cloth down. And because his face went blank, with no readable expression, she was puzzled and vaguely hurt.

"Aren't you going to say anything? Is it so startling that you can't?"

"Well, it is a bit of a surprise."

Naturally, he would be remembering the day when she had come here with tear-swollen eyes and a pathetic story of trouble at home. But that was past. This baby was testimony to the start of a new understanding, a whole new era. And she said lightly, almost frivolously, "Why? I'm not that old."

"That's not what I meant."

"Oh, that! That's old business. It's over, Bruce, completely healed."

"Josie and I only want you to be happy, Lynn."

"I am happy."

"Then let me congratulate you." He gave her a quick hug. "I'll tell Josie the minute she comes in."

When she got back into the car, he was still watching her with that first blank look on his face. And as the car moved away, she heard him call after her, "God bless you, Lynn."

Now came a time of bloom. Nausea went as abruptly as it came. She felt strong and able, animated by good health. Because it had been so unexpected and because she was older, this new life seemed more marvelous than any of the others had. When, after amniocentesis, the doctor asked her whether she wanted to know the sex of the baby, she declined. She wanted to have all the delights, the suspense, and the surprise.

Once Robert told her she looked "exalted." He had come upon her in a quiet moment listening to music, and she had laughed, making light of her own profound feeling.

"It's only hormones," she had answered.

In the garden, working through a drowsy noon, and in the beautiful new kitchen, she often sang. From time to time she had a recall of that almost mystical experience when, on the top of the cliff, she had stood looking out upon the silence of sea and sky.

For Josie and Bruce's anniversary Robert proposed taking them to the dinner dance at the country club. This suggestion surprised Lynn because it was always she who arranged their social times with the Lehmans, and she remarked upon it.

"Well," he replied, "they were so nice to the girls while we were away, so it's only right to do something for them in return. I don't like being indebted. Wear that white dress again," he said. "Maybe it was the dress that got me started on Robert junior one of those nights."

"You really do want it to be Robert junior, don't you?"

"Or Roberta, or Susie, or Mary, will be just as wonderful. Wear the bracelet, too, will you?"

"Of course." For the first time she clasped it on without any ugly memory. After all, it was stupid, it was almost superstitious, to let such memories persist. Chicago was long past. Her heart—or whatever it is that makes a person different from every other person on earth—was glad. And Robert owned it.

But she never entered the club without feeling a small dread of encountering Tom Lawrence. The very thought made her face burn. And for some inexplicable reason she had a premonition that tonight was to be the night.

So it was. They had just sat down when she saw him in the dining-room doorway. Unaccompanied, he hesitated as if he were looking for somebody. She could only hope that Robert would not catch sight of him, but of course, Robert was too alert to miss anything.

"I was standing there hoping I'd see somebody I know," Tom said when Robert hailed him. "My date had to leave town in a hurry, a family illness, and at the last minute I thought I'd come alone anyway. How are you all?"

His light, skeptical eyes roved around the table, skimmed past Lynn, who was doing her best to look indifferent, and came to rest on Bruce, who replied. "I can answer for Josie and myself. It's our anniversary and we are feeling absolutely great, thank you."

"Congratulations. How long?"

"Twenty years."

"That's marvelous. Nice to hear that in these days."

I wonder, Lynn thought, whether he is remembering my invitation to our fiftieth?

"Do you care to join us?" Robert asked. "Since you and Bruce are old friends, or I should say old jogging companions, at least."

"Yes, pull up a chair," Bruce said.

The evening was ruined at the outset. Unless she could contrive to keep her eyes down on her plate, she would be looking straight at Tom, who now sat across from her. And she was furious with him for foisting himself upon them; surely he knew what he must be doing to her.

When the three men took over the conversation, the two women subsided into listening. First came the usual generalities about the state of the economy; then almost imperceptibly, talk veered to the personal as Robert skillfully led it where he wanted it to go.

"I understand you're related to our boss, Bruce's and mine."

"Yes, we're good friends," acknowledged Lawrence. "I don't see him that often unless I happen to be in San Francisco or I'm invited to their Maine camp in the fall, which I generally am. They like to go for the foliage season. There isn't much of a foliage season in California, as we all know," he finished agreeably.

"I have to admire a man like Monacco," Robert said, "working his way up from the bottom to where he is today. These modern heroes amaze me, these men who create jobs, make the country strong, and let people live better. Heroes," he repeated.

No one contradicted him, and Robert continued, "I heard him speak in New York not long ago and was vastly impressed. He talked about what we're all concerned with, the future of the European community, especially the new eastern republics. I've been exploring a lot of ideas myself. The rapidity of change is astounding. Who could ever have predicted it?"

Lawrence said that no one could have, not to this extent, anyway.

"Establishing a company, a brand name, isn't going to be as easy as some think. We're talking about a huge, backward area with poor transportation, and it's all so fragmented. Czechoslovakia is different from Hungary, and they're both worlds removed from Romania. Worlds apart." And Robert made a wide gesture. "But I find it all fascinating, a history book in reverse, the future unfolding before your eyes. Fascinating."

Lawrence agreed that it was.

Lynn could only wonder about the thoughts that Tom must be having as he listened, with head politely inclined toward Robert. And Robert, all unaware of the other man's opinion of him, continued smoothly.

"I'm having fun with some ideas of my own. One thing I'm doing is studying Hungarian, and that's not the easiest language in the world."

"Where do you get the time?" asked Lawrence.

"It's not easy. I have to squeeze it in somehow, mostly on Saturday mornings."

"That's when I go jogging with your colleague here." Lawrence motioned toward Bruce. "We're out conditioning our flab, while you're in town conditioning your brain." He laughed.

Bruce defended Robert. "He watches his flab, too, as you can see. He watches everything. He's known for it in the firm."

Tom said, "You've got a fine name there yourself, Bruce. Monacco's aware of it. I told him you were my jogging partner, and he recognized your name, your good name."

"Thanks," Bruce said. "I like my work, but I also like to forget business over the weekend, stay home or go out into the country, picking up old furniture. Then I spend Sunday afternoon puttering around restoring it. I'm teaching myself to weave cane. Maybe I should have been a cabinetmaker. Who knows, I might end up being one when I retire."

"You can't be serious," Robert said.

For the first time Josie spoke. "He could be. I guess you still don't know Bruce that well."

Here we go again, Lynn thought. What is it about those two? Impatiently, she twisted in the uncomfortable chair while trying to avoid Tom Lawrence's eyes.

"Well, maybe I don't know Bruce." And Robert demanded of him, "Do you mean to say you'd leave one of the biggest firms in the world to become a cabinetmaker?"

"Probably not," Bruce replied mildly. "Just a thought. But there is something rewarding about working with your hands. I love the feel of old wood. It almost comes alive under your fingers." And he looked around the table with his wide, slow smile.

And Lynn thought, as always, So cheerful, never in a hurry, and still he gets things done.

"I have never been especially ambitious," Bruce said as if he were thinking aloud. "I just keep going step by step."

"For someone who's not especially ambitious, I should say you've come mighty far," Josie remarked, with the combination of affection and gentle rebuke that was so typical of her.

For answer Bruce took her hand, and they sat united, content with each other. He is thankful that she's here, Lynn knew. She's had four good years. If you can get through five, you're home free, they say.

When the dance band struck up, Bruce rose. "Excuse us. It's not the anniversary waltz, but it will do just the same."

Tom's eyes followed them. "I like them," he said simply.

Robert acknowledged the remark. "Yes. Salt of the earth."

"You two go and dance. Don't mind me." For the first time Tom addressed Lynn. "I always do seem to lack a partner, don't I?"

Compelled to make some reply, she gave him a faint smile. Then Robert said hastily, "Why don't you dance with Lynn? I want to make some inquiry about the cake I ordered for the Lehmans and check on the champagne."

"You're sure you don't mind?" asked Tom.

Asking Robert whether he minds, as though I were an object that can be borrowed or lent! She was hotly indignant.

"No, no. Go ahead," Robert said. And a second later she was on the dance floor with Tom Lawrence's arm around her waist.

"Why are you doing this?" The final word emerged with a hiss. "It's not even decent, what you're doing tonight."

"Why? I want to apologize, that's all."

"What? Not again?"

"Yes. I've been making too many bad mistakes involving you. When I left you at the pool that day, it didn't take me long—as a matter of fact, I was only halfway home—to realize that I had said some horrendous things. I've been hoping to meet you so that I could tell you I'm sorry. I hurt you. I interjected where I had no business to be."

"No, you didn't have any business."

"I am dreadfully, dreadfully sorry."

He drew far enough away so that he could look into her face, and she saw in his an expression of genuine contrition and concern. She thought wryly, I've had so many apologies these past months, Robert's and now this. And she wondered, too, whether it could be the body contact while dancing that made it easier for people to make these intimate revelations. Who would think now that these two people, strangers to each other, were saying such serious things to the tune of a society dance-band?

"In my work I seem to have acquired a kind of intuition. It works like a flash, and as a rule I find I can depend on it. But that's no excuse for using it. I must learn to keep my mouth shut even when I'm sure I'm right."

"But you were wrong that time. Your intuition failed you. Look at me," she commanded with a proud lift of her head. "How do I look to you?"

"Very, very lovely, Lynn."

"Robert treats me very, very well, Tom."

"Does he?"

"I'm going to have a baby."

The skeptical eyes looked straight into hers while two pairs of feet moved expertly, not missing a step. Then the music stopped and Tom released her.

"God bless you, Lynn," he said.

The blessing jolted her. It was what Bruce had given her when she had brought him the news, and it had seemed fitting on his lips. But on Tom Lawrence's it seemed ironic.

Nevertheless, the evening turned out not badly after all.

Bruce and Josie received their cake and their champagne toast. At Robert's request the band played "The Anniversary Waltz," Bruce kissed Josie, everyone applauded, and then they all went home.

"Very smooth, that Lawrence," Robert remarked on the way back.

"Does that mean you don't like him?"

"I can't make up my mind."

"That's unusual for you. You generally know right away what you think about people."

"Maybe that's a failing. Maybe I shouldn't be so sure of my judgment. Oh, he's sharp as a tack. Congenial, a thorough gentleman, but somehow I can't make up my mind what he thinks about me. I almost think he dislikes me. But that's absurd. Why should he? Oh, but that Bruce! He makes such an idiot of himself with his remarks about furniture when, if he were more attuned to what's going on, he should have seen that I was leading the conversation somewhere. I looked up Lawrence's law firm. They have offices in Brussels, London, and Geneva. You never know what might come of that. Besides, the connection with Pete Monacco is no bad thing. Good Lord, a man has to keep his eyes wide open! That's Bruce's failing. I saw it the first day he came to the St. Louis office. Remember when I came home and told you? A lightweight, I said. A nice guy who'll never get very far. Oh, he's done all right, but he's stuck where he is. Stuck."

"That's not what Tom Lawrence said. Remember? He said Bruce has a very good name in your firm."

"Fine. But I'm there on the spot and I think I should be a better judge than Lawrence is."

Jealous. Jealous of Tom because I was foolish that night, and of Bruce because he is a handsome man. He wants to be the only handsome man, I suppose. Lord, men can be such babies!

"All the same," Lynn said amusedly, "if I had a brother, I'd want him to be like Bruce."

"As long as you wouldn't want your husband to be like Bruce. Or like anyone else, including Tom Lawrence. Right, Mrs. Ferguson?"

"Right," she said.

Josie telephoned with thanks for the anniversary celebration.

"It was lovely, perfect. They even played our songs, our specials."

"That was Robert's doing. You know he never forgets anything."

They gossiped briefly, and then Josie said, "Tom Lawrence really admires you."

"How can you know that?"

"He told Bruce."

"Oh, he admires my cooking."

"No, you."

"Well, that's generous of him."

"He's a generous person."

"I didn't realize you knew him that well."

"I don't know him *that* well. He stops in for a cold drink or a hot drink after he's met Bruce on the track. I find him interesting. Hard to pin down, like quicksilver. But very decent, very honorable."

"How can you know if you say you don't know him well?" Lynn asked, wanting for some reason to argue the point.

"I just know. It's not important either way. I only wanted to pass on a compliment."

When the conversation ended and she hung up the phone, she sat for a moment or two staring into the mirror on the opposite wall. An odd little smile flickered over her lips.

A few weeks later Robert telephoned from the office at midday. He never called from the office, and she was startled.

"Is anything wrong?"

"Wrong? I should say not." There was glee in his voice. "In a million years you'd never guess. I got a call from California from the big boss. I almost fell off the chair."

"Not Monacco? He called you?"

"Himself. I can't imagine what Tom told him about me. He seems to have described me as some kind of genius, some sort of phenomenon. So, Monacco says he'd like to meet me and have a talk. We've been invited for the weekend to his place in Maine. His wife will call you."

Robert was chuckling; she knew that he was wearing an enormous smile and that his eyes would be brilliant with excitement.

"I haven't mentioned it to anyone here. It's a bad policy to seem boastful. Being casual about it is much the better way."

"Does that mean not to tell Josie?"

"Oh, they'll know. We'll have to ask them to keep an eye on the girls again, anyway, won't we? But, uh, keep it light, as if it's nothing much. It'd be nasty to rub this under Bruce's nose, since he wasn't invited. Now I'm beginning to get nervous. I do have some good ideas, it's true, but I hope the man won't be expecting so much from me that I'll fall flat on my face. Well, at least you'll be there to help charm him. I think you must have charmed Lawrence."

"Don't be silly."

Robert laughed. He was absolutely euphoric. "In a nice way, I meant."

"I didn't charm him, any way, nice or not. I danced with him once, at your behest, if you remember, and we hardly spoke."

"Okay, okay. Don't keep the phone tied up too long in case Mrs. Monacco should call."

When she hung up, her feelings were mixed. Of course this was a marvelous thing for Robert, an unprecedented summons to the man's home. Small wonder that he was ecstatic. She could only be glad for him, and she was glad. Yet at the same time she was slightly vexed and vaguely troubled.

She made excuses to avoid the country club, although she knew Robert liked to go there for dinner. But apparently Tom Lawrence also liked to go there. . . .

Robert urged her. "As new in the community as we are, it's important to keep being seen. Otherwise, people forget you're alive."

"Your name's all over this community, on practically every committee. They couldn't forget you if they wanted to," she told him.

"Speaking of remembering people, we really should show some appreciation to Tom Lawrence. Let's have him over for dinner one night. I mean, when have you heard of anyone's doing such an extraordinary favor for a man he scarcely knows? Of course I called him at once to thank him, and I mentioned that we'd like to have him come over soon."

"I will, but first I want to get a few things out of the way. That root canal's been bothering me, which means a few visits to the man in the city. And I want to get the baby's room finished, too, before I get so big that I won't want to go into the city. But I will," she promised.

It disturbed her to think of seeing Tom again; it was disturbing in itself that she should feel that way. She was a literal person, one who needed a clear explanation for everything, even for the workings of her own mind. So it was with some dismay that one afternoon not long afterward she encountered him on a New York street. Having done her errands, she was on the way to Grand Central Terminal and home. She had stopped in front of a small picture gallery, attracted by a painting of sheep on a hillside, as well as by the name above the entrance: Querida. An unusual name. The name of Robert's first wife. It gave her a small, unpleasant flutter. And then, turning away from the window, she had seen Tom Lawrence.

"What are you doing in the city?" he inquired, as though they were old friends who reported their doings to each other.

She replied casually, "I go to a dentist in the neighborhood. And today I bought nursery furniture."

"That must be a happy thing, although I wouldn't know, would I?"

Again, she had a sense of being brightly, although not disagreeably, scrutinized.

"You're looking wonderful. They tell me there are women who actually thrive on being pregnant. Are you buying pictures?"

"No, just admiring." And wanting to divert that scrutiny, she remarked, "These sheep are lovely."

"She does have nice things. I've priced some, and the prices are very fair, but she's a cranky kind of oddball. Are you on your way home? Yes? So am I. We'll go together. Are you walking or cabbing?"

"I always walk as much as I can when I'm in the city."

"Yes, it's wonderful this time of year. Everything seems to be waking up. And the shops! I can see why women go crazy in the shops."

Tweeds and silks, silver, mahogany, and burnished leather made a passing show of the windows as they walked down Madison Avenue. The most brilliant blue, as deep as cobalt, overhung the towers, and where distance disguised grime, the towers shone white.

"Am I going too fast for you?" Tom asked.

"No, I'm fine."

They were keeping an even pace. Always with Robert she had to hurry to keep up with his long strides, but then, she thought idly, Robert was half a head taller than this man.

"I never take the train home this early," Tom explained, "but I made myself take time off to do some shopping today." He went on making small talk. "My days are pretty long. I take the seven-thirty every morning, so I guess I'm entitled to treat myself now and then."

"Robert takes the six-thirty."

"He's a hard worker."

And suddenly she cut through the small talk, saying, "I must thank you for that incredible invitation to Maine. I know Robert's told you how much it means to him."

"Oh, that. It was all Pete's idea. He says there's never much time during his flying visits to New York, what with all the meetings and stuff, so Maine's a much better place to talk."

"I didn't mean Maine, specifically. I meant the whole business." She raised her eyes to Tom, inquiring directly, "Why did you do anything at all for Robert? Did he," she asked, not flinching, "did he by any chance ask you to?"

"Lord, no. Don't you know he wouldn't do that? But I knew he wanted something all the same."

Troubled, she went further. "Was he so obvious?"

"I suppose not really. I guess maybe it was my famous intuition that I told you about," Tom said rather mischievously.

"No, really. I'm serious. Because you don't like Robert."

"Robert's very smart, very competent, very diligent. I knew I wouldn't go wrong by recommending him."

"But Bruce wasn't invited."

"I didn't mention Bruce."

"Why not? You like him very much. You said so; I heard you."

"Ah, don't ask so many questions, lady!"

Embarrassed, she murmured only, "It was awfully good of you."

In the train Tom read the newspaper, and Lynn read her book, until the train had passed the dark brown tenements in the uptown reaches of the city, then the cheerful towns with their malls and parks, and crossed the Connecticut line. At that point he laid the paper aside and spoke.

"Lynn . . . I have another apology to make."

"Oh, no, not another! For what this time?"

"For that first night at my house. If your husband could have read my thoughts, which fortunately he couldn't, he'd have had a right to be furious." Tom paused. "The truth is, I was hoping that you and I'd get together. Oh, not that night," he amended quickly, "of course not. But I thought perhaps the next time."

She turned her face away toward the window to hide her exasperating blush. Naturally, it was flattering to be propositioned after all these years, to know that she could tempt someone else beside Robert. She supposed, though, that she ought to feel angry; whatever had made this man dare to think that she would be open to his proposition? And she felt guilty because she was not angry.

Rather mildly, she said, "But you knew I had Robert."

"I made a mistake. I misread you, which I don't usually do. Maybe it was the wine or the spring night or something. Anyway, a sexual attraction doesn't have to disrupt a man's or a woman's other life. Do I shock you?" For she had turned to him and saw now his rueful smile. "Yes, of course I do. You'd eat yourself alive with guilt if you ever—you'd say 'cheated.' Well, I respect that. Maybe someday you'll feel different about it."

"Never." She shook her head decisively. "Robert and I are permanent." She looked down at her little swollen belly and repeated, "Permanent."

Tom followed her glance. "I understand. And I've made my apology for my thoughts and intentions that night. I wanted to clear my own mind. So—" She remembered that he had that funny way of saying "so" when he changed the subject. "So. You'll have a good time in Maine. Pete and Lizzie are easygoing, not formal at all. Paper-plate people like me. And it's beautiful this time of year. Over near the New Hampshire line the mountains turn red and gold. I'll be sorry to miss it."

She was surprised. "You're not going?"

"No. I've too much on the fire at the office."

She was not sure whether she was sorry or glad that he would not be there.

Robert laid careful plans for the weekend. "We'll need a house gift, you know."

"Wine?" she suggested. "Or I'll find something suitable for the country, a rustic bowl for flowers or fruit or something like that."

"No, definitely not. That's banal. Besides, they already have their own wine and no doubt a couple of dozen bowls or whatnots too."

"Well, what then?"

"I'll tell you what. An enormous box of your best cookies. Those almond things, you know the ones, and the lemon squares, and some chocolate brownies. Everybody loves them. That will be just the right gesture, friendly, simple, and elegant. As for clothes: sweaters, naturally, and heavy shoes. They'll probably take us tramping through the woods. And raincoats, and don't forget an umbrella. Something silk for the two nights in case they dress for dinner."

"They won't dress for dinner up in the woods, and besides, I haven't a thing that fits anymore. I never did show this early, but I do show now."

He regarded her thoughtfully. "You look like a woman who needs to lose a little weight around the middle, that's all."

"That's just it. My things don't fit around the middle, and it's too early for maternity clothes."

"Well, buy something. For myself, tweed jackets, not new. A relaxed, used look." Robert unfolded his plans systematically. "We'll start the afternoon before and stay overnight on the road. Then we'll arrive rested and fresh before noon. And we'll take the station wagon. The Jaguar might look—I'm not sure, but it might look overdone. If the boss drives one, it certainly will. Yes, the station wagon."

In midmorning they arrived exactly as planned. A long log house set about with cleared fields lay on a rise above a small lake. At the side were two tennis courts. On a wide veranda looking down on a bathhouse and a dock was a row of Adirondack chairs. The driveway was a rutted dirt road with a worn, grassy circle for parking; half a dozen cars were already there, station wagons, plain American sedans, and not an import in sight.

Lynn looked at Robert and had to laugh. "Are you ever wrong?" she inquired.

"Ah, welcome, welcome," cried Pete Monacco, descending the steps. "How was the trip?" His voice boomed, his handshake was painful, and his smile showed square teeth that looked as granite hard as the rest of his large body. "Beautiful scenery here in the East. I wouldn't miss this for the world. California is home and we love it, but for color you've got to see New England. Just look out there! My wife, she's Lizzie and I'm Pete, we're all first-name folks when we're up here, has taken everybody sailing, but they'll be back for lunch. Here, let me give you a hand with the bags."

In their room Robert beamed. "I don't know what the hell that fellow Tom can have said about me. Call him 'Pete'! You wouldn't guess he's the same man as the one who flies in with an entourage like the President's, gives a talk that's part pep and part scolding, leaves his commands, shakes your hand in the reception line, and then flies back across the Mississippi. Well, here we are. Can you believe it?"

He looked around the sparsely furnished room. A rag rug covered the floor, the walls were pine, the bed had Indian blankets and a huge comforter folded at the foot. The only ornament was the view that was framed by the single window.

"There's a sailboat coming in," Lynn said.

Robert peered over her shoulder. "Pretty sight, isn't it? Yes, all you need is money. Well, and taste too," he conceded. "Knowing how to use it."

"We ought to go down and meet everybody," she said as Robert began to unpack.

"No. Tidy up first. It'll take five minutes, if that. Let's get a move on."

Hot coffee and doughnuts were being served on the veranda when they came downstairs. Lizzie Monacco, in jeans and a heavy sweater, shook hands.

"Excuse my freezing hands. There's a real wind out there. But it's great fun. Would you people like a ride around the lake this afternoon?" Like her husband she was voluble, with curly gray windblown hair and a candid expression. "My goodness, how young you are! Lynn, isn't it? You are the youngest female here, and we shall all feel like old hags next to you."

"No, no." Lynn smiled. "I have a daughter who'll be going to college next year."

"For goodness' sake, and you're pregnant too. I hope it's not a secret, but Tom told me, anyway. I hope you're feeling well, but if you're not, don't feel you have to keep up with our crazy pace. Just take a book and relax."

Robert answered for her. "Lynn's in good shape. She plays a great game of tennis too."

"You do? Good. We're all tennis freaks here. So maybe after lunch and a hike—there's a lookout place just down the lake where you can climb and see for miles, really splendid—maybe when we come back, we can play."

"This is what you love. Busy, busy, busy," Lynn murmured later to Robert.

"I know. It makes me feel like a kid. And the air, the pine smell. I feel great."

These men came from the company's top echelon, chiefly from Texas and points west of Texas. If there were any women in the top echelon, they weren't at this party; these women were all wives. They didn't, Lynn noted, wear the same anxious look that she had so often seen on the women at the country club, whose husbands were still on the way up and always fearful of falling back down. These people seldom fell back or fell very hard if they did; there was always a golden parachute. She listened as the older women talked of volunteering, of the Red Cross and the United Way. Those slightly younger had gone to work in real estate or travel agencies and were pleased with themselves, since they did not have to work and yet did so.

"Tom told me that you're a fabulous cook," said Lizzie Monacco, drawing Lynn into the conversation. "I took a look at that gorgeous box of cookies. We're going to serve them at dinner tonight. It was darling of you."

Lynn was thinking: Tom has surely done a lot of talking. He had put effort into this weekend. Pete Monacco was not a man who was readily open to suggestion, that was obvious. So Tom must have been very, very persuasive.

After the hike, tennis, and cocktails, they dressed for dinner. Lizzie had been most tactful.

"We do change for dinner. But nothing fancy, just anything you'd wear to your club on a weekday night. Anything at all." And she had given Lynn her candid smile.

"You were right again," Lynn said as she took a dark red silk dress off the hanger. She laid a string of pearls and the bracelet on the dresser.

"Don't wear that," Robert cautioned.

"Not? But you always want me to."

"Not here. It looks too rich. The pearls are enough. Modest. Sweet. I'm sorry you wore your ring, come to think of it. Ah, well, too late."

"You beat him at tennis. Should you have?" she asked.

"That's different. People respect a winner. They respect sports. It may seem silly, and I suppose it is when you really think about it, but the idea of excelling in a sport sort of stamps a man. He won't forget me." With his head tilted back he stood knotting his tie and exuding confidence. "That's what I keep telling the girls. That's what I shall tell him." He pointed at her abdomen, laughed, and corrected himself. "Sorry, I don't want to be sexist. But I don't know why I'm sure it's a him. Come on, you look lovely as always. Let's go down. I'm starved."

In the long dining room on a pine sawbuck table, pewter plates were set on rough linen mats. The utensils were plain stainless steel. But the candles were lit, and the dinner was served by two maids in uniform. A pair of handsome golden retrievers lay patiently in a corner.

"The great thing about the airplane," Lizzie said contentedly, "is that you can bring your household across country, dogs and all."

The airplane? No, the private company jet, thought Lynn, and was amused. A variety of conversations crossed the table, and she tried to catch some of them. There was talk of travel, not to London or Paris, but to the Fiji Islands and Madagascar. One couple had been on an expedition to the South Pole. It was like peering through a crack in the door, to a new world. Robert wanted to push the door open and walk into that world. It seemed to her as she overheard him at the other end of the table that he had already gotten one foot through the crack.

His rich voice and his eager expression were very attractive. At any rate, three or four of the men were paying attention, leaning to catch his remarks, which were addressed, of course, to Monacco.

"—we should, I've been thinking a lot about it, and we should train our own people in languages before we send them over. We should do our own public relations. Our outside PR in one office alone costs twenty-five thousand a month, minimum, and it won't be any less over there. I've been getting some figures together. Seems to me we know our own product best and should be able to do our own PR."

Then Monacco asked something that Lynn, caught in the crossfire of conversations, could not hear. But he had asked a question; that meant he was listening carefully.

"—met a German banker recently from Stuttgart. He's just the man to give us the answer to that. He travels all through the new republics. Yes, he's a good friend of mine. I can get in touch with him as soon as I get back to the office."

"Oh, that house where the light's on?" Lizzie was saying. "Across the lake, you mean. That's the caretaker's light." Through the autumn dusk there sparked one point of fire; it danced in the black water. "They left, and the place is for sale. We had a real scandal around here," she explained to Lynn. "This perfectly wonderful couple—we've known them for years and their place is really beautiful—well, she left him. It seems he knocked her around once too often. All those years it had been going on and none of us ever had the faintest suspicion. Isn't that amazing?"

Lynn's neighbor, with eager eyes and voice, supplemented the story. "They were a stunning couple. How could we have guessed? He had the best sense of humor too. He absolutely *made* a party. You'd never think to talk to him that he could do things like that."

"Well, it goes to show, doesn't it? You never know what goes on behind closed doors."

"No," said Lynn.

Her heart had leapt as though a gun had sounded. Now, just calm down, she said to herself. Just stop it. That business is all past. It ended months ago on the island. It's finished, remember? Finished.

Robert's voice sounded again over the chatter. "Of course, advertising's cheapest during the first quarter of the year, we know that. Television and radio are hungry then. I think we should find out how that works abroad before we make any definite commitments."

Almost unconsciously, Lynn glanced toward him, and at that very instant he glanced toward her, so that she caught his familiar, endearing smile. Things are going well, it declared.

"Oh, here come your marvelous cookies," cried Lizzie.

"You didn't make these yourself?" asked Lynn's neighbor.

"Yes, she did. I know all about her. She's professional."

Lynn corrected her. "No, no, I'd only like to be."

"Well, why don't you? I have a friend whose daughter—she must be about your age—makes the most exquisite desserts for people, bombes and—"

"Lynn's pregnant," Lizzie interrupted. "She'll have other things to do."

"Really? Congratulations! You have a daughter ready for college and you're having another. That's marvelous."

All eyes were on her. An earnest woman said, "You set an example, starting again just at the age when practically everybody's breaking up. Your baby's lucky."

"I hope so."

"One thing's sure, between you and that handsome husband of yours, it'll be good looking."

Presently, everyone got up and went into the living room for drinks. A vigorous fire flared under the great stone mantel, drawing Lynn to stand and gaze at it.

"You're looking thoughtful," said Pete Monacco.

"No, just hypnotized. Fountains and fires do that, don't they? And this has been such a lovely day."

He raised his glass to her as if making a toast. "We're glad you came. Robert's got interesting ideas. I'm glad he was brought to my attention. Unfortunately, some very bright guys get lost in the crowd—not often, but it can happen. He'll be making his mark in the firm. Hell, he has made it."

"I think I've left an impression," Robert said later. They were in bed under the quilt. "He asked me to put some of my ideas in writing and send them to him. What was he saying to you?"

"Nice things. That you were going to make your mark on the firm."

The window was low. When she raised her head, she had a clear view far down to the lake, where the diamond point of light still glistened from the vacant house that belonged to "the perfectly wonderful couple."

Robert stroked her stomach. "It won't be long before this fellow will be kicking you."

"Who is he? What will he be?" she wondered. She had also begun to think of the baby as "he." "It's all so mysterious. When I look back upon where we've been and then look ahead, even only as far as a year from now . . . Yes, it's all so mysterious."

It had grown very cold outside, and the wind had risen, sounding a melancholy wail through the trees. Even under the quilt it was cold, and Robert drew her close.

"Listen to that wind," he whispered. "It's a great night for sleeping, all snug in here. And it's been a great day. Things are really looking up for us, Mrs. Ferguson." He sighed with pleasure. "I love you, Mrs. Ferguson. I take it you're aware of that?" He chuckled, drawing her even closer.

"I am," she answered, thought following swiftly: It is absurd to let a piece of gossip affect me. What have Robert and I to do with those people? I know nothing about them, anyway. I am I and Robert is Robert.

He yawned. "Can't keep my eyes open. Let's sleep. Tomorrow'll take care of itself."

That was certain. They unfold, those unknown tomorrows, with their secrets curled like the tree that lies curled within the small, dry seed.

They started home right after dawn on Sunday. That way, Robert said, they'd be back before dinner with some time left over to be with the girls.

The house was deserted when they arrived. There wasn't even a light on.

"Ah, poor Juliet! They left her in the dark," said Lynn as the dog came forward into the dark hall. "They're probably over with Bruce and Josie. I guess they didn't expect us back this early."

"I never asked you what Josie said about our going up to Monacco's place."

"She didn't say much."

"I wonder what they really thought. You can't tell me there isn't some sort of envy, in a nice way at least."

"I don't think so. You know Josie is the last person to disguise her feelings, especially to me. So I'd know if there were."

"Did you know we've been invited to Monacco's in Maine?" Lynn had asked her, wanting no cat-and-mouse game between them, no dishonesty posing as tact.

And Josie had replied that yes, Robert had told Bruce, and she had said, "Don't feel uncomfortable on account of Bruce. I know you." She had smiled. "Bruce wasn't made to shine or sparkle. He knows himself."

That was true. You could see that Bruce knew who he was and didn't need to measure his worth by other people's accomplishments.

"Robert's exceptional," Josie had said. "He works like a demon and deserves whatever he may get."

Robert said now, "I did feel a little sorry, a little uncomfortable, when I told him."

"Well, you needn't have. Josie told me you deserve whatever you get."

Robert laughed. "One can take that in two ways."

"They mean it in one way only."

"Of course. Just a joke." He started upstairs with the two suitcases. "Come on, let's unpack before they all come home."

"I'll do it in the morning."

"You always say that. Who wants to wake up and find suitcases staring you in the face? Never put off till tomorrow what you can do today. That's my motto."

She followed him. The first room at the top of the stairs was the new nursery, and she couldn't pass it without peering in. The furniture had arrived, the crib and dresser in light yellow; the walls matched; there were large Mother Goose pictures in maple frames and spring-green gingham curtains, a refreshing change from pink and blue. A large, soft polar bear sat in one corner of the crib. At the window there was a rocking chair, where she would sit to nurse the baby. The thought of doing this again brought a renewal of youth, an affirmation of womanhood. None of the theories that one read, with all their political or psychological verbiage, could come within miles of describing the real sweetness of the fuzzy head and the minuscule splayed fingers against the breast.

In the bedroom, where Robert had already begun to unpack, the telephone rang. He was standing by the bed holding the phone when she came in.

"What? What?" he said. A dreadful look passed over his face. "What are you saying, is she—"

And Lynn, seeing him, turned ice cold.

"We'll be there. In the parking lot. Yes. Yes." He put the phone down. He was shaking. "That was Bruce. Emily's had a hemorrhage. From menstruation, he thought. She's in the hospital. Hurry. He'll meet us there."

The car squealed around the corner at the foot of the drive.

"Take it easy, Robert. Not so fast. Listen, listen, it was just her period, that's all it was. . . . But why a hemorrhage?" She babbled. "But it can't be anything too bad. She's in perfect health. . . ."

"They don't admit people to the hospital for nothing at all," he said grimly.

She wrung her hands in her lap and was quiet, while, in a frenzy, they rode through the town and into the hospital parking lot, where Bruce was waiting. Robert slammed the car door and began to run toward the entrance.

"Stop, I have to talk to you first," Bruce cried. "No, no, she's not—you're thinking she died, and I'm breaking it to you easily—but no, no, she's upstairs and she'll be fine, only she's terrified." The kind, earnest eyes matched the kind, earnest voice. "The fact is—well, I have to tell you, Emily had a miscarriage."

There was a total silence, as when the sounds of the world are drowned by a heavy snowfall. Traffic on the avenue and bustle in the parking lot all receded, leaving the three in that pool of silence, looking from one to the other.

"She's terrified," Bruce repeated, and then begged Robert, "don't be hard on her."

"How—" Lynn began.

Bruce resumed steadily. "She telephoned us around noon. She was more worried about Annie than about herself. She didn't want Annie to know. So Josie took Annie to our house, and I brought Emily here. The doctor says"—Bruce laid his hand on Lynn's arm—"he said she was in the third month. Are you all right, Lynn?"

Robert groaned, and at the piteous sound she turned to him. So he had been justified, more than justified, in his fears. And she cried inwardly: Oh, Emily, I trusted you! And she cried: Was this my fault? Robert will say it's my fault.

"Shall we go?" asked Bruce.

On the long walk from the parking lot she rallied. I'm the one who is good in emergencies, remember? Say the mantra: Good in emergencies . . . Her legs were weak, yet they moved. Then it seemed as if the elevator would never come. When it did, they shared space with a patient on a stretcher; so Mom had been carried that day with the white sheet drawn up to a drained white face. No one spoke as they ascended, then stepped out into a foreboding wave of hospital smells, of disinfectant and cleaning fluids. Ether too? No, it couldn't be, not in a corridor. But it sickened her, whatever it was, and she swallowed hard.

"I asked for a private room," Bruce said when they stopped at the end of the corridor. His voice rose half an octave, cheerfully. "Emily, your dad and mom are here."

A hot sunset light lay over the bed where Emily lay. Her body made only a slight ridge under the blanket, and the one arm that was exposed was frail; nothing of Emily had ever before seemed frail.

Lynn took a cold, sweating hand in hers and whispered, "We're here. Darling? We're here."

She wanted to say, It's going to be all right, it's not the end of the world, nor the end of you, God forbid. There's nothing that can't be solved, can't be gotten over, nothing, do you hear me? Nothing. She wanted to say all these, but no sounds came from her dry lips.

Emily's beautiful eyes wandered toward the ceiling. Tears rolled on her cheeks. And Robert, who had been standing on the other side of the bed, said faintly, "I have to sit down."

He's going to be sick, Lynn thought, while Bruce and the nurse, who had been at the window, must have had the same thought, because the nurse shoved a chair across the room, and Bruce took Robert's arm.

"Put your head down. Sit," he murmured.

Robert laid his head on Emily's coverlet, and the others walked toward the door out of his hearing.

"Poor man." The nurse clucked her tongue. "It's funny how often men take things harder than we do. She's going to be fine, Mrs. Ferguson. Mr. Lehman called Dr. Reeve. He's the chief of gynecology here, you couldn't get better."

Lynn's voice quivered. "I'm so scared. Tell me the truth. She looks so awful. Please tell me the truth."

"She's very weak, and she's in quite some pain. This is like giving birth, you know, the same pains. But there's nothing to be afraid of, you understand? Here, rest till the doctor comes back."

Rapid steps came purposefully down the hall. Dr. Reeve looked like a doctor, clean shaven, compact, and authoritative. He could play the part in a soap opera, Lynn thought hysterically; a foolish laugh rose to her throat and was silenced there. Were they really in a hospital room talking to this man about Emily?

Robert stood up. "Bruce you talk, you do it," he said, and then sat down again.

Bruce conferred briefly with the doctor, who then turned back to the parents.

"She's losing a lot of blood," he said, wasting no words. "We'll need to do a D and C. She says she hasn't eaten since breakfast. Can I rely on that? Because if she's had food within the last few hours, we'll have to wait."

Lynn replied faintly, "I don't know. We've been away. We just got home."

"You can rely on it," Bruce said.

"Fine. Then we'll take her up right away." Dr. Reeve looked keenly at Robert and Lynn. "Why don't you two go out with your brother and—" Bruce prompted. "I'm just a friend."

"Well, take them out and get something to eat." He looked again at Robert, who was wiping his eyes with the back of his hand. "Have a drink too. You can come back later in the evening."

"A good idea," said Bruce, assenting. "We'll do just that."

"No," Robert said. "I'm not leaving here. No, we'll stay."

"All right," Bruce said quickly. "There's a sun parlor at the end of the hall. We'll sit there. And if you need us for anything, Doctor, that's where we'll be."

"Fine. I suggest you go there now, then." The professional smile was sympathetic, but firm.

He means, Lynn knew, that we are not to stand here watching them wheel Emily into the operating room. It's plain to see that Robert can barely cope with this. Poor Robert. And she took his hand, twining her fingers through his as they went down the hall with Bruce.

In restless, forlorn silence they waited. Bruce and Lynn thumbed through magazines, not reading, while Robert stared through the window wall at the treetops. It was long past visiting hours, and steps were few in the hall, when a familiar, distinctive clicking sound approached: Josie's high heels, worn because Bruce was so much taller than she.

"I got permission to come in," she whispered. "I tracked Eudora down, and she went straight to your house, so I could bring Annie back there. Eudora's a princess. Annie was having her bath and getting ready for bed when I left."

Josie was wise. She gave no comforting words, no warm hug that would have brought on tears. She simply did whatever was needed.

Robert, with head in hands, was huddled in the sofa. All six feet four of him looked small. Lynn got up and caressed his bent head.

"Our beautiful girl, our beautiful girl," he moaned, and clearly she recalled his cry when Caroline's tiny body lay before them. Our baby. Our beautiful baby.

"She's going to be fine. I know. Oh, darling, she will."

"I'd like to get my hands on that rotten little bastard. I'd like to kill him."

"I know. I know."

Time barely moved. Eventually it grew dark. Bruce stood up and turned on the lights, then returned to sit with Josie. They spoke in whispers, while Lynn and Robert sat hand in hand. No one looked at his watch, so no one knew what time it was when Dr. Reeve appeared in the doorway. He looked different in his crumpled green cotton pants, with a pinched face and circled eyes. Authority had come from the suit and the tie and the brisk walk. Now he looked like a tired workman. Such scattered thoughts went through Lynn's head as he came toward them.

"Your girl is all right," he said. "She's in the recovery room, but she'll be back in her own room shortly. Mr. Lehman asked for a nurse through tonight and as long as needed. Good idea if you can afford it. Now, I suggest that you go home and come back again in the morning. Emily won't know you for hours, and it's already close to midnight." He glanced at Robert. "If—it's highly unlikely—if it should be necessary to call anyone, shall—" He glanced toward Bruce.

Robert got up. It was as if the news had brought him back to life. "No, we're the parents. We're over the first shock, and we can handle whatever comes next. You can imagine what a shock it was, being away and finding this when we got home."

"Of course. But it must be good to have friends like these to handle an emergency for you."

"We appreciate them. Bruce and Josie are the best."

"Well," Bruce said brightly now, "all's well that ends well. What I suggest is that we get something to eat. I personally could eat shoe leather at this point."

Josie went considerately on tiptoe through the corridor. "Darn heels sound like hammers," she whispered. "Listen. We're all too tired to go home and forage for food. What about the all-night diner on the highway? We can get a quick hamburger or something."

When they were settled in a booth, she explained, "I told Annie that Emily had a sick stomach, a little problem. She was scared at first, but then she accepted my story and seems fine."

"She mustn't ever know, of course," Lynn said.

"I knew you would feel that way about it, and that's why I told her what I did."

The emphasis on *you* prompted Lynn to ask, "Why? Wouldn't you feel that way?"

"I'm not sure. Kids know much more about what's going on around them than you may think."

"I'm sure Emily didn't tell her about—about what was going on between herself and Harris, for God's sake!"

"I'm sure Emily didn't, but as I said, kids are smart, and Annie is especially so. Smart and secretive," Josie added. "Annie could say a lot of things if she wanted to or dared to."

Robert, who had said nothing since he sat down, now burst out. "Never mind what Annie knows or doesn't know! It's Emily who's tearing me to shreds. The thought of her—" He turned upon Lynn. "I want you to know, I blame you as much as Emily. I told you when she was only fifteen years old that you were too lax with her. You have no backbone. You let people walk all over you. And you're not alert. You don't look around and watch what's going on. You never did."

Caroline, Lynn thought, and her will ebbed hopelessly.

"Now here we are," Robert said. "Yes, here we are."

"That's hardly fair, Robert," Josie protested angrily, "and not true. I don't know of a wiser, more caring mother than Lynn. You mustn't do this to her."

"I don't care. This was all avoidable. Is this what I work for, to see my daughter ruined, thrown away on a penniless bastard? Ruined—ruined."

The fluorescent bulbs above them glared on Robert, turning his exhausted face dark green.

Bruce said quietly, "You mustn't think of Emily as being ruined, Robert. This is a terrible thing, I know it is, but still, at seventeen she has a wonderful long life ahead. You mustn't," he said more sternly, "allow her to think otherwise."

Robert flexed his fingers. "I want to get my hands on the bastard. I just want to get my hands on him."

Despair sank like a stone in Lynn's chest. A few hours before they had been feeling—or she had been feeling on Robert's behalf—the glow of his success. They had been driving home through the bright fall afternoon with music on the radio, the new baby on the way, and—

"I could kill him," Robert said again. "Home now, sleeping like a log, not giving a damn, while Emily is—" He broke off. "Does the bastard even know, I wonder?"

"Of course he does," Bruce said. "He's quite frantic. He wanted to go to the hospital, but I told him he couldn't. I told him to call me for information. As a matter of fact, I will telephone him when we get home. He's waiting up."

Lynn was inwardly saying her mantra again: Good in emergencies. Now she made inquiry. "The third month. What was she—what were they—intending to do? Did she say? I don't understand," she whispered.

Bruce answered her. "On the way to the hospital Emily told me that she hadn't known really what to do. She had intended to get up courage to talk to you both this week, but she didn't want to spoil her father's important trip to Maine, to get him upset before the big meeting."

Robert made correction. "It wasn't a big meeting. I don't know where she got that idea. It wasn't that important."

"Well, anyway, that's the story. They were, I gather, quite beside themselves this last month, the two of them. They didn't know where to turn."

Lynn burst into tears and covered her face. "Poor baby. The poor baby."

Bruce and Josie got up. "Let's go. Get whatever rest you can," Josie commanded. "I have to go to work in the morning, although I suppose I could phone in."

Lynn recovered. "No. Go to work. You've done enough. You've been wonderful."

"Rubbish," said Bruce. "If you need either of us, you know where we are. You two will come through this all right, though, and so will Emily. Only one thing: Be kind to each other tonight. No recriminations. This is not your fault. Not yours, Robert, and not Lynn's. Have I got your word?" he asked, leaning into the car where Robert had already started the engine. "Robert? Have I got your word?" he repeated sternly.

"Yes, yes," Robert muttered, and grumbled as he drove away. "I don't know what he thinks I'm going to do to you."

That you are going to go on blaming me, she said to herself. That's what he thought. But now you won't, thank God. I don't think I can bear a harsh word tonight. And yet, was any of it my fault? Perhaps. . . .

Home again, she walked restlessly through the house. Setting the table for breakfast, she thought: Disaster strikes and yet people eat, or try to. She let the dog out and, while Juliet rummaged in the bushes, watched the stars. The sky was sprinkled with them; far off at a distance beyond calculation, could there be some living, thinking creature like herself, and in such pain?

She went upstairs to Emily's room, wanting to feel her presence, wanting to find some clue to her child's life. The closet and the desk were neat, for Emily was orderly, like Robert. There hung the shirts, not much larger than a hand towel. There stood the shoes, sneakers next to a pair of three-inch heels. On the bedside table lay a copy of *Elle* and a book: *Studies of Marital Abuse.*

Lynn opened the book to the first chapter: "The Battered Woman in the Upper Middle Class." She closed the book.

Are we now marked by this forever? Is it engraved on Emily's mind forever?

"Come," Robert said from the doorway. "This won't do you any good." He spoke not unkindly. "What's that she's reading?" And he took hold of the book before Lynn could hide it. "What the devil is this trash? The battered woman! She'd have done better to read about the pregnant high school girl."

"The one has nothing to do with the other."

Yet perhaps it had. Things are entwined, braided into each other. . . .

"Somebody comes out with a 'study,' " Robert scoffed. "Then somebody else has to write another. It's all a money-making, publicity-seeking lot of trash. Exaggerations. Lies, half of it. Throw the damn book out."

"No. It belongs to Emily. Don't you touch it, Robert."

"All right," he grumbled. "All right. We've got enough trouble tonight. Come to bed."

Neither of them slept. It began to rain. Drops loud as an onslaught of stones beat the windows, making the night cruel. Turning and turning in the bed, Lynn saw the hall light reflected upward on the ceiling. Robert would be sitting downstairs in his usual corner, his "mournful" corner, alone. If anything were to happen to Emily, it would kill him. But she had poor Annie—why did she always think "poor Annie," as if the child were some neglected misfit, disabled and deserted, when she was none of these? And then there was this baby, the boy Robert wanted. But nothing would happen to Emily, the doctor had said. He'd said it. Her thoughts ran, circled, and returned all night.

The doctor was just leaving Emily's room after early rounds when Robert and Lynn came down the hall. He spoke to them quickly in his succinct, flat manner. For after all, Emily could mean no more to him than another problem to be solved as skillfully as he could.

"She's still in some pain, but it's lessening. She has anemia from the blood loss, and we've just given her a transfusion, so don't be shocked when you see her. It's all to be expected." He swung away, took a few steps, and turned back. "I have a daughter her age, so I know." He stopped. "She'll have her life," he said then with an abrupt smile, and this time walked away.

A lump in Lynn's throat was almost too painful to admit speech, but she called after him.

"Thank you for everything. Thank you."

The nurse, who had been sitting by the bed, stood up when, with questioning faces, they entered the room.

"Come in. She's not sleeping, just resting. She'll be glad to see you."

Lynn stood over the bed. Glad, she thought bitterly. Glad, I doubt. Bruce said she was terrified.

The girl's face was dead white, frozen, carved in ice.

Robert said softly, "Emily, it's Dad. Dad and Mom."

"I know. I'm very tired," Emily whispered with her eyes shut.

"Of course you are. Emily, we love you," Robert said. "We love you so." His voice was so low that he repeated the words. He wanted to make certain that she had heard him. Kneeling on the floor, he brought his face level with hers. "Emily, we love you." Then he put his face down again on the coverlet.

Everything spun too fast. The way life moved and sped was extraordinary. It was fearful. One was, after all, quite helpless. First there was Emily trying for Yale with all the honors. And then there was this scene. A sudden vertigo overcame Lynn and she grasped the back of the bed to steady herself.

The nurse whispered, "She'll sleep now. The night nurse said she was up most of the night in spite of the medication."

So they waited all day in the room. Late in the afternoon Emily awoke and stirred in the bed.

"I'm better," she said clearly.

And indeed, some faint color flowed under her skin, and her eyes were bright, their pupils large and dark as after recovery from fever.

Next she said, "You're very angry."

They spoke in unison. "No, no."

She sighed. "You need to be told."

"Not now," Robert said. "You don't need to talk now."

But Emily insisted. "I want to." In a tone of bewilderment, as if she were telling a stranger's story, one that she did not really understand, she began. "At first I didn't know. I didn't think, it was only about the middle of the second month. I didn't know. And after that, I was so scared. I couldn't believe it."

Her thin hands clung together on the coverlet. On her little finger she wore the initialed gold ring that had been too large even for her middle finger when it was new. She had been eight, seven or eight, Lynn thought; my sister gave it to her for her birthday; we had a clown at the party, I remember.

"I—we didn't know what to do. We kept talking about what to do. I was going to tell you, honestly. I just couldn't seem to get my courage up."

And Lynn thought of the day she had learned about the baby who, it now seemed, was at this minute making its first movements within her, of how she had brought the news home and the house had turned into a holiday house.

"I didn't want an abortion, I couldn't do that."

"What then would you have done?" Robert asked softly.

"We thought—I'll be eighteen this month, we'll be in college next year. They have married couples in college, lots of people marry that young. We'd want to be married, we'd want the baby to have proper parents." Emily's eyes turned toward the ceiling for a moment, reflecting. "You see, we're not that modern. Maybe I am, but Harris isn't. He comes from a very religious family. They go to church every Sunday. He does, too, and they'd want things done right. They're very good people, really. Harris wouldn't be what he is if they weren't."

Robert raised his head, looked across the bed toward Lynn. His lips formed a sneer; she understood the sneer. But he said nothing. And she herself was as yet incapable of making any judgment at all.

"You won't believe this," Emily said, "but it was only one time. I swear it." When neither parent answered, she continued, "I loved him. I love him now. So it happened. It was one day when we were going to the lake, and—"

"No." Robert spoke roughly. "No. We don't have to hear about that."

He did not want to imagine his daughter with a man, to think of Emily and sex at the same time. Well, that was understandable, Lynn supposed.

Now Emily reached for her hand. "You know, Mom," she said. "You understand about loving, even when there are times one shouldn't." And she gave her mother a serious, meaningful look, holding her so long with that look that Lynn, struck by painful memory, was the first to turn away. It was as if Emily wanted to remind her of something, as if there were some complicity between her daughter and herself.

Then the nurse came back. It was five o'clock, dinnertime, and visiting hours were over until the evening, she said, apologizing.

"Anyway, now that Emily's doing fine, you must feel better yourselves."

"You must be awfully tired, Mom." Emily smiled. "You're starting the fifth month, aren't you? Go home and rest."

When they were halfway home, it occurred to Lynn that Emily had not spoken one direct word to Robert.

A car was parked in front of their house when they entered the driveway. Two men got out and walked toward them. One was Harris in his neat chinos, and the other, of equal height, with the same thick brown hair, but older and broader, was undoubtedly his father, wearing a policeman's uniform.

"Oh, no," Lynn said aloud.

Robert heard her and gave an order. "Be quiet. I'll handle this."

They met beside Robert's car. The boy, like Lynn, was afraid, but his father came forward frankly.

"I'm Lieutenant Weber. My son has come to talk to you. Speak up, Harris."

Robert gave a stop signal with his raised hand. "There is nothing you can tell me that I want to hear. Nothing."

The boy flushed. The blood, surging from neck to scalp, looked as though it must burn him.

"I'd like to beat you to a pulp," Robert said, making a fist with the raised hand.

"Mr. Ferguson," the father said, "perhaps if we go inside and talk together—"

"No. My little girl is in there, and anyway, I don't want you—him—in my house. I don't want to talk to him."

"Let him speak here, then. Please, Mr. Ferguson. It'll only take a few minutes."

"I just want you to know," Harris said, "it's hard to find the words, but —I am so terribly sorry, I'll never forget this as long as I live." His whole body was shaking, but he raised his head and threw his shoulders back. "I'm ashamed. I am so terribly ashamed, and so sad for Emily because I love her. I don't know what else to say, Mr. Ferguson, Mrs. Ferguson." He gave a little sob, and his Adam's apple bobbed. "You've always been so nice to me, and—"

His father continued for him. "I have always told him, always since he was grown, that he had two little sisters and that he must treat girls as he'd want somebody to treat them."

Robert interrupted. "Look, Lieutenant, this is all very sweet talk, but there's no point in it. Talk can't undo the facts or make us feel any better. The facts are that Emily came close to dying—"

"No, Robert," Lynn said softly. "No, don't make it worse than it is."

"My wife's a sentimental woman. She doesn't want to hear the truth spoken. It's all right for you to talk sweetly, young fellow. You're not the one lying in pain."

Harris's eyes glistened, and with her eyes Lynn tried to communicate with him. Certain thoughts were taking shape in her mind. He hadn't raped Emily, after all. And it did take two.

Lieutenant Weber said it for her. "It does, after all, take two," he reminded them gently. He gazed out toward the hill where darkness already lay on the trees. "And it's not the first time this has happened, God knows."

A dialogue spun itself out between the two men while Lynn and Harris stood by.

"That doesn't concern me. I'm only concerned about this time."

"Of course. As the father of girls I surely understand. The question is, what is to happen now to these young folks?"

The man was sorrowful and yet not humble, Lynn saw. Somehow the onus is always put on the boy, so it must be hard to be standing in his shoes. Yet he does it honorably. And Robert was making it harder, offering no way for minds to meet.

"He's heard plenty from me and his mother, too, about this, you can bet, enough so he'll never forget it," Lieutenant Weber persisted.

"He didn't hear enough. If he were my son, I'd break his neck."

The father laid his hand on his son's arm. "What good would that do?"

"Let him suffer a little, that's what."

"Don't you think he is suffering? He's a good kid, same as Emily. She's been at our house, and we know her well. She's a fine girl, the finest. They made a mistake, a bad one, but not the worst. Now it's up to us to help them."

"I'm going inside," Robert said coldly. "We've been through hell, my wife and I, and we're wasting our strength listening to drivel. If you'll excuse us." The gravel crunched under his heel as he moved.

"I'm sorry you think it's drivel, Mr. Ferguson. Harris came here like a man to face you. In our family he's been taught to have respect. Never mind this modern stuff. He goes to church, he's not the kind who goes banging—pardon the expression"—this with a bow toward Lynn—"every girl he—"

Robert's anger blazed. "No," he said, "not every girl. Only a girl from a family like this one, a home like this one." He waved his arm toward the house. "Not such a dumb idea to come snooping and sneaking around a place like this so he can raise himself up from the bottom."

Lynn cried in horror. "Robert! Robert!"

"You stay out of this, Lynn. People like him there think they'll better themselves by creeping in where they don't belong."

"Now, wait a minute, Mr. Ferguson. Don't you take that superior tone with me. I won't stand for it."

"Dad! For God's sake, don't! Please don't argue," Harris pleaded.

"Don't you worry, son. You go sit in the car. Go now. I won't be long."

When the boy was out of hearing, he resumed. "I came here like a gentleman with my son. I planned to go into your house so your neighbors across the road wouldn't recognize me in my uniform. I wanted to spare you again, the way I spared you before. I wasn't going to tell you this, for Emily's and Harris's sakes I wasn't, but you've asked for it. On the bottom, are we? You're hardly one to talk."

"Explain yourself," Robert said. "And lower your voice while you're at it."

"Yes, that would be a good idea," replied the other man, and lowered it. "It would have been better for you if you had lowered yours that night a while back when you were battering your wife."

"Oh, Lieutenant, oh, please," Lynn begged.

"Mrs. Ferguson, I'm sorry, but I have to. I'm a man too. Maybe it's just as well that Mr. Ferguson hears the truth."

Lynn's heart raced. It crossed her mind that even at her age, one could have a heart attack. How fast could a heart beat before it gave up?

"Let me tell you," Weber said, "I was called here, I was on duty, when a call came a while back in the summer. The people across the road were out taking an evening walk when they passed your house and heard something going on. So they phoned the station, and up I came. I stood in the dark, and I heard enough to know what it was, all right. I could have taken you in right then and there. But I wasn't about to make trouble for Emily. I figured she already had enough because it can't be the greatest thing for a girl to grow up here, grand as it is."

Robert was breathing heavily, and Weber continued.

"We're very fond of Emily. We know what she is. True blue. I wouldn't hurt her for the world. So I told the people across the road that it was a mistake, and back at the station I buried the record. Buried it. So don't you talk to me about fine family, Mr. Ferguson, or coming up from the bottom." He turned to Lynn, who was crying. "I know you're expecting, Mrs. Ferguson, and this isn't good for you. I'm awfully sorry about it. About everything. If there's anything I can ever do for you, you know where I am, where we are, Harris and—"

"Yes, you can do something," Robert said. He was shaking. "You're a lying bastard, cop or no. You saw nothing when you were here, and you know you didn't. You're trying to intimidate me. Well, it won't work. Now get out of here, you and your precious son. And never come back, either one of you. That's what you can do, and that's all I have to say."

"That's just what I intended to do all along, Mr. Ferguson. Good night, Missus."

For a minute the two were speechless. Lynn was as shocked and immobile as in that first second when Bruce had told them about Emily. The sound of Weber's chugging old engine died away down the road before Robert spoke.

"Stop crying. Cry about Emily, not about that garbage." He bent down in the dusk to stare at her. "Don't tell me you're feeling sorry for that wretched kid. Yes, I wouldn't be surprised. I suppose you are."

"Yes, Robert, I am."

"It figures. That's you."

"Maybe it is."

Pity, like a wave, flooded over her, pity for everything, for a child lost in the crowd and crying for its mother, for a shivering dog abandoned on the roadside, for Emily, so afraid, so ashamed, and for that young fellow, too, with his scared eyes, paying such a price for his few moments of a natural passion. And now, unmistakably this time, the baby moved within her, flexing its tiny arm or leg, stretching and readying itself for a hard world.

"We've seen the last of them, at any rate," Robert said as they went toward the house. "If he ever comes here, you're to throw him out. But he won't dare." They went inside, where Robert poured a drink. His hand was shaking. "My heart's pounding like a trip-hammer. This sort of thing doesn't do you any good, that's for sure."

"No," she said, wiping her wet cheeks.

There was a terrible shame in the room, as if two strangers, a man and a woman, had blundered into a place where one of them was naked. It was not quite clear to her who the naked one was here, Robert, so painfully proud, or she herself, who had for the first time seen another human being stand up to Robert and win. For Weber had won; there could be no doubt of that.

He swallowed the drink and went to the foot of the stairs, calling Annie.

"We're home, honey. What are you doing?"

"Homework," came the answer.

"What homework?"

"Geography."

"Have you got the atlas up there with you?"

"Yes."

"Good. Good girl. Well, stay up there and finish it."

Returning, Robert said, "We need to talk before she comes down."

"About what?"

"About what we're going to do, naturally. I'd like to take her out of that school. Put her in private school, where she won't have to see him. I don't want her to see him even passing in the halls."

"You can't do that to her, you can't break up a term in senior year, Robert!"

He considered, then conceded, "I suppose you're right. But I'm going to have a talk with Emily—oh, don't worry, I see the worry on your face. It's going to be very peaceable, with no recriminations, because she's been through enough. But I'm going to make things quite clear, all the same. I want her to rest at home for a week or so, and when she goes back to school, she'll say she had the flu." He walked back and forth across the room with steps so firm that the crystals on the wall sconces made a musical tinkle as he passed. "I want you to keep a strict watch over her free time, Lynn. I want to know where she's going, with whom, and when she'll be home, and no nonsense about it. You get the idea." He increased his pace so that the crystals complained. "Damn! Damn! And life was looking so good. The fates just can't let you enjoy what they give without taking something away at the same time, or so it seems. However, there's no use lamenting about the fates."

Lynn agreed that there was not, and he continued, "I want to keep up with what I started in Maine, keep up the momentum. If it weren't for all that, I'd like to take the lot of us away over Thanksgiving and again at Christmas, and again in February, spend every damn school vacation away from here. But as it is . . . well, we'll have to find other things to do, a ski weekend, theater tickets, Saturdays in the city, anything to keep that girl out of harm's way."

So he walked the length of the room like a general organizing his campaign. That which had been darkly, safely buried, that which Weber had dug up and brought into a cruel glare, had been dismissed from Robert's mind: It was an outrageous lie, it had never happened.

At least, Lynn thought wryly, at least Weber's done one thing; he's had a sobering effect; Robert hasn't said anything more about my being to blame for Emily's trouble.

The words repeated themselves in pitying silence: Emily's trouble.

"I am so terribly tired," she said involuntarily.

Robert gave her a glance. "Yes, you do look done in. Go to bed. I'll see how Annie's doing."

She moved heavily. It was an effort to raise her arms and slip the dress over her head, to pull the spread back and get into the bed. Yet it was not long before she fell into a thick, dark sleep. Toward morning when the windows turned gray, she dreamed. She tumbled, hurling from some great height while grabbing in terror at the empty air, while below, sharp, pointed things—knives, sticks, thorns?—were aimed at her open eyes, and there was no way, no way she could—

She screamed, screamed, and was jolted awake. Robert was holding her, saying softly, "What is it?"

"Nothing, nothing," she whispered.

He comforted her shaking body, stroking the back of her neck. "Nerves. Nerves. And why not? You've been through too much. Take it easy. I'm here. I'm here."

"Then I have your promise, Emily?" Robert asked.

"I have already given it to you," she answered, lying back on the pillowed sofa.

"It is for your own good, Emily. You've had a very narrow escape. As terribly hard as it was, the miscarriage"—here he seemed to gulp over the word—"was easier than the other way would have been. Your whole life, your ambition, everything, would have turned inside out." He made a gesture of hopeless dismissal. "So now the rest is up to you," he said, standing up and producing a smile meant to encourage. "I have to run for the late train. My desk must be loaded." At the door he turned back again. "Oh, yes, I meant to tell you, I've bought tickets to the opera, Saturday matinees. But you'll be able to squeeze in your homework all day Sunday. And Annie will too."

"He's so well oiled," said Emily when Robert had gone. "Everything planned. You press a button and the answers to all your problems just pop out. Quick and easy."

"That's nasty, Emily. Your father means so well. You never thought he'd be so understanding, now, did you?"

"Does he think I don't see through him? Do your homework all day Sunday, meaning, Don't leave this house. I'm keeping an eye on you."

"That's not true. You heard him say you should go out with other boys."

"I don't want to go out with other boys. I want to be with Harris. I want to be trusted."

Lynn raised an eyebrow. "Trusted? Well, really, Emily."

"It happened once, Mom. We're hardly ever alone together in the first place. All summer we were at the lake with a crowd, you know that. You believe me, don't you?"

Her blue eyes, moist as petals, are so beautiful, that it's a wonder he could resist her at all, Lynn thought.

"You believe me?" the girl repeated.

"Yes. But you see what happened from just that once."

"We want to get married."

"Oh, my God, Emily, you're much too young."

"Eighteen! You were only twenty."

"That was different. Your father was older."

"My father? Yes, and look what you got."

Lynn, choosing to ignore the sarcasm, said only, "Harris, or you, or both of you, may change your minds, you know."

"Not any more than we'll change our minds about medical school. And it was horrible, what Dad said about Harris wanting to better himself because our family has more money," Emily said bitterly. "It was a cheap and cruel and stupid thing to say. Harris phoned me at the hospital just before you got there to take me home, and he told me."

"Your father was beside himself with worry over you. I've never seen him so desperate. People say things when they're desperate."

Lynn felt as if she were being driven toward a trap. But Harris had not been present, he had been sent to wait in the car when his father had talked about that night last spring. Her mind moved swiftly in recollection. Obviously, then, Weber hadn't wanted Harris to hear that part. He was a decent human being who had done his best to conceal what had happened. "I buried it," he had said. "Buried it." No, he would not have told Harris. And Lynn's fear subsided.

"Harris said his parents have told him he mustn't see me, that he must even avoid me in school."

"They're right, Emily. It's wiser that way."

"It's all Dad's fault. It goes back to him."

Lynn protested, "There's no logic in that remark. I don't understand it at all."

"Don't you? I could tell you, but you wouldn't want to hear it. There's no use talking when you won't be open with me, Mom."

Lynn, folding her hands on her lap, looked down on the backs that had been covered with puncture wounds. What Emily wanted was a confirmation, an admission about those wounds, now long healed. But she was not going to get it. A mother hides her private pain from her children. For their own good she does this.

For my own good, too, she thought. Abruptly a tinge of anger colored her feeling for Lieutenant Weber. He should not have said those things! He should have known how they would hurt. But then, there were the things that Robert had said . . . Her head throbbed.

"I'll tell you, Emily," she said somewhat crisply, "I can't play verbal games with you. You say you're a woman, so I'll talk to you as one woman talks to another. I'll tell you frankly that I'm not feeling my best right now, and I don't want to argue about anything. I only want to help you, and I want you to help me too."

Emily got up and took her mother into her arms. "All right, Mom, we won't talk about this anymore. Just have a wonderful, healthy baby and be well." She smiled at Lynn. "Don't worry about me. I'll work hard the rest of the year and graduate with honors too. You'll see. And I won't make any trouble for anybody. I've made enough already."

"W HAT'S the matter with Emily?" Annie asked again. "Why won't anybody tell me?"

"There's nothing to tell. She's just working terribly hard these days. She has to keep her grades up if she wants to get into Yale," Lynn answered cheerfully.

"She cries a lot. Her eyes were red last night." Annie's own small, worried eyes were suspicious. "Didn't you see?"

"She has a little cold, that's all."

The weight of Emily's sadness lay heavily on Lynn. Of course she cried, why wouldn't she, poor child? The double shocks, to the body and to the spirit, had aged and changed her. Hardened her too? she wondered.

She hesitated at the door of Emily's room. Conscious of her own pregnancy's pronounced visibility, she could not help but think of its effect on the wounded girl.

But she opened the door, and in the cheerful, artificial tone that had by now become a habit, inquired, "Busy? Or may I come in?"

Emily put the book down. "I'm busy, but come in."

"I don't want to disturb you. I thought—you've been isolated lately with all this studying. Of course, it's necessary, I know." Floundering so, she came suddenly to the point. "Tell me. Do you need to talk about your feelings, about Harris? Because if you want to, I'm here. I'm always here for you."

"Thanks, but there's nothing to talk about."

Emily's shoulders appeared to straighten, and her chin rose a proud inch or two. This small display of pride seemed to shut Lynn out, and she repeated gently.

"Nothing?"

"No. We stay completely away from each other, so if that's why you're worried, don't."

"I'm not worried about that. I know you'll keep your word."

"He sent me a birthday card with a lace handkerchief in it. And we do talk on the phone." Emily paused as if, Lynn thought, she expects me to protest about that. When no protest came, Emily said proudly, "He works every day. He even has a Sunday job. I suppose it's part of his punishment."

"Oh! I shouldn't think punishment was necessary. I mean . . . Our feeling is that you should have fun, you know that." And when Emily was once more silent, Lynn continued, "I know boys call you."

"Because they know Harris and I are through."

"But you never accept."

Emily gave her a twist of a smile. "If I wanted to, and I don't, there wouldn't be time, would there? My days are filled up. Aren't they?"

Indeed. True to his word, Robert had provided an activity for every available hour; they had gone to the opera, to country fairs, and the local dog show; they had skated on the season's first ice at Rockefeller Center and seen the exhibit at the Metropolitan Museum. Vigorously, tenaciously, he fulfilled his plan, and with equal tenacity and her new cool courtesy, Emily had complied.

But how she must ache!

So the autumn passed, a long, slow season this year, the ground covered with black leaves rotting under steady rain, a season sliding downhill toward a frozen winter, as if the chilly gloom wanted to reflect the cold that underlay the sham politeness in the house.

By tacit agreement the trouble was covered over. At meals Robert led the talk to current events, the day's headlines. Alone with Lynn the talk was chiefly about the firm. It was as if, for him, nothing else of any import had happened or was happening.

"They're thinking of sending me abroad," he told her one night. "There's a group from the West Coast going, from Monaco's office, and they want me to go with them for a meeting in Berlin. After that I go alone to meet the people whom we've contacted in Budapest." Excited, stimulated, he paced the bedroom floor and came to rest behind Lynn, who was brushing her hair at the mirror. "It'll take two weeks probably, if

I go. I'm pretty sure I will, though. It'll be some time in December. I hate to leave you." He studied her face. "You look tired."

"I'm fine. We'll be fine."

"You're pretty heavy this time, that's what it is. By March you'll be yourself again."

She agreed. "I'm sure."

Yet she felt a weakness that she had never felt before. It was hard to get out of bed in the morning, and so hard to keep running between activities, the train to New York, the car to the country fair, going, going all the time. With Robert away there would at least be some rest.

Josie said, "It's not the pregnancy. You're emotionally wrung out. Emily's trouble was enough to do it, God knows."

But you don't know the half of it, thought Lynn. Involuntarily, she sighed.

Josie remarked the sigh. "You never went back to my friend—Dr. Miller, I mean." The tone was accusatory.

"No." Go back to tell him about Lieutenant Weber and—and all the rest? Wake that up yet again? And for what? What could he do, that man, except make her feel like two cents, sitting there? And biting the thread with which she was mending Annie's skirt, she remarked only, "That child tears everything. She's always bumping into things."

"How do she and Robert get along these days?"

"All right. No problems."

Not on the surface, anyway. He kept them all too busy, she thought. But perhaps that was healthy? Healthy and wholesome. You want to think so . . . but is it?

"Robert's leaving for Europe on Tuesday, you know," she said, feeling slightly awkward because Bruce was not leaving. Yet to ignore the fact before Josie would be more awkward.

"Yes, I know."

No more was said about that. Then Josie asked about Emily.

"She never mentions Harris, and I don't ask anymore. 'It's over,' she told me. So maybe Robert was right when he said it would pass and the scars would fade. I guess so. I don't know." She reflected. "Anyway, she's working long hours, half the night, for the science fair. It's all voluntary. I think she's doing too much, but Robert says I should leave her alone. Well, of course, he's so proud of her achievement. And I am, too, but mostly I want her to be happy. I feel"—Here Lynn put the sewing down and clasped her hands—"I feel so terribly sorry for her, Josie, and for the boy too."

"Bruce has seen him a few times when he passes the soccer field on the way to the jogging track. He asks about Emily."

"Yes, I'm sorry for him," Lynn repeated, and, with a little laugh, added, "You can imagine that Robert isn't. His anger over this has gone too deep. There's no forgiveness in it."

"Robert's an angry man to begin with," Josie said. "Listen, Lynn, I don't want to come after you with a sledgehammer, but I wish you would listen to me. You *need* to talk to somebody. Keeping your secrets—and I know you do—will only harm you in the end. God only knows what may happen." And she repeated, "Robert is an angry man."

Her comments only offended Lynn; Josie's comments always had. They were exaggerated, and anyway it was unseemly to disparage a woman's husband to her face, no matter what you thought.

Yet this was the only flaw in the long friendship. She had always to consider that. And she had also to consider the nasty things Robert said about Josie. So she made her defense a calm one.

"Robert has always worked under very high pressure. Right now he's got his heart set on building a future for this baby, for the son he's convinced it is."

"Oh, naturally he'd want a son."

"Well, we already do have two girls, Josie. Anyway, Robert's a workaholic. I worry sometimes that he'll work himself to death."

"If he does, it'll be by his own choice."

"Oh, no, he plans to live and rear this boy. He's got such plans, it's really amazing to hear him; you'd think having a baby was the grandest thing that can happen. Well, I guess it is, after all." Stricken with embarrassment before this barren woman, she stopped.

Josie's response was quick. "Don't be sorry about me. I've long accepted that other women have babies and I don't. You have to face the realities, one right after the other, all through life."

Lynn was immediately sober. "Well, you surely face them," she amended. "I remember how you were when you had your operation. You were amazing." She smiled. "Thank goodness, you're fine now."

"Is that a statement or a question?"

"Well, both, I guess." Lynn was startled. "You are fine now, aren't you?"

"You can't know that positively," Josie answered quietly. "Can you ever know anything positively?"

"I suppose not. But are you telling me something—something bad about yourself?"

"No. I'm only telling you that facing reality isn't the easiest thing for most of us to learn."

There was a silence until Josie rose to depart. She left a vague discomfort in the room, a hollow space, a chilled draft, an enigmatic message. Lynn felt as if she had been scolded.

On Monday, the night before he was to leave, Robert came home early. He had bought new luggage and laid it on the bed ready to pack. His passport and traveler's checks were on the dresser, the new raincoat hung on the closet door, and his list was at hand.

They had dinner. He was euphoric, filled with a sense of novelty and adventure.

"This is much more than a question of profits, you understand. The world's peace, its future, hang on whether we can make the European Community work. We need to take all these eastern republics into some sort of attachment to NATO. That's why it's so important to lay an economic foundation." He talked and talked. His eyes were brilliant.

Upstairs again after dinner, he went on talking while folding and packing; he would not allow Lynn to do it for him, preferring his own method. As he called out, she checked off the list.

"Notebook, camera, film, dictionary. There, that's it." He turned to her. "God, I'll miss you."

"You'll be too busy to miss anyone."

"Only you," he said gravely. "Hey, I guess the girls have gone to bed. I'll kiss them good-bye in the morning unless they're still asleep."

"They'll be up."

"I'm leaving at the crack of dawn. Where's Juliet?"

"Right there on the other side of the bed. I'll go put her out."

"No, no, I will. Come on, girl, let's go," he said as the dog, stretching and yawning, lumbered behind him.

It was not half a minute later when Lynn heard the voices exploding in the kitchen, and she raced downstairs. Robert was standing over Annie, trembling in her nightgown, with a face all puckered in tears. In front of her on the kitchen table was a soup bowl piled high with ice cream, whipped cream, fudge sauce and salted almonds; the base of the tower was encircled by a ring of sliced bananas, and the peak was adorned with a maraschino cherry.

"Look! Will you look at this!" Robert cried. "No wonder she can't lose weight. You're a pig, Annie. You're worse than a pig because you're supposed to have some intelligence. You're disgusting, if you want to know."

Annie sobbed. "You—you've no right to say things like that. I haven't murdered anybody. If I want to be fat, I'll be fat, and it's my business."

Lynn mourned, stroking the child's head. "Oh, Annie. You had a good dinner. You were supposed to be in bed."

Robert interrupted. "Stop the coaxing and caressing. That's been the whole trouble here anyway. No discipline. No guts. Anything they want to do, they do."

He snatched the soup bowl, Annie snatched, too, and the contents slopped over onto the table.

Annie screamed. "Don't touch it! I want it!"

"Oh, this is awful," Lynn lamented. "I can't stand this! Robert, for heaven's sake, let her have a spoonful, a taste. Then she'll let you throw it away, I know she will."

" 'Let' me? What do you mean? Nobody 'lets' me do anything in this house. I'm the father. Here," he shouted with the bowl now firmly in his grasp, "this is going where it belongs, into the garbage pail."

The lid clanged shut, and Annie howled. "That was mean! You're the worst father. Mean!"

"I may be mean, but you're a mess. A total, absolute mess. A disappointment. You'd better get hold of yourself."

Lynn protested, "Robert, that's cruel. It's true that Annie needs to watch her weight, but she is not a mess. She's a lovely girl, and—"

"Lynn, cut out the soft soap. It's sickening. I gag on it."

"Don't you yell at Mommy! Leave Mommy alone!"

The two confronted each other, the trim, tall man opposed to the square little girl whose stomach bulged under her nightdress and whose homely, pallid face was mottled red with rage. Lynn summoned every ounce of control.

"Come upstairs with me. Come to bed," she repeated quietly. "There's no sense in this."

When she had pacified Annie and seen her into bed, she went to her own bedroom, where Robert was reading.

"Well," she said, "a nice good-bye on your last night. Very nice to remember."

A stack of Christmas cards waiting to be addressed lay on a table beside his chair. He held up a photograph of the Ferguson family, standing in front of the holly garlands on the living room mantel; they were all

smiling; even Juliet, with lolling tongue, looked happy. Then he snapped
the card back onto the pile and mocked:

"The perfect American family. There they are. Perfect."

"Losing your temper like that over a dish of ice cream," she protested.

"You know very well it was more than that. It was the principle of the
thing, the disobedience, her defiance."

"You called her a 'mess.' That was unforgivable. Brutal."

"It's the truth. I work with her, you see how much time I spend trying
to lift her out of her slovenly habits, I try my darnedest, and still she
comes home with C's on her report card. I don't know what to say anymore."

Robert stood up, walked to the dresser, where he arranged his combs
and brushes in parallels, then walked to the window, where he brought
the shade even with the sill.

The baby made a strong turn or kick inside Lynn. Its weight pulled her
so hard, she had to sit down.

"I can't stand this," she said.

"Well, what do you want me to do? Go around pussyfooting, pretend-
ing not to see what I see? Maybe if you kept better order here—"

"Order? What's disorderly? Do you mind giving me an example other
than the ice cream tonight?"

"Okay. That business last week when she went to school with a ten-
cent-store ring on each finger. She looked ridiculous, and I said so, but
you let her do it anyway."

"Oh, for heaven's sake, it's the style in her grade. So it looks ridiculous
—what difference? So I let her do it, and now I'm a failure as a mother."

"Don't put words in my mouth. I didn't call you a failure."

But you've thought it. I know. Ever since I let the baby drown.

"You implied it," she said.

"What's all this quibbling? What are we doing here?" Exasperated, he
punched his fist into his palm.

She should really not argue with him. Just don't talk back, she told
herself. He's tense, he has to leave early in the morning, he needs his
rest. Annie will forget about this, I'll forget, and it will all pass if I just
keep quiet.

Yet a quick answer leapt from her mouth. "I don't know what you're
doing, but I know what I'm doing. I'm trying to cope."

He stared as if in astonishment. "You? You are? Coping? While I'm
working my head off on the brink of the biggest opportunity of my life—
of our lives—calmly keeping myself together and doing an expert job in

spite of the disaster here at home, the disaster that you allowed to happen—"

She sprang up. "Back again to Emily, are you? This is too much. It's insane."

"Insane? You don't want to hear it, I know. And if you notice, I haven't talked about it. Purely out of consideration for your condition, Lynn. Purely."

"Louder! Speak louder so she'll be sure to hear this."

He strode to the door, closed it, and said in a lower voice, "I warned you and warned you about her and that bastard, but in your laissez-faire way you did nothing. You didn't watch her, you ruined a beautiful girl, you ruined her life."

Lynn's anger mounted. "Listen here, you with your phony accusations. I could have done some accusing, too, in my time if I'd wanted to, and my accusations wouldn't have been phony either. You know darn well what—"

Robert sprang up, grabbed her arms, and shook her. "If you weren't pregnant, I know what I'd—"

"Take your hands off me, Robert. You're hurting me. Now, you let me alone, you hear?"

"Goddamn crazy house," he muttered, walking away. "I'll be glad to get out of it in the morning."

She lay down, hoping for sleep. Anger was disaster. Some people throve on it, but it sapped her; some bodies just were not programmed for anger. She lay awake while Robert undressed and did his small last-minute chores. She heard his shoelace break as he sat on the side of the bed removing his shoes; she heard him fumble in the weak lamplight, searching for another lace.

When at last he got into bed, she did not turn to him, as was their custom, nor did he turn to her.

In the morning when she woke, he was gone.

It was a brilliant morning. It turned the view from the kitchen window into a Japanese print: Brittle black branches on the hill's crest cut patterns against the sky. Lynn stared at it, unseeing; on this day it could give her no pleasure. Nothing could. A faint nausea rose to her throat, and she pushed her cup away. Too much coffee. Too many heavy thoughts.

The house was quiet, and the hum of its silence was unbearably mournful. She got up, moving her clumsy body to the appointment book on the desk. There was nothing much for today except the monthly visit to the obstetrician, who would scold her for not having gained weight;

years ago they used to scold you for gaining it. Other than that, there were just a few little errands and marketing. Lunch with Josie had been crossed out because Josie had a cold, and that was just as well, for she was in no mood for sociability.

Dr. Rupert having been called away, Lynn was to see an associate, a young man, younger than she, his curly hair hanging almost to shoulder length over his white coat. The look had gone out in the eighties, but now, in the nineties, it was apparently coming back. Wrapped in white sheeting, she sat on the examining table observing him while he read her record.

"Nausea last month, I see. How is it now?" he asked her.

"I still have it now and then."

"It's not usual in the sixth month."

"I know. I didn't have it the other times."

"It says here that you feel unusually tired too."

"Sometimes." She didn't feel like talking. If he would just get on with it and let her go! "I'm much larger than I was with my other babies, so I guess there's just more to carry."

He looked doubtful. "Could be. But your blood pressure's up this morning. Not terribly, but definitely up. Is there any reason that you can think of?"

Alarmed, she responded quickly. "Well, no. Is it bad?"

"No. I said not terribly. Still, one has to wonder why it's up at all. Has anything upset you?"

His smile wanted to persuade her, but she would neither be persuaded nor tricked into any admission. Yet, some answer had to be given.

"Perhaps it's because my husband has just left for Europe, and that worries me a little. I can't think of anything else."

He was looking straight into her eyes. His own were shrewd, narrowed under eyebrows drawn together as they might be if he were doing a mathematical computation or working a puzzle.

"I was wondering," he said slowly. "Those marks on your upper arms—"

"Marks?" she repeated, and glancing down, saw above her elbows the blue-green spots where Robert's thumbs had pressed last night.

"Oh, those." She shrugged. "I can't imagine. I bruise easily. I'm always finding bruises and can't remember how I got them."

"Symmetrical bruises. Somebody made them," he said, flashing the same easy smile.

As if she didn't see through him! His deliberately casual manner, coaxing, as if he were speaking to a child!

The father said to the new bride, "Somebody made those marks. Lynn, I want to know."

"Is there something you want to tell me?" the doctor asked her now.

Thinking she heard a note of curiosity in his voice, she felt the hot sting of indignation. It was the new style these days; you got it on television and in print, people saying whatever came into their heads without manners or tact, prying and snooping with no respect for privacy; *just let it all hang out.*

"What can you mean?" she retorted. "What should I possibly want to tell you?"

The young man, catching her expression, which must have been fierce, retreated at once.

"I'm sorry. I only asked in case you had something else on your mind. So, that's all for today. Next month Dr. Rupert will see you as usual." And he turned back to the chart.

Her heart was still pounding when she left the office. Meddler. Officious busybody. She wondered whether he would write, *Two bruises, upper arms,* on the chart.

Even as she pushed the cart through the supermarket a little while later, she was still aware of her heartbeat. Then, in the parking lot as she was unloading the cart, she caught sight of Harris Weber and his mother in the next row of cars. And her heart began its race again. They hadn't seen her yet, and she bent lower over the bags so that they might leave without noticing her. This avoidance was not because of any ill feeling toward them, for she had almost none toward Harris and certainly none at all toward his mother; it was because the unknown woman knew things about her, about her and Robert. . . . And she wanted to hide, not to look the woman in the face and have to see there—what would she see there? Curiosity? Pity? Contempt?

But they were taking so long that by now the boy must have recognized her car and would know she was leaning ostrichlike over the groceries in order to avoid them. Something told her to look up, not to hurt the boy.

"Hello," she said, and raised her arm in a slight wave.

He gave her his bright, familiar look, that candid look with the masculine sweetness in it, whose appeal she had felt from the very first.

"Hello, Mrs. Ferguson."

"How are you?" she called across the car's hood.

"Fine, thanks. And you?"

She nodded and smiled; the mother nodded and gave in return a smile that said nothing; it was merely polite and perhaps a trifle shy. That was all. And they drove away, the old car sputtering out of the parking lot.

There, Lynn told herself, that wasn't so bad. It had to be done. Yet the little encounter had given her another kind of sadness—not for herself, but for Emily. She went home, put the groceries away, sat down to read the mail, mostly bills and Christmas cards, and with the sadness still in her, listened to the drowsy hum of the silence.

The telephone rang. She must have been dozing, for it startled her, and she jumped.

"Hello," said Robert.

"Where are you?" she cried.

"In London. I told you, we took the day flight so we're staying the night here, and we leave for Berlin in the morning. It was a fine flight."

"That's nice," she said stiffly.

"Lynn, it's night here, but I couldn't go to sleep without talking to you. I waited till you'd be back from the doctor's. How are you?"

"How is my health, do you mean, or my state of mind?"

"Both."

"My health is all right. The other is what you might expect."

"Lynn, I'm sorry. I'm so awfully sorry. I said it was a good flight, but it wasn't, because I kept thinking about us all the way. About us and Annie. I didn't want to hurt her feelings, God knows. I never do."

"You hurt her because she isn't Emily. She isn't beautiful, and—"

"No, no, that's not true. I do everything for her, everything I can. But I'm not as patient as you are, I'll admit that. I always do admit when I'm wrong, don't I?"

She wanted to ask: Shall I count the times you do, the times you don't, and give you the ratio? But that kind of hairsplitting led nowhere. It was like jumping up and down on the same spot.

She sighed. "I suppose so."

"I get frustrated. I want so much for her, and she doesn't understand. Annie's not easy."

There she had to agree. Yet she fenced with her reply, saying sternly, "Nobody is, Robert."

"That's not so. You are. You are the kindest, the gentlest, the most reasonable, sensible, wonderful woman, and I don't deserve you."

Was this the frowning, hostile man who had shouted last night in the kitchen, hurt her arms, and turned his back on her in the bedroom? Yes, of course he was. And somewhat scornfully she admonished herself: Don't tell me again that you're surprised.

"Lynn, are you there?"

"I'm here, I'm here."

"Tell Annie I'm sorry, will you?"

"Yes, I'll tell her."

"The whole thing was stupid, the way we turned away from each other without saying good-night as we always do, or without saying good-bye this morning. What if one of us should have an accident like the Remys and we were never to see each other again?"

The Remys, who had lived across the street. Linda and Kevin. The words pierced her. She could still hear Linda's terrible cry when they called to tell her of the accident; the sound had rung down the block so that people had come running, and Linda had gone mad.

"He left for work an hour ago!" she screamed, and had kept screaming. "He left for work an hour ago!"

"That angry night would have been our last one. Think about it," Robert said.

A heart attack. A plane crash, or a car crash on a foreign road in fog and rain. His mangled body. They would return it to America. He would never sit in that chair again.

"Lynn, are you all right? What is it?"

"I'm all right."

But he had pierced her. It felt like internal bleeding. She was seeing herself in the house alone—because what are one's children, more than an extension of oneself? These vulnerable girls, this unborn infant to care for, and he not coming back. No man's voice, no man's dependable step coming up the stairs at the end of the day. No man's strong arms.

"I guess my nerves wore thin," she said. "I should have brought you and Annie together before night. But I was just plain mad. And then, I'm not twenty years old anymore," she finished ruefully.

"Yes, you are, as you were when I met you. You'll always be twenty. Tell me you love me a little. Just tell me that, and it'll hold until I come back. Tell me you're not angry anymore."

Her very flesh could feel the vibrations in his voice, the quiver of his pain.

"I love you all so much, but you first of all. I'm nothing without you, Lynn. Forgive me for the times I've hurt you. Forgive me, please."

"Yes. Yes."

The marks on the arms, the hot-tempered words so dearly repented of

—what are they in the end compared with all the goodness? Nothing. Nothing.

Thousands of miles apart, we are, and still this tie renews itself as if he were in this room or I in that strange room in London, and we were touching one another. Astonishing!

So her anger dissolved. It lifted the chill that had clung like a wet pall all that day, and comfort began to warm her.

"And you love me, Lynn?"

"Yes, yes I do."

In spite of everything, I do.

"Take care, then, darling. Give my love to the girls. I'll call again in a couple of days."

Relief was still flooding, and she was still sitting there cradling the plastic instrument in her hands as if it could still hold some essence of that relief, when it rang again.

"Hello, this is Tom Lawrence. How are you?"

"I'm fine, thank you." And she actually heard the lilt in her own voice.

"I'll tell you why I'm calling. I wonder whether you can do me a favor. My sister's in town with her daughter. They live in Honolulu, and she thought it was time for Sybil to see what lies beyond Hawaii. Sybil's twelve. Don't you have a girl about twelve?"

"Yes, Annie. She's eleven."

"That's great. May we borrow her? Do you think she'd like to go into the city? We'd see a show, maybe a museum or maybe the Statue of Liberty. How does that sound?"

"It sounds lovely."

"Well, then, we'll pick Annie up tomorrow morning, if that's all right, and we'll take the train in."

"Annie'll be thrilled. She loves New York."

"It'll be a new experience for me, with two ladies that young. My sister wants the morning off by herself to do the shops, so I'll be on my own with the girls for a while."

"You'll do very well, I'm sure."

"She'll like Sybil. A nice kid, even if she is my niece."

A faint worry passed through Lynn. For some reason she imagined the sister to be like the excessively smart young women whom she had seen at that party in Tom's house. She would be incredibly thin, and her daughter would be, too, dressed in French clothes, and looking sixteen years old. There were plenty of girls like that, but Annie was not one of them.

So it was with some relief that she greeted the party at the door the next morning. Tom's sister, who might have been his twin, was pretty and proper and friendly. Sybil, like her, was neither thin nor fat, although not as pretty as her mother. Annie would have a good day.

Lynn's prediction turned out to be right. Annie had a wonderful Saturday. At dinnertime she repeated triumphantly, "I had chocolate cake with raspberries and cream. I told them my father says I'm too fat, and Tom said when I'm older I'll want to diet and not to worry too much in the meantime."

" 'Tom'? You called Mr. Lawrence 'Tom'?"

"He told me to. Because Sybil calls him 'Uncle Tom.' "

Light snow, mixed with rain, had begun to freeze. In the moment of quiet it could be heard tinkling on the windowpanes.

"It's nice eating here in the kitchen," Emily said. "Cozy."

It was true. In the dining room with only four at the table, it always seemed that ten or twelve more were missing, for the table, an original Sheraton, was long enough to seat eighteen. The room always seemed to echo. Robert said, though, that a dining room was meant to be dined in.

Annie was still full of her day. "I told him I hate my hair, it's so kinky. And he said I can have it straightened if I want to. I said my father won't let me, and he said I could do it when I was grown up because I could do whatever I wanted then. He said he knew a lady who had it done, and she loved it afterward." Annie giggled. "I'll bet he meant one of his wives."

Lynn and Emily glanced at each other. And Emily scoffed, "You don't know anything about his wives."

"Yes, I do. Sybil told me. He's had two. Or maybe three, she thinks." Annie, looking thoughtful, stopped the fork midway to her mouth. "You know what? If you ever divorce Dad, I think you should marry Tom."

"Why, Annie! As if I would ever divorce Daddy."

"I should think you would pick Uncle Bruce," Emily remarked. "You love him so much."

She had a twitch at the corner of her mouth as she spoke, that might have been humorous, or cynical, or both. Lynn looked away.

And Annie said seriously, "Yes, of course I love him, silly, but he has Aunt Josie."

Lynn rebuked them. "This is all silly. And don't you dare say anything as idiotic as that in front of Daddy either. He's coming home the week after next on Wednesday."

"Eleven more days. Only eleven more days," Annie said. "I thought he was going to stay longer."

"Well, he'll be finished with his work by then," Lynn explained, "so it will be time to come home."

Annie grumbled. "He just left. What's the use of going away when he just turns around and comes right back? He can't be doing very much. I hope they give him a bigger job next time."

"Go let Juliet out. She needs to go," Lynn said.

On the Monday, when school reopened, Emily came home without Annie, grumbling, "That kid! She missed the bus again. Now I suppose I'll have to get in the car and go back for her. And she'll be soaked, too, standing outside in this mess."

Lynn looked out of the window where sleet was slanting as if it, too, like the trees, were leaning against the wind. A high, dangerous glaze lay on the white slope.

"No, I'll go, Emily. The roads are slippery, and you haven't been driving long enough to manage."

Emily looked at her mother's enormous belly. "And if the car gets stuck and you have to get out and you fall? No, I'll go, Mom. I'll be careful."

When you come down to it, she is still the most responsible girl, Lynn thought as she watched the car move cautiously down the drive, slide into the road, and move almost inch by inch out of sight. Nevertheless, she remained at her anxious post by the window, mentally timing the trip to the school and return.

When the telephone rang—always at the most inconvenient moments, it seems, the telephone has to ring—she picked it up. An unfamiliar voice came over the wire.

"Lynn Ferguson? This is Fay Heller, your sister Helen's neighbor in St. Louis. Do you remember me?"

Lynn's insides quivered. "Yes, yes. Has anything—Where's Helen?"

"Helen's fine. The whole family's away on a ski trip. I'm calling because they're away, and your little girl Annie's here at my house."

Lynn sank down onto a chair. "Annie? There with you? I don't understand."

A very calm, soothing voice explained. "Don't be frightened. She's quite all right, unharmed. She arrived in a taxi around three o'clock. I saw her ringing Helen's bell, and naturally getting no answer, so I went over and brought her here. She doesn't want to explain herself, and so I haven't pressed, but—"

Oh, my God, she's run away. What else is going to happen? To run away makes no sense. . . .

"I can't imagine whatever got into her head!" Lynn cried, the trite words coming automatically, while her thoughts ran opposite. You don't have to imagine, you know. Robert is coming home. . . .

The ice cream episode had been horrible, and yet . . . To run away . . . Annie, Annie . . .

Her head pounded. Her sweaty, cold hand shook, holding the receiver.

"Kids do surprise us sometimes, don't they?" The woman was trying to make light of the affair, trying to console. "I guess we did the same to our parents in our time."

Lynn's thoughts were racing. However had Annie bought a ticket and gotten onto the plane? An unaccompanied child, going all that distance? They would never sell her a ticket.

"May I talk to her, please?"

"I did suggest that she call you right away, but she was a bit upset, naturally, so I thought it better not to insist."

"She's not afraid to talk to me? Tell her I won't scold her. I only want to know how she is. Tell her, please, please."

"Well, the fact is, I wouldn't say she's afraid, but she was really awfully tired, and I sent her upstairs to lie down. After she ate, I mean. She was hungry."

Now the woman is being tactful. The truth is, Annie doesn't want to talk to me.

"She wants to go home. Do you want me to see whether there's a plane we can get her on this evening?"

So she does want to come back! Oh, thank God for that.

"No, in the circumstances, I don't want her to fly alone. I'll find out how I can fly from here instead."

"Actually, the weather's very bad on this end. Why don't you let me keep her overnight? It's late in the day now, anyway."

Tears were gathering; Lynn's throat was tightening. And the other woman, apparently sensing this, said gently, "You're thinking she's a trouble to us, but she isn't. And she's quite fine here. You remember my three, don't you? They're grown and gone, but I still know what to do with a young girl. So don't worry."

A little sob broke now. "I'm terrified thinking what might have happened if it hadn't been you who discovered her. God knows who else might have come along."

"Well, no one else did. Wait a minute, my husband's saying something.

Oh, I'm right. Nothing's flying out of here tonight. You'll have to wait till tomorrow."

"All right, then, I'll take the first plane in the morning. And, oh, I want to thank you. How can I even begin?"

"Don't bother. You would do the same for someone. Just get a good night's sleep if you can."

She must wipe her eyes and compose her face before Emily came back. The mother is strong in emergencies, not shaken. A mother hides her fears and hurts. But she hadn't been able to hide them from the doctor that morning. . . .

In the back entry Emily stamped snow from her boots and called, "Mom? Mom? She wasn't there. I looked all over. The darn kid must have gone home with one of her friends. You'd think she could at least call up. Why, what's the matter?"

"What on earth do you think that foolish child has gone and done?" Lynn wanted to express, instead of her total dismay, a kind of mock exasperation as if to say, with hands thrown up, What will she do next?

But Emily did not respond in kind. "She's very frightened. Her dark thoughts frighten her," she said gravely.

The two women looked at each other. It occurred to Lynn that they, too, were exchanging such rather enigmatic looks quite often lately. It occurred to her, too, that it was always she herself who first dropped her eyes or turned away.

"Annie was never an easy child, not like you," she said, since a comment of some kind was needed.

That, of course, was just what Robert had said when he called from London. And Emily's reply was the very one that she, Lynn, had given to Robert.

"Nobody's easy."

She was not up to a philosophical argument, not now. "I'll fly out tomorrow on the first flight I can get." Since Emily still stood there looking uncertain, she added, "I remember the Hellers. They're good friends of Aunt Helen's. So let's try not to worry too much."

Emily said only, "Well, I've a ton of work. I'd better get to it."

Sometimes, not often, it can seem that there's no comfort in Emily, Lynn thought. In fact, she even has a way of making me feel uncomfortable, almost as if, right now, I'm the one who made Annie run away.

The dog whined to go out. She stood at the kitchen door while Juliet ran to the shrubbery, where each twig was now glassy with ice. The dog squatted, ran back, and shook the wet from her fur, sprinkling the kitchen floor. On sudden impulse, oblivious of the wetness, Lynn knelt and hugged her. She needed living warmth.

"Oh, God," she said, letting the dog lick her hand.

But she needed words, too, warm words, and these the animal could not give. So she went to the telephone. She had to tell Josie.

"Are you all right?" asked Josie when she had finished her short account.

"Yes, yes, I only needed to talk. I'm sorry to be dumping on you when you're sick."

"It's only this nasty cold that I still can't shake, and you are not dumping. Hold on a minute. Bruce is here and he wants to know what this is all about."

First Lynn heard them conferring in the background. Then Bruce came to the telephone.

"Lynn, take it easy," he said. "I'll go bring her back. The weather's bad, and you can't risk a fall. I'll go in the morning."

She protested, was overruled with utmost firmness, and, suddenly exhausted, went upstairs to lie down on the bed.

In a rowboat, alone and terror stricken, struggling and straining somewhere on turbulent high seas with no land in sight, she suddenly saw the flare of light and heard someone speak. Emily was standing beside the bed.

"Mom dear, wake up. You've been asleep for more than an hour. You've got to eat something. I've made dinner."

In midmorning Tom Lawrence called with an invitation to Annie for a good-bye dinner with Sybil, who was going back home. The normalcy of this request, made in Tom's jocular way, but arriving in these abnormal circumstances, made Lynn's answer choke in her throat.

"Annie's not here." Her voice slipped into a high falsetto. "Annie's run away."

There was a pause. What should, what could, anyone reply to news like that?

He asked her quietly whether she could tell him anything more.

"Yes. She went back to St. Louis to my sister. Only, my sister wasn't there—" Her voice broke, and he had to wait for her to resume. "Bruce has gone to bring her home."

"Robert's not back, then?"

"No. The day after tomorrow."

"Who's with you, Lynn?"

"Nobody. I made Emily go to school, and Josie has a terrible cold, flu or something. And I don't want anyone else to know."

"Of course not. You shouldn't be there by yourself, though. I'm coming over."

"Oh, no! You needn't. I'm all right, really."

She must look frightful, a pregnant elephant with dark circles under the eyes. . . . Strange that she should care at all, at a time like this, how she would appear before this man. "Your work, your office—"

"I'm coming over."

The pile of logs in the fireplace was ready to be ignited. For a moment she regarded it uncertainly, feeling a little foolish for even having the thought, as though she were being a hostess preparing for guests. Then, deciding, she lit the fire, went to the kitchen to prepare coffee, took a cup of violets from the windowsill and put it on the tray with the cups and the coffeepot. By the time Tom arrived, the fire was lovely, the coffee was fragrant, and a little plate of warm muffins lay on the table before the fire.

In jeans and a flannel shirt he looked like a college boy, belying his years. Robert never wore jeans. Her thoughts were disconnected.

"Do you want to talk about it?" he asked. "Or shall we talk instead about the day's headlines? Or shall we not talk at all?"

She put out her hands, palms up, expressing confusion, and began to string together the adjectives that seemed to come automatically with every description of Annie. "I don't know how to say it. . . . She's a difficult, secretive, moody child." She had to stop.

Tom nodded. "She's a great little kid, all the same. My sister couldn't get over how much she knows compared with Sybil."

And Robert complains that she's stupid.

"She's a sweet little girl, your Annie."

There was a very gentle compassion in Tom's face. His eyes were leaf shaped; funny, she had not noticed that before.

"You gave her a wonderful time. She loved it."

He took a muffin. "Banana. It's different. What's in it?"

"Orange peel. I thought I'd try it. Is it any good?"

"Wonderful. I told you, you ought to be in business. But of course, this is hardly the time."

The fire crackled, drawing them with its ancient lure to watch its tipsy dance. Presently, Tom spoke again.

"May I talk frankly? Annie's worried about herself, isn't she? About her weight and her hair?"

"Yes, you were very kind to reassure her."

And as she remembered Annie saying, "You should marry Tom," a tiny smile, in spite of herself, quickly came and went.

He opened his mouth and closed it.

"You were going to say something, Tom."

"No, I changed my mind."

"Why? Please say it."

He shook his head. "I got in a lot of trouble with you once, remember?"

"Yes, because you said things that weren't true."

She had to tell him that. Had to. Framed in silver on the table beside the sofa, Robert was regarding her gravely. On his hand the wedding band showed prominently. It had been his idea to wear joint rings.

Tom had followed her gaze. And, as if he had made a resolve, continued. "I was only going to say that Annie repeated several times that her father was upset about her weight. That's all I was going to say. I thought it might be a useful clue to what's happened."

Upset. That dreadful scene. *You're a mess.* The child's blotchy, tear-smeared face. And then: *I would never hurt her feelings. I love you all.*

"I don't know what to think," she murmured, as if Tom weren't there.

He took a swallow of coffee, put the cup down, took it up again, replaced it once more, and then said, "I'm your friend, Lynn. We haven't known each other very long or closely, but I hope you feel that I'm your friend."

Clearly, he was trying to pull from her some admission, some confession of need, and some appeal for his help. Even in the midst of this day's turmoil she was alert enough to be aware of that. Yet she felt no resentment toward him for trying, which was strange, and because it was necessary to respond to his generosity, she murmured, "I know you would help if you could. The fact that you're sitting here is enough to tell me that."

"And you're sure I can't help?"

She shook her head. "It is something we shall have to work on with patience. Robert always used to talk Annie out of her—her moods—but lately, they've been having their troubles. Well, she's growing up, and growing up is harder for some children than it is for others."

"Oh, yes. Well, I wouldn't know, not having had any children, only wives."

She leapt toward the change of subject. "How many, may I ask?"

"Two and a half."

"A half!"

"Yes, I lived with one for a year. You might call that having half a wife." He laughed. "Oh, it was all very friendly. We made a mutual decision to call it quits."

Lynn thought: If I had him, I don't think I would, or could, easily let him go. And she remembered how when she first had seen him, she had felt a kind of lightness about him, a bright illumination, shedding happiness.

He gave her now a quizzical look, saying, "You don't approve?"

"I? I don't judge. But Robert wouldn't—" And she stopped.

That was wrong. Her mention of Robert's trouble with Annie was wrong. One kept one's problems to oneself, within the family. And she looked again at Robert's photograph, which, although it was of ordinary size, dominated the room. This time, Tom followed her glance.

"I talked to Pete Monacco the other day. He wanted me to know how much they're all impressed with Robert. Of course, he thinks Robert and I are very close friends."

At the "close friends," Lynn flushed. She said quickly, "Well, Robert's impressive. I don't know where he gets all his energy. In addition to everything else he does, he's taken on a new project, fund-raising for AIDS research."

"Incredible energy."

There was a pause, as if they had both been brought up short at a line that neither one must cross. Then a telephone call came, easing the moment.

"Yes, Bruce? Oh, thank God. Yes, hurry. Don't miss it." She hung up. "That was Bruce, phoning from the airport. They're on the way home. Annie's cheerful, and I'm not to worry." She wiped her eyes. "Not to worry. Imagine."

"But you do feel a lot better."

"Yes. I'll talk to Annie very, very seriously. As you say, she's a bright girl. We'll talk heart to heart. I can reach her." As she spoke, it seemed to her that this was a reasonable attitude. You talk things out, you reached understanding. True, Annie had run off on a crazy impulse, but she had come back; it was not the end of the world.

"Yes, I do feel better," she repeated.

He stood up, saying, "That being the case, I'll leave you. It's my sister's last day."

"Of course. You were wonderful to come at all."

"You're a lovely woman, Lynn. But you're all out of style. Oh, I don't mean your clothes. When you're a normal shape you look like Fifth Avenue. I mean, you still have a sort of old-fashioned, small-town trustfulness. I'm not making myself clear, am I?"

Answering his smile, she said, "Not really."

"What I mean is, trust is out of fashion now."

He took her hand and raised it to his lips.

"Something I learned last year in Vienna. They still do it there. 'I kiss your hand, honored lady.' "

At the front door, puzzled and slightly embarrassed, she could think of only one thing to say, and repeated, "It was wonderful of you to come. Thank you so much."

"I'm here for you anytime you need me. Remember that," he said, and went down the path.

She was left with the same puzzlement. Was this just unusual kindness on his part, or was there anything more to it? She was, after all, so inexperienced. She had hardly spoken to another man or been alone in a room with any man but Robert since she was twenty years old. But she let herself feel flattered anyway. For a pregnant woman with a burdened mind it was a pleasant feeling.

"Well, here we are," cried Bruce when Emily opened the front door.

Lynn held out her arms, and Annie rushed into them, hiding her face against her mother's shoulder. Bruce looked on, his smile combining triumph with relief, while a gleam of moisture fogged his glasses.

"Why did you do it, darling?" Lynn cried. "You scared us all so terribly. Why? You should have talked to me first!"

"Don't be angry at me. I was scared too." Annie's plea was muffled in Lynn's sweater. "I was scared when I was on the plane. I wished I hadn't done it, but I couldn't get off the plane, could I?"

"No, no, darling, not without a parachute." And Lynn pressed the child closer. Then she cried, "How ever did you get a ticket at your age?"

"There were some big girls going to college and they let me say I was their sister. Then when I got there I wanted to go back again, only I didn't have enough money. I used up everything in my piggy bank for one way. So I had to go to Aunt Helen's house. And I rang the bell, and nobody was there, and"—the recital ended in a wail—"I wanted to go home!"

"Of course you did. And now you are home."

But the courage of the child! To make this plan, to carry it out by herself, took brains and courage.

Annie drew away, wiped her running nose with the back of her hand, and shook her head. Tears had streaked her face. Her rumpled collar was twisted inside the neck of her coat. If the girl were beautiful, Lynn told herself in that instant, one would not feel quite so much anguish, such protective pity. And she repeated softly, "Why didn't you tell me, Annie, whatever it was?"

Annie burst out. "You wouldn't answer. Anyway, it's awful here. It's so full of secrets in this house. You're sick—"

At that Lynn had to interrupt, protesting, "Darling, I'm not sick. Sometimes when a woman is pregnant, her stomach acts funny, that's all. That's not being sick. You know. I've explained it to you."

"But that's not the kind of sick I mean. And besides, there's something wrong with Emily too. She's different. She's always in her room. She hardly talks to me anymore."

Now it was Emily who interrupted. "That's not so, Annie. I have to study in my room. And anyway, I do talk to you."

"You won't let me come in, and I know why. You're crying, and you don't want me to see it. Nobody ever tells me the truth. When you went to the hospital, you said it was something you ate, infectional flu or something."

"Intestinal flu," said Lynn.

"And that's all it was," said Emily.

"I don't believe you! Do you want to know what I think? It was something Dad did."

"Oh, what a dreadful idea!" Lynn cried.

Perhaps they ought to have listened to Josie and told the truth to Annie. These days kids knew everything. They knew about abortions and miscarriages, homosexuality, AIDS, everything. But Emily would not have wanted it. And it was Emily's life, after all.

"How can you think such a thing?" Lynn cried out again.

"Because he's mean, that's why. You never want anybody to say things about him, but I don't want him to come home. I don't. I don't."

And this was what his tumultuous angers had produced. What mattered all his steady, persistent efforts to teach tennis or piano? Lynn wanted to cry again, but knew she must not.

Like strangers on an unfamiliar street, uncertain which way to turn, the little group stood hesitantly in the hall.

Bruce broke into the uncertain silence. "Let's get our coats off at least and sit down."

"You must be hungry," Emily said promptly. "I can fix something in a couple of minutes."

"No," Bruce answered. "We had dinner on the plane. I think we should talk instead."

They followed him into the den, where Lynn had kept the fire burning all day. He walked toward it and stood with head down and an intent expression, as if he were seeing something hidden in the fire's ripple and flare. Then he turned about and, still with the same grave face, began rapidly to speak.

"We had a few words about all this on the flight home. But then I realized it wasn't the place for the things I wanted to say. So let's have an open talk now. What I want to explain to Annie is something she has already found out, that people, every one of us, are a mixture of all the people who came before us. This one's eyes and hair, that one's talent for the piano, another one's sense of humor or short temper or patience or impatience."

Except for the jingle of Juliet's collar as she scratched herself, the room had gone very still. Not used to seeing him so solemn, they were all drawn to Bruce.

"And when you get people together in a family, in the same house, you come up against these differences every day. In my house Josie thinks I'm messy, and I am. I get sawdust on my clothes and in my pockets. Then I come in and sit down on the sofa and leave sawdust between the pillows. Josie can't stand that. I think she makes too much of a fuss because I don't think the sofa is that important, but she does, and she thinks I ought to see that it's important. So we're just different, that's the way we are."

He paused with his eyebrows drawn together and looked them over keenly. "And every one of you here does things that the others can't stand." He raised his hand as if to halt anyone who was about to speak. "No, I'm not looking for confessions. I just wanted to make my point. Annie, have you any idea what my point is? I mean, why Josie and I don't pull each other's hair out over the sawdust? Or one of us doesn't run away?"

Annie gave a small smile.

"Makes you want to laugh, doesn't it? Tell me. Why do you think we don't?"

"I guess," she said weakly, "because you love each other."

"You guessed right, Annie. That's the whole answer. You say your father's 'mean.' Maybe he seems so, but I'm not here, and I don't know.

But if he does say mean things, the truth is he also says very good things, too, doesn't he? And does good things for you too?"

Receiving no answer, Bruce pressed again. "Come now. Doesn't he?"

"I guess so."

"Ah, Annie, you know so. I've been here often enough. I've seen you two play piano duets together, and that's wonderful. I've watched him teach you to play tennis, too, and I've met you both at the library on Saturday mornings, getting books. Do you think he does all those things because he's mean?"

Lynn had seldom heard Bruce speak at such length and with such intensity; he was known for his brevity. When they were together, it was Josie who, earnest and positive, did most of the talking.

"So maybe, I'm not saying he has, but you say he has a terrible way of scolding. But, Annie, what can you do about it? He isn't likely to change. People rarely do, Annie. Most of us stay pretty much the way we're made. So running away won't help. This is your home, here's your mother, here's your sister. You'll have to make a go of it right here."

Emily was looking straight ahead. Her face held sadness; the parted lips were tired. And what were the thoughts that had drawn a line across her forehead? Lynn's own head was heavy with scattered recollections. Did Bruce really mean what he was saying?

"It comes back to love, as you just said about Josie and me. You have to remember that people can scold and yell and still love. Your father loves you, Annie. He would do anything for you. Always think of that, even if it's sometimes hard to do. Try not to let words hurt you, even if they seem unfair and perhaps really are unfair. If it's his way to speak harshly sometimes, well then, that's his particular fault, that's all, and you'll have to live with it."

All this time Bruce had been standing, and now he sat down, wiping his forehead as if he had been making a great effort. Again Lynn saw the gleam of moisture behind his glasses. Today is a day, she thought, that I'd like to forget. This desolate day. And yet, he has managed to put some heart into it.

"I was wondering," he said now slowly, his remark directed at Lynn as much as to Annie, "whether it might not be a good thing for Annie to have someone to talk to when she feels troubled? There's a Dr. Miller, a friend of Josie's—"

"It would be a wonderful help to you, Annie," Lynn said. "I agree with Uncle Bruce."

Immediately, Annie objected. "No! I know what you mean. A psychologist. I know all about that, and I'm not going, not, not, not!"

Lynn waited for Bruce to respond. It seemed quite natural to trust the decision to him.

He said gently, "You don't have to decide this minute. Think about it carefully, and when you change your mind let your mother know."

"I won't change my mind," Annie said.

This defiance sounded exactly like Robert. Curious thought. If Annie should agree, though, there would be another tussle, strong objections from Robert, almost impossible to override. And yet, Lynn thought fiercely, if need be, I will override them.

"Okay, okay," Bruce said. "Nobody's going to force you to do anything. We're just glad you're home. Your family can't get along without you, Annie, even Aunt Josie and I can't. We depend on you for those Sunday mornings when you help with the furniture."

Bruce had a project, repairing old furniture that had been donated for the needy, a quiet project that brought no acclaim. And Lynn recalled again, as she so often did, her father's old expression: He is the salt of the earth.

The fire had died into a pile of white ash, yet its friendly heat seemed to linger. Bruce was standing before it with hands outstretched toward the warmth. And a bizarre thought flashed into Lynn's head: What if I were to get up and put my arms around him? Bizarre! Have I lost my mind? The man is Josie's husband, for God's sake. And I am Robert's wife. And it is Robert whom I love.

She said cheerfully, "You're hungry, no matter what you say. Stay a minute. I made vegetable soup this afternoon while I was waiting for you."

"That sounds good after all," Bruce admitted. "Airline food leaves you hollow."

So they came to a little spread in the kitchen, soup and biscuits, a dish of warm fruit and a plate of chocolate chip cookies. To Lynn's surprise Annie refused the cookies. Could it be that when sweets were freely offered, Annie found that she didn't want them as badly as when they were refused? One had to ponder that.

At the front door she took Bruce's hand between both of hers.

"This is the second time you've been a lifesaver. Do you realize that?"

"It's what friends are for, Lynn."

"I am so very rich in friends." And for no known reason she told him that Tom Lawrence had come that morning too. "I was so surprised."

"Why? He thinks the world of you," Bruce said. "But then, we all do."

When he had gone and Annie was upstairs, Lynn asked Emily, "What was Bruce saying while I was in the kitchen?"

"Nothing much."

"You all suddenly stopped talking when I came in. Don't hide anything from me, Emily."

"Okay. He only said that you need us at this time. That it's not right for you to be under stress, not good for you or for the baby."

Lynn frowned. "I hate to seem like an invalid, for heaven's sake. As if you shouldn't feel free to express yourselves naturally. I don't want that."

"Is it true about the baby?"

"I don't really know. They say it may be."

"I've never seen him so stern," Emily said. "He seemed almost angry at us."

"Why, what do you mean?"

"He said we are to keep this house peaceful no matter what anyone—what anyone says or does. Ever. We are to keep things smooth and happy." Emily reflected. "It's true, I have never seen him so stern. He actually commanded us. It didn't seem like Uncle Bruce talking." She laid her cheek against Lynn's. She was taller than Lynn, who had not been aware until this instant how much taller. "We—both of us—took him very seriously. Annie won't do anything wild again. He helped her a lot. Don't worry, Mom."

"If you say so, I won't."

"Promise?"

"I promise."

But it is all too simply said, Lynn told herself. How many of Bruce's own words he really believed, she thought again, or what he truly thought, she could not know.

Nevertheless, when Robert came home, it was as if the two previous days had been wiped out of memory.

Having been delayed at customs to pay for all the gifts he had bought, he was late in arriving. It took two men, the driver and Robert, to maneuver a tall carton up the walk and set it down in the hall.

"Why, what on earth have you brought?" Lynn cried.

"You'll see."

His eyes sparkled; the long trip, the exertions, had only lifted his high spirits. He had hugs and kisses for them all. For an instant, as Annie was pulled to him, Lynn, watching and inwardly imploring, thought she saw refusal in her eyes, but it vanished, and perhaps she had only imagined it. Laughing, he held Lynn's hands and stepped back at arm's length to examine her.

"Oh, my, you've grown! Look at your mother, girls. I swear it looks as if she had twins in there, or triplets. If so, we'll have to build an addition onto this house, or move. But how are you, darling?" And not waiting for an answer, "How is she, girls? Has she been feeling well? Because she'd never tell me if she hadn't been."

"She's been fine," Emily assured him.

"Then you've been taking good care of her." He rubbed his hands together. "It's freezing outside, but nowhere near what it is in Central Europe. Oh, I've got a million things to tell you. It's hard to know where to begin."

"How about beginning with dinner?"

"Ah, dinner! Ah, good to be home."

Lynn had prepared a feast of rich, hot food for a winter's night: mushroom soup, brown slivers floating in the golden broth, duckling with dark cherries, spinach soufflé with herbs and onions, and apple pudding in wine sauce. Champagne stood in a nest of ice, and everyone drank except Annie, who tasted and made a face. Even Lynn, in spite of her pregnancy, took a sip. The table was set with the best china and the Baccarat crystal that Robert had bought. In the center Lynn had arranged a low cluster of white roses. All this excellence did not go unappreciated.

"Your mother!" Robert exclaimed. "Your mother. Just look at all this." He was exultant.

"What a fantastic experience! Of course, it was hard work, late hours, talking and translating, meeting all sorts of people, some cooperative and eager, some stubborn—but that's life, isn't it? All in all, though, I should say it was a great success. Budapest, as you walk through the old quarter, is somewhat dark and dingy to our eyes, but wonderfully quaint, all the same. And then suddenly you come up against a modern glass tower. The company's office is as modern as anything we have in New York. You walk away, and there's a Chinese restaurant, next a pizza place, and there you see what's ahead, you see the future."

Robert paused to cut off a piece of duckling, swallowed it, and could barely wait to continue his tale.

"Hungary is a full democracy now. Knowing some history of its past, you can only feel the marvel of what's happening. Eventually, they'll be in NATO, or in some sort of association with it. No doubt of that. What the country needs now, what all these countries need, is management training, and that's where the West, where we, come in. Oh, say, I almost forgot. I brought a real Hungarian strudel. I bought it yesterday morning. It's in my carry-on. Well, we can eat it tomorrow. It'd be too much with this dessert too. You should see the little coffeehouses, Lynn. All the pastries! You would get recipes galore. I sat in one of them and looked out onto a square with palaces and a huge Gothic church. Marvelous. You're going to love it, girls."

"What about college?" Emily asked anxiously.

"Don't worry, just you get into Yale. Nothing's going to interfere with that." Robert smiled. "You'll just fly over whenever there's a vacation. I'll be earning enough to afford it, don't worry."

"And what about me?" inquired Annie.

"Don't you worry. We'll have a fine school for you, with diplomats' children and all sorts of interesting people and—"

He had brought home his full vigor and his old magic. It was contagious. And in her daughters' faces, Lynn saw that they were feeling the contagion too.

"And of course we won't be limited to Hungary. It's so quick and easy to get around Europe, and you'll have a chance to see it all. You'll see Greece and the Parthenon, and you'll know why I wanted you to study the Greek gods, Annie. Rome, Paris, of course, and"—he made a wide sweep of his hand—"the world! Why not?"

After dinner they opened the packages. Standing in the center of a circle of chairs, Robert unwrapped and displayed his finds. He had bought with care. For Annie there was a cuckoo clock. "I remember you said once that you wanted one, and this one's a beauty." For Emily there was a watercolor of a castle on a hill. For Lynn there were Herend figurines, all in green and white and large size: a kangaroo, an elephant, and a unicorn.

"I thought awhile about whether I should get them in the red or the green. What do you think, did I do right, Lynn?" he asked.

And without waiting for her reply he set them on the mantelpiece, then stepped back, regarding them with a slight frown. "No, not that way." He moved them. "They should be clustered at the side. Symmetry is boring."

Lynn remarked, "I don't know where you got the time for shopping."

"I don't know myself. When you want to do something, you make the time. That's about it."

The evening went on long past Annie's bedtime and usurped Emily's homework hours.

". . . and we should have at least a few days' skiing in Chamonix. From what I've read the French Alps have a special charm. Oh, I'll manage to get days off." Robert laughed. "The boss of the office can always wangle a few days, especially when he's overworked all the rest of the time. Say, look at the clock. All of a sudden jet lag has got to me. Shall we go up?"

In their bedroom as he undressed, Robert said, "Things are looking so good, Lynn, so good. You know what they say about getting sand in your shoes, so you'll want to return? Well, there may not be any sand over there, but I can't wait to go back."

As he emptied the suitcase and sorted the contents, he moved fast and spoke fast, leaping from one subject to the next.

"I faxed a report to Monacco and got a very pleased reply. . . . I noticed something different about Emily tonight. That sort of remote look she's been having is quite gone. She seemed warmer toward me. Yes, as I predicted, she's gotten over that fellow. Thank God. . . . And Annie, too, was really sweet, I thought. . . ."

He hung his ties up on the rack and, turning, suddenly exclaimed, "Oh, but I missed you all so much, hectic as it was. Did you miss me as much, Lynn?"

She was telling herself: He's bound to find out, so I might as well get it over with now. So as briefly as possible she began to relate the story of Annie, making sure not to disclose any of Annie's remarks about him.

Robert was startled, vexed, and dismayed, all together.

"Good God," he said, "the minute my back is turned some disaster befalls my children."

Lynn's heart sank.

"I didn't want to spoil your homecoming, and I hope this hasn't, because, as you see, we're all right now." And she improvised, for to tell the tragic story with complete accuracy would only provoke an argument. "It seems she had been worried about me. Well, I suppose it's only natural for her to have mixed feelings about this pregnancy. And then she was upset about Emily last summer. She thought Emily was terribly sick and we were hiding the truth. It all seems to have been preying on her mind, and so she just—"

And why am I hiding the truth myself? she asked now as she fell suddenly silent. Am I still so torn about Caroline that I fear to take any more blame for anything? He has already said that Emily's trouble was my fault. . . .

Robert had sat down heavily. "And Bruce brought her home," he said.

"Yes, it was wonderful of him, wasn't it?"

He slumped in the chair. In the weak light of the lamp on the bedside table, his face went sallow, as if the vigor had just drained out.

Anxiously, Lynn explained, repeating herself, "He was wonderful. He talked to Annie, to both of them, so beautifully."

"What did he talk about?"

"Oh, life in general, meeting challenges, optimism, understanding one another. He did them a lot of good."

"That may be, but I'm not happy about it."

"No, there's nothing to be *happy* about. I really do believe, Robert, that Annie should have some help, some counseling. And so should we."

"That's nonsense. I've told you my opinion of that stuff. Anyway, Annie's not the first kid who got a notion in her head and ran off. It happens all the time. I'm sure she was sorry before she was halfway there."

Well, that much was true. . . .

"But I'm thinking about Bruce. He's my subordinate in the office, and he knows my family's most private affairs, Emily's mess last summer, and now this. Dammit all."

"He was very kind," Lynn said, and then, wanting to clear the record entirely, she added, "Tom Lawrence was very kind too. He came over that morning."

"Oh, for God's sake, he too? How did that happen?"

"He didn't want me to be alone when he heard. You shouldn't mind, Robert. These are good friends."

"Good friends, but they know too much."

"They're fine men. They would never talk about our children. You know that."

"The fact that they themselves know is enough," he grumbled.

As she leaned to take off her shoes, she could barely reach her feet. Seeing her struggle, he got up to help her. The baby was active; its movement under her sheer slip was visible to him, and she saw that he pitied her; he would not argue.

"Poor girl," he said. "What a time you've had with me away! Poor girl. Now I'm home, you relax and let me take care of things."

The baby turned and turned. Through these last frantic days she had scarcely been able to give thought to it, but now awareness of its imminent arrival shocked her. Only another eight or nine weeks from now, it would be separated from her, separated and yet in another way closer, because of its demands, which would and should come before any others. She must, she must, keep calm and hopeful for its sake.

Calm and hopeful. All right, then. Relax and let Robert take care of things. He wants to, anyway.

Robert V. W. Ferguson, Jr., was born early on a windy morning in between winter and spring. Rough and tough as he had been in the womb, his exit from it was remarkably easy. He weighed nine pounds, came with a full head of hair, and was the first of the Ferguson babies not to be bald. His hair was sandy like Lynn's; his face gave promise of length and would probably be aquiline like Robert's.

"All in all a nice compromise," said Robert. He stood against a background of spring bouquets arrayed on the windowsill. "Have you counted the flowers? That basket of green orchids on the end is from Monacco. He wired it from California." He watched his son feeding at Lynn's breast. "What a bruiser!" he cried. "What a bruiser. Just look at that boy."

Scarcely containing his jubilation, he made Lynn feel like a queen.

Back at home she lay in bed like a queen.

"You're going to take it easy, you're going to rest and be waited on at least till the end of the week," Robert insisted.

The bassinet, skirted in white net, stood beside the bed, and Lynn thanked Josie for its blue bows.

"The minute we heard from Robert that it was a boy," Bruce said, "she came over here. And I want you to know that I'm the one responsible for the bows being blue."

"So sexist," Josie said.

"You surely weren't going to put pink ones on, were you?" asked Lynn.

"Why not?" was Josie's cheerful reply. "Still, I did what my husband ordered."

Their funny mock bickering amused Lynn. The short hour that she had been home had already filled her with a fresh sense of well-being. New books in their bright jackets were stacked on the bedside table, next to the box of chocolates—now no longer on the forbidden list—and a cluster of lilies of the valley in a tiny cup. Husband, friends, and daughters, all of them fascinated by the baby in his soft wool nest, were gathered around her. Annie and Emily spoke in whispers.

"You don't have to whisper, darling," Lynn told them. "Talking won't disturb him a bit."

Annie asked anxiously, "When can we hold him?"

"When he wakes up, I'll let you hold him."

And shyly, Annie said, "Isn't it funny? I don't know him at all, but I love him already."

Lynn's eyes filled. "Oh, Annie, that's lovely."

"Why? Did you think I wouldn't love him? I'm much too old to have sibling rivalry with the baby."

Everyone laughed. Bruce patted Annie on the back, and Emily said, "Annie, where are the boxes that came this morning?"

"Right here, behind the door. Open them, Mom. They're probably more sweaters. He's got seven already. And there's a big box downstairs that came yesterday. I haven't opened it."

Robert went down and a few minutes later returned with a child-size wing chair upholstered in needlepoint.

"Queen Anne! Isn't that adorable? A formal chair for our living room," cried Lynn. "Whoever thought of that?"

"Tom Lawrence's card, with best wishes." Robert frowned. "Why such a lavish present? We hardly know him. He's not an intimate."

Lynn, feeling the rise of heat, hoped it wouldn't flow out on her cheeks. Tom had outdone himself; the gift was original, in perfect taste— and expensive.

As if Bruce had read her mind, he came to the rescue.

"It's not so lavish for a man in Tom's position. Expense is relative. And obviously he likes you both."

"Well, it's only that I don't like feeling beholden," Robert explained.

A puzzled look crossed his face. Lynn knew that he was thinking back to the weekend in Maine, and to all the things Lawrence had done for him, the good words he had put in for him.

"You'll have to write to him tomorrow at the latest, Lynn."

"I don't feel up to it. I'm more tired than I thought I was," she said untruthfully.

A letter to Tom, if indeed he had any ideas—and the more she thought, the more certain it appeared that he might have some, even though she had certainly made her own position quite clear—might be unwise. The situation was a little bit exciting, but it was also disturbing. No, not a letter.

"You write," she told Robert, "and I'll sign it along with you." And she turned to Emily as if she had abruptly remembered something. "Hasn't Aunt Helen even phoned?"

Annie, Emily, and Robert all looked around at each other.

"No? How strange. I don't understand it."

"Oh," Robert said, "it was supposed to be a surprise, but we might as well tell you. They're on the way, both of them. They should be here in an hour or two. They're renting a car at the airport."

"Darwin too?" Lynn was touched. "How good of him to take the time!"

"His time." Robert laughed. "Bathtubs and toilets. Important business."

"I shouldn't care to be without either one," Bruce remarked, laughing.

Josie said firmly, "I like Darwin. I always did. He's kind."

"Oh, kind, yes," Robert agreed. "A diamond in the rough."

If only Robert would not always, always, say things like that!

And Robert said, "I might as well break the news. Aunt Jean has taken it into her head to come too."

"Don't look so glum! I think it's darling of her to want to see the baby. I'm glad she's coming, and I'm going to show her I'm glad." But then immediately Lynn worried. "Where's everybody going to sleep? And what's everyone going to eat? They'll be here for a couple of days, I'm sure, and—"

"Not to worry." Emily assured her. "I've fixed a nice bed in the little third-floor room for Aunt Jean, Uncle Darwin and Aunt Helen will have the guest room, and we've a ton of food. Uncle Bruce went marketing with us this morning before you got home, to help carry all the stuff. Enough for an army."

"And the dinner table's set already," Annie said. "We even made a centerpiece out of the flowers you brought home."

So they all came and went, up and down the stairs all day, in and out of the room where the queen lay back on embroidered pillows, the best set, kept for sickness in bed and so, fortunately, never used before.

Annie brought Juliet up to let her sniff at the bassinet. "To get used to the baby's smell," she explained. Robert brought a supper tray. "Don't I make a good butler?" he asked, wanting praise. And then came Helen and Darwin, he as pudgy and beaming as ever, she as welcome as ever.

"I feel as if I haven't seen you for a century," Lynn cried as they hugged each other.

"Well, it's been almost two years. No matter what they say about planes getting people back and forth in a couple of hours, it's a big trip. It's traveling."

"This family's going to get used to traveling," announced Robert, who in his pride was standing with a hand on the bassinet. "This little boy is going to see the world." And when Helen looked blank, he asked, "Do you mean to say Lynn hasn't told you? Yes, we're going to be living abroad for a while. Two years, three, five—who knows?" And he gave an enthusiastic account of his project.

"How is it that you never told me about all this?" asked Helen when the two were alone. Then, before Lynn could reply, and in her quick, penetrating way that so much resembled Josie's way, said, "You had too much else on your mind, that's why."

"Well, it wasn't the easiest pregnancy, I'll admit. But isn't he darling? His head is so beautifully shaped, don't you think so?"

Helen smiled. "He's lovely. Mine looked like little monkeys for the first month or so. But I wasn't thinking of the pregnancy. I meant—you must know that I meant Annie."

Lynn had no wish to reveal the doubts and worries that, even though Annie did seem to be much steadied, still flickered in her consciousness. She especially did not want to admit them to Helen. So she spoke lightly, in dismissal.

"Annie's over all that."

"Yes, until the next time."

Helen was always reaching for clues, for signals and alarms; of course it was because she had never liked, and still didn't like, Robert. But she was too decent to say so.

There was a note of petulance in Lynn's voice when she replied. She heard it herself and even knew the reason for it: I've said things are different now, but I've said it often enough before too; I don't want to be reminded of that today; I just want a little time to be purely happy with my baby.

"Annie's fine, Helen. Delighted about Bobby. Can't you see?"

Helen's silence told Lynn that she did not believe her.

"You can ask Bruce if you don't trust me," Lynn added stubbornly. "He knows Annie well."

"I want to trust you," Helen said, her lips making the tight pucker that always gave a shrewd look to her pretty face. "I want to. But I know that if things were bad, you would never admit it."

Probing, probing, Lynn thought resentfully.

"You've always been so secretive. One has to worry about you."

Lynn's impatience mounted. "Look at me. What do you see? Look around at the house. What do you see?"

"I see that you look the same as ever and your house has everything of the best."

From downstairs there came the sounds of a piano accompanying lively song.

"That's Robert playing, and the girls are singing. They made up a funny song to welcome me at the door when we came home from the hospital. Doesn't that tell you anything?" demanded Lynn.

"Well . . . It tells me that we all love you." And Helen, apparently accepting defeat, changed the subject. "Do you know what? I'm starved. I'm going down to see what there is to eat."

"May I come in, or will I tire you?" Jean hesitated, as was her way. At least it was her way when she was in Robert's house.

"Of course come in. I'm not the least bit tired and it's ridiculous for me to be lying on this bed, but the doctor said, 'Two days rest, positively.' "

When Jean had admired the baby for the second time, she sat down in the rocking chair by the bed. For a few moments she said nothing, merely smiling at Lynn with the expression that Robert called "meek"; instead Lynn had always seen, and saw now, not meekness but a stifled sorrow.

Jean folded her old, brown-spotted hands together; lying in her flowered lap—did she never wear anything but flowers?—they were patient and strong.

"It's nice to have a time alone with you, Lynn," she said. "And this is likely to be the last time. I'm moving to Vancouver."

"But so far away! Why?"

"I'm going to live with my brother. We're both pretty old and all we have is each other."

"You have us. You could move here, near us."

"No, dear. Let's be truthful. Robert doesn't like to have me around."

There was nothing meek about the statement. It had been delivered with a rather stern lift of the curly gray head and an expression that, although grave, was yet without rancor.

The statement demanded an honest reply. Or a more-or-less honest reply.

"Robert can be irritable sometimes with anyone, Aunt Jean, when he's in the mood. But you must know, his bark is worse than his bite."

"I know. He was a darling little boy, and so smart. We used to play games together, checkers and dominoes. He loved to beat me, but, oh, his temper was terrible when he lost! We had fun together . . . but things change. It's a pity, isn't it? After my sister was gone, and he moved away. . . . You would have liked Frances," Jean said abruptly. "She was a gentle person. And she would have loved having you for a daughter. You've always reminded me of her. You're soft and you're kind, like her."

Very much touched, Lynn said simply, "Thank you."

The rocking chair swayed; there was a quaintness in its regular creak, an old-fashioned peacefulness as in the presence of the old woman herself.

"I'm sorry you and I haven't seen more of each other, Lynn. But I'm glad to see how well things are going for you. They are going well, aren't they?"

"Why, yes," replied Lynn, wondering.

"And Robert is still a good husband to you."

Was that a question or a statement?

"Why, yes," Lynn said again.

Jean nodded. "I'll think of you here in this lovely house and it will be a pleasure to me. I've put that photo of Emily and Annie into a flowered frame. I like to have flowers everywhere. I guess you've learned that about me, haven't you? I do hope you'll send me a nice photo of Bobby sometime."

"As soon as he grows some more hair. I promise."

"And that you'll still call me every week—even in Vancouver."

"Of course we will. You know that."

"I like your sister," Jean said, "and your friends Josie and Bruce. There's something special about him, although I don't know yet what it is."

Lynn smiled. "You like everybody, I think."

"No, not everybody. But I do try to find the good in people if I can. Frances was like that—too much so for her own good—oh, well, tell me, does the baby need an afghan for his carriage?"

So the conversation veered away from people into the neutral area of things, things knitted, woven, cooked, and planted. The comfortable ease that Jean had brought into the room was ever so vaguely troubled when she left.

I wish people wouldn't be so—so enigmatic, Lynn said to herself.

Now Emily came and sat on the edge of the bed.

"Mom, you're so especially beautiful when you're happy," she said.

She had a charming way of widening her eyes to express emotion. Today her hair was twisted and piled on top of her head; she wore the heart-shaped gold earrings that Robert had given her on her last birthday. Just to look at her brought an undiluted joy that Lynn needed just then.

"I'm happy when you all are." The baby grunted in his sleep. "Turn him onto the other side of his face for a change," she said.

"Oh, Lord, I don't know how. I'm scared to touch him."

Lynn laughed. "I know. When you were born, I was afraid to pick you up, afraid you'd break. Just raise his head gently," she directed, "and turn it. He's not that fragile."

"He sighed," Emily said. "Did you hear him? It sounded just like a sigh when I turned him."

"He's probably worrying about the international situation," Lynn said cheerfully.

But Emily was grave. "Mom," she said, "I never realized what a serious thing it is."

"Serious?"

"To care for a baby, I mean. A person should think about it very, very long before doing it."

She spoke very low, not looking at her mother, but away toward the window where a dark blue evening was coming on. And Lynn understood her meaning: that what had happened last summer must not happen again.

Still speaking toward the darkness, Emily continued, "All the plans you must have for him, his health and his school, the cozy room that he was brought to, and the quiet home. You have to plan, don't you? And keep to the plan."

Lynn was putting herself into her daughter's place, trying to imagine her remorse, to feel the fright that must still be hers when she considered some of the turns her life could have taken. And hesitating, she said softly, "There will be a right time for you, Emily. You know that now, don't you?"

Emily turned back to her. "I know. And I'm fine, Mom. I really am. Believe me."

She was an achiever, competent and strong. A young woman with purpose, Lynn thought as always, certainly not your usual high-school senior.

"Yes," she said. "Yes, I do believe you." And then to relieve the poignancy of the moment, "But have you had your dinner?"

"Half of it. I thought you might not like being alone."

"I don't mind at all. Go down and finish. Just hand Bobby to me first. He's going to be hungry in a minute, I can tell."

And sure enough, the boy woke just then with a piteous wail.

"Turn on the lamps before you go. Thanks, darling."

When Emily walked out she left no suspicions and no enigmas behind to fog the air. Lynn took a deep, pure breath. From belowstairs came the pleasant buzz of talk. She could imagine them sitting at the table; Robert at its head was carving and serving the meat in the old-fashioned style to which he kept. The back door banged; somebody was letting Juliet out. Someone was walking through the halls; heels struck the bare floor between the rugs. These were the sounds of the family, the rhythms of the house, the home.

Let Helen peer and delve; she means well, but never mind it. And never mind poor, dear old Jean's *And Robert is still a good husband to you?* It is the natural curiosity of a lonesome woman, that's all it is.

These last few days, these last few months, had been so rich! Before then it had been a cruel year, God knew, but was pain not a part of life too? Miraculously now, a new spirit seemed to have come over them all, over Robert and the girls, and because of them, over herself.

And she lay with the hungry baby at her breast. Little man! Such a little creature to have, by his simple presence, brought so much joy into this house! Lynn was feeling a cleansing gratitude, a most remarkable peace.

PART FOUR

◇

Spring 1989–
Fall 1990

5

THE enormous room was packed. Every table had been taken, and, reflected in the mirrored wall of this somewhat typically gaudy hotel ballroom, the audience was impressive in its size.

"This man," said the mayor, "this man on whom we gratefully bestow the Man of the Year Award, has accomplished more for our community in the few years he has been among us than many, including myself, who were born here, have done for it."

Affectionate and friendly laughter approved of the mayor's modesty. Nevertheless, thought Lynn at the pinnacle of pride, it is true.

"The list of his activities fills a long page of single-spaced type. There's his work on behalf of the hospital, the cancer drive, the new library, so sorely needed, for AIDS, education, for the whole recycling program that has set an example to the towns around us. I could go on and on, but I know you are waiting to hear from Robert Ferguson himself."

Robert had grace. Beside him on the podium the town's dignitaries, three men and a pleasant-faced woman with blue-white curls, looked nondescript. It was always so. Wherever he went, he was superior.

"Mayor Williams spoke of a list," he said. "My lists are much longer. They contain the names of the ones who are really responsible for the success of whatever good causes I have been helping. It would take hours to tell you who they are, and I might miss some, and I mustn't do that. So I'll simply tell you that we owe a debt of hearty thanks to all those people who manned telephones, gathering the funds we needed, who stuffed envelopes, gave benefit dinners, wrote reports, and stayed up nights to get things done."

His voice was richly resonant, his diction clear and pure, but unaffected. There wasn't a cough or whisper or creaking chair among the audience.

"And above all, I must give full credit to the company of which I am fortunate to be a part, to General American Appliance, of whose magnanimous gifts, not only here in our community but all over the country, you are certainly aware. The extraordinary generosity of such great American corporations is the wonder of the world. And GAA has always been outstanding for its public service. *We care.* And here in this relatively little corner of the United States, you have been seeing the fruits of our caring.

"And so I thank my superiors at GAA for encouraging my little undertakings here and covering for me whenever necessary, so making it possible for me to find the time I need.

"Last—my family. My wonderful wife, Lynn—"

All eyes turned to Lynn in her daisy-flowered summer dress; Robert had been right to insist on a smashing new dress. Across from her at the round table sat Bruce and Josie, flanked by town officials. Bruce smiled as he caught her eye; Josie, who seemed to be regarding the chandeliers, had no expression. And a thought fled through Lynn's mind: Robert has not mentioned Bruce.

". . . and my lovely daughters, Emily and Annie, who never complain when I have to take some of the hours I owe them to go to a meeting. Emily will be graduating from high school on Tuesday, and entering Yale in the fall."

Emily, serene in white, inclined her head to acknowledge the applause with the simple dignity of a royal personage. Her father's dignity.

". . . and our Bobby, four months old today, has been very cooperative too. He tolerates me—"

Laughter followed, then more applause, a concluding speech, a shuffling of chairs, and the emptying of the room. In the lobby people crowded around Robert; he had charmed them.

"How about a drink? Come back to our house. It's early yet."

"Thanks, but my wife's a real mother, a nursing mother, and Bobby's waiting," Robert said.

He was glowing. It was as if there were a flame in him, heating his very flesh. She felt it when she stood beside him at the crib, watching the baby settle back to sleep after feeding. And surely she felt it when afterward in bed he turned to her.

"All those months we've missed because of the baby," he whispered. "We have to make up for them."

In the close darkness of the bed, without seeing, she yet knew that his eyes were thrilled, that their blue had gone black with excitement. She put her hand out to feel his racing heart, the heat and the flame.

The graduates, in alphabetical order, came marching down the football field through the lemon-yellow light of afternoon.

"Good thing that kid's name begins with *W*," Robert whispered.

He may be at the end of the line, Lynn thought, but he's still the valedictorian.

It was the finality of all this ceremony that was so moving. Childhood was indisputably over. These boys and girls would all disperse; these young ones, a little proud, a little embarrassed in their gowns and mortarboards, would be gone. The bedroom would be vacant, the customary chair at the table unoccupied, and the family diminished by one. Nothing would ever be the same. Two weak tears gathered in Lynn's eyes. Reaching for her purse to find a tissue, she was touched on the arm.

"Here, take mine," said Josie. "I need one too."

Josie knew. Bruce knew, too, for he had taken Josie's other hand and clasped it on his knee. Last year at this time things had looked rather different for Emily, alone and desperate with her secret. Now they were calling her name, handing the rolled white document: "Emily Ferguson, with highest honors."

But Robert was chuckling, bursting. His girl. His girl. He was the first to scramble down from the benches to take her picture and rejoice.

Everywhere were cameras, kissing and laughing and calling. The PTA had set up tables on the grass for punch and cookies. People crowded in knots and got separated, parents making much of teachers, younger brothers and sisters finding their own friends.

Lynn, as she stood at a table to replenish her cup of punch, heard Bruce's voice a few feet away.

"Yes, of course it's a science and an art. You're lucky at your age to be so sure of what you want to do."

"Well, it's useful," she heard Harris say. "That and teaching are the only truly essential things"—and then, so apologetically that she imagined his fair skin flushing—"I don't mean that business isn't useful, Mr. Lehman. I don't express myself very well sometimes."

"Don't apologize. I quite agree with you. If I'd had the ability, I would have wanted to be a doctor or perhaps a teacher of some sort."

They caught sight of Lynn, who had filled her cup. Sure enough, Harris was brick-red.

"Congratulations, Harris," she said.

"Thanks. Thanks very much. I seem to have lost my folks. I'd better run."

They watched him dart back into the crowd.

"It touches you to see a boy like him. You just hope life will be good to him," Bruce said.

"I know. I feel the same."

"Robert would slaughter us if he heard us."

"I know."

She oughtn't to have agreed; it was complicity with Bruce against Robert. And as they stood there drinking out of their paper cups, she avoided his eyes. It occurred to her suddenly that they had never had a dialogue; they were always in a foursome or more.

Presently, Lynn said, "Emily's having a little party tonight. Want to come and supervise the fun? They're all over eighteen, and Robert's allowing one glass of champagne apiece. One small glass."

"Thanks, but I think not. We'll call it a day."

That was strange. She was wondering about the refusal, when she met up with Robert.

"Did you see Bruce talking to young Weber?" he demanded.

"Only for a second."

"Well, I watched. Bruce deliberately sought him out. Your fine friend. I consider that disloyalty. Unforgivable."

Not liking the sarcasm of "your fine friend," she answered, "But you'll have to forgive it, won't you, since there's nothing you can do about it."

"More's the pity."

"It's all over, anyhow. Emily's started a new chapter. Let's go home for her party."

The next day in the middle of the afternoon, Bruce telephoned, alarming Lynn, who thought at once of Robert.

He understood. "Don't be frightened. It's nothing to do with Robert, and I'm not at the office. I didn't go in today." His voice was clearly strained, as if there were something wrong with his larynx. "Josie was operated on this morning. I'm at the hospital in her room. She's still in recovery."

"Why? What is it?" Lynn stammered. "It's not—"

"Yes," he said, still in that strangled voice. "Yes. The lymph. The liver. It's all through her."

A wave of cold passed through Lynn. *Footsteps on my grave,* my grandmother had used to say. No, Josie's grave. And she is thirty-nine.

She burst into tears. "I can't believe it. You wake up suddenly one morning, and there's death looking into your face? Just like that? Yesterday at the graduation she was so happy for Emily. She never said . . . There's no sense in what you're telling me. I can't make any sense of it."

"Wait. Hold on, Lynn. We have to be calm for her. Listen to me. It wasn't sudden. It's been going on for months. All those colds she said she had, that time I went to St. Louis last winter to fetch Annie, all those were excuses. She was home, too sick to move; she almost didn't get to the graduation yesterday. She wouldn't have chemo—"

"But why? She had it before and came through it so well!"

"This is different. We went to New York, we went to Boston, and they were all honest with us. Try chemo, but without much hope. That's what it came down to, underneath the tactful verbiage. So Josie said no to it, and I can understand why, God knows."

Lynn asked desperately, "Then why the operation now?"

"Oh, another man saw her and had an idea, something new. She wanted to refuse that, too, but you grasp at straws and I made her try it. I was wrong." And now Bruce's voice died.

"All these months. Why did she hide it? What are friends for? You should have told us, Bruce, even if she wouldn't."

"She absolutely wouldn't let me. She made me promise not to worry you. She said you had enough with the new baby and . . ." He did not finish.

"But Josie's the one who always says you should face reality."

"Your own reality. She's facing hers, and very bravely. She just didn't want to inflict *her* reality on other people as long as she could face it alone. Don't you see?"

" 'Other people'! Even her best friend? I would have helped her. . . ." And afraid of the answer, Lynn murmured the question, "What's to happen?"

"It won't be very long, they told me."

She wiped her eyes, yet a tear slipped through and dropped on the desk, where it lay glistening on the dark leather top.

"When can I see her?" she asked, still murmuring.

"I don't know. I'll ask. Maybe tomorrow."

"Does Robert know?"

"I called him this morning at the office. They needed to cancel my appointments. I have to go now, Lynn."

"Bruce, we all love you so, Emily and Annie. . . . I don't know how to tell Annie."

"I'll talk to her. Annie and I, you know we have a special thing."

"I know."

"I have to go now, Lynn."

She put the receiver back and laid her hand on the desk, saying aloud, "I am heartsick." And the words made literal sense, for her chest was heavy, and the cold tremble would not stop. Josie, my friend. Josie, the sturdy, the wise, fast moving, fast talking, always there. Josie, aged thirty-nine.

She might have sat in a fog of sorrow all that afternoon if Bobby's cry had not rung through the fog. When she had taken him up from his nap and fed him, she carried him outdoors to the playpen on the terrace. With a full stomach and content in his comfortable, fresh diaper, he lay waving a rattle. Dots of light flickering through the emerald shade seemed to please him, for every now and then his babble broke into something that sounded like a laugh. At four months! She stood looking down at his innocence, knowing that there was no way on earth he could ever be shielded from heartbreak.

After a while she rolled the playpen over to the perennial border, where he could watch as she knelt to weed. A different reaction had begun in her, a need to move, to assure herself of her own vitality.

From a tough central root, purslane shot its multiple rubbery arms and legs like an octopus, crawling like cancer among the phlox and iris, peonies and asters, all the glad and glorious healthy life. With fierce hatred she dug out the roots and threw them away.

The sun had gone behind the hill, and the grass had turned from jade to olive when tires crunched the gravel. Robert, on his way from the station, had called for the girls at the pool, and the three were coming toward her as she rose from her knees. By their faces she saw that he had given the news to the girls.

"Is she going to die?" asked Annie, never mincing words.

The truth was as yet unspeakable. She could think it and know it, but not say it. So Lynn answered, "We don't know anything except that she's very sick."

"Perhaps," said Emily, "the operation will have cut it all away. My math teacher in junior year had cancer when he was thirty-five, and he's old now."

"Perhaps," said Robert. "We shall hope."

Alone with Lynn he gave a long, deep sigh. "Poor guy. Poor Bruce. Oh, if it were you . . ."

"Are we maybe rushing to a conclusion?" She clasped her hands as if imploring him. "Is it really hopeless?"

"Yes. He told me the only hope left is that it may go fast."

Measured by the calendar it went fast, covering as it did only the short span of summer. And yet it seemed as if each day contained twice the normal count of hours, so slowly did they move.

Once on a weekend they tried bringing Josie home. She was so light that Bruce, carrying her, was able to run up the steps into the house. At the window, where she could look out into the trees, he set her down and brought an ottoman for her feet. The day was warm, but she was shivering, and he put a shawl around her frail shoulders.

The cat bounded onto her lap and she smiled.

"He hasn't forgotten me. I thought maybe he would have."

"Forgotten you? Of course not," Bruce said heartily.

We are all acting, thought Lynn. We know we dare not show tears, so we talk loud and briskly, we fear a moment's silence, we bustle around and think we're being normal.

A fine rain had begun to fall, so that the summer greenery was dimmed behind a silvery gray gauze. Josie asked to have the window opened.

"Listen," she said. "You can hear it falling on the leaves." And she smiled again. "It's the most beautiful kind of day in the most beautiful time of the year."

This time next year, Lynn thought, and had to look away. She had brought a dinner, light, simple food, white meat of chicken in herbs. Josie took a few mouthfuls and laid the fork down.

"No appetite," she said, apologizing, and added quickly, "but as always, your food is marvelous. Someday you'll do something really big with your talent. You should be trying it now."

Robert corrected her. "She has her hands full at home. Right, Lynn?"

"I don't know," said Lynn, thinking that Josie's skin, her lovely skin, was like old yellowed newspaper.

"But I know," said Josie, wanting her way.

In the evening she asked to go back to the hospital, and Bruce took her.

Her flesh fell off, leaving her eyes sunken into their round bony sockets and her teeth enormous in the cup of her jaws. Yet in a brief spurt of energy a lovely smile could bring harmony to this poor face. More often, it seemed as though the medication was loosening her tongue. Indeed, when she was lucid, she admitted as much.

"Yesterday I said something I perhaps should not have said," she told Lynn one afternoon. "I remember it now quite clearly, isn't that odd?"

"I don't remember anything," Lynn assured her, although she did remember and quite clearly too.

"It was when I showed you the roses that Tom Lawrence brought. I was so surprised. I didn't expect a visit from him. We don't know him all that well."

"He likes Bruce, that's no mystery."

"That's what you answered me yesterday. I said, 'No, he likes you, Lynn.' We are his contact with you, since he can't very well see you when Robert's not there, and he doesn't want to see you when he is there. That's what I said, and it upset you."

"Not at all. Why should it upset me, since it's so silly?"

"It's you who know the answer to that. But you would never tell me what you think about Tom. You would never tell me anything that really touches you in the deepest part of your heart. You're too secretive, Lynn."

"Secrets, Josie?" Lynn queried gently. "What about you? You've been sick for six months and never said a word."

"There was nothing you could do!" And as Lynn began to protest, she cried, "Now, don't scold me again about that!"

The plaintive tone, so unlike Josie's clear, brisk way of speaking, was hopeless and, like the wasted hands on the coverlet, helpless.

And Lynn burst out, "Was I so wrapped up in myself, my new baby, my own life, that I didn't see what was happening to you? How can I have been so blind to your need?"

"Lynn dear, no. I had good days and bad ones. I just didn't let you or anyone see the bad ones. And you are the last person to be accused of self-absorption. It would be better for you if you did think more about yourself."

"But I do," Lynn protested.

"No, you don't. You've built a wall around yourself. Even your sister knows that. No one can really get through to you. But a person can't do what you're doing forever." Josie turned in the bed, seemed to find a more bearable position, and resumed, "That's why I wish—I wish you had a man like Tom. I could die knowing that you were being treated well. That you were safe. . . ."

"Josie, Josie, I'm fine. I'm safe, dear. And don't talk about dying!" And don't talk about Robert. . . .

"Yes, now I must. There's a right time to speak out. Six months ago it wasn't necessary. Now it is."

Lynn looked at the walls, the depressing hospital-green walls that, if they could talk, would tell of a thousand griefs and partings. Now here was another. It was too hard to imagine a day on which she would pick up the telephone to call Josie and have to tell herself that Josie was no longer here.

"You've been my support," she said, ready to weep. "Whenever I'm worried about Annie, and I worry so about her, you're my support. You've borne all my troubles."

Josie's wan smile was faintly bitter. "No, not all. You skirt around the truth about Robert."

"About Robert?" Lynn admonished gently. "But we are very happy, Josie. . . . Everything's fine now."

"No, no." Josie's head rolled back on the pillow. "I'm a social worker, you forget. I see things you could never imagine. I see things as they really are." Suddenly her fingers clawed at the sheet, and her body writhed. "Oh, why can't you be honest with me when I'm in such pain, when I have to die and leave Bruce? Oh, God, this pain!"

Lynn's heart was bursting. "I'll get the nurse," she said, and ran, and ran.

Even now, half raving, Josie probes, she thought on the way home.

Josie and Helen.

It was all too much to contend with. Her deep thoughts ran like an underground river.

The summer plodded on, creating its own routine. At Robert's insistence Bruce came almost every evening for dinner before going to the hospital.

"He must have lost fifteen pounds," Robert had observed. "We can't let him go on like that. It's a question of decent responsibility. He's part of the firm of GAA, after all."

Annie left for scout camp, and Lynn said, "I'm glad she's gone. It would be too hard for her when—" and glancing at Bruce, she stopped.

He finished for her. "When the end comes? Annie and I have had some very truthful talks about that, and I don't think you need to worry about her. She's quite prepared," he said firmly, "as I must be." He smiled. "And am not."

No one at the table spoke until Emily said gravely, "This makes everything else in the world seem small, doesn't it?"

A heat wave, striking the countryside, struck the human body with intent to draw its breath out. Petunias went limp in the border, and birds were still. Even the dog, after a minute or two outside, panted to get back into the house. And in the air-conditioned house the air was stale. It was as if the very weather had conjoined with events to stifle them all.

"It takes too long to die," said Emily.

And then one morning at breakfast Emily had something else to say, something very serious.

"You'll be shocked. I'm scared to tell you," she began.

Two startled faces looked up from their plates.

"I don't know how to begin."

"At the beginning," Robert said impatiently.

The girl's hands clung to the table's edge as if she needed support. Her eyes were darkly circled, as if she had not slept. She gulped and spoke.

"I'm not going to go to Yale."

Robert stood up, his chair screeching on the floor, and threw his balled napkin onto his plate.

"What? What? Not going to Yale?"

"I wrote to them. I want to go to Tulane."

My God, Robert's going to have a stroke, Lynn thought, while into her own neck, the blood came rushing. She could see the beat of the pulses at his temples and put her hand on his arm to warn him.

"Tulane? Why," he said, "of course, it's the southern climate, isn't it? You like that better. Oh, of course, that must be it." And he made an elaborate sweep of his arm in mocking courtesy.

Emily said quietly, "No, Dad. It's because Harris got a scholarship there." And she looked without flinching at her father.

Robert stared back. Two pairs of steady eyes confronted one another, and Lynn glanced toward the girl, so frightened yet firm, and back to the furious man and back to the girl. How could she be doing this to them? She had given her word. How could she be doing this to herself? After all that had been said, all the reasoned explanations, the kind, sensible advice; had it all passed into deaf ears and out again?

As if she were reading Lynn's thoughts, Emily said, "I have not lied to you, since that's what you must be thinking. I have not seen him even once since—since what happened. We do talk on the phone. You know that, Mom."

"What?" cried Robert. "You knew they had telephone communication and you allowed it!"

His anger, like a diverted stream, now rushed torrentially toward Lynn. She braced herself. "Why, yes. I saw no harm in it." His eyes were hot and were cold; the cold burned like dry ice. "I thought, I mean—"

"You didn't think and you don't know what you meant. It's just another example of your ineptitude. This whole affair was mismanaged from the start. I should have done what I wanted to do, sent her away to a private school."

"A school without telephones?"

"That could have been managed," Robert said grimly. He picked up the ball of napkin and hurled it back onto the plate. If it had been hard, it would have shattered the plate. "Dammit, I don't know how I manage to keep my head. A thousand things on my mind, and now this! If I should have a stroke, you'll have a lot of questions to ask yourselves, both of you. That's all—"

"No. Don't blame Mom," Emily said, interrupting. "That's not fair. The fault is mine. The decision is mine. Dad, I'm nineteen. Please let me have some say in my own life. I'm not trying to defy you, I only want to be happy. We don't want to be away from each other for four years. No, please listen to me," she said hurriedly. "There won't be a repeat of what happened last year. I understand that's what you're afraid of. We'll be very careful, we'll be so busy keeping our grades up, that we'll keep all that to an absolute minimum, anyway—"

Robert roared. "I don't want to hear about your sex life."

"We haven't had any for a year. I only meant—"

"I'm not interested, I said!"

"This is disgusting!" Lynn cried.

She closed her eyes. How ugly, the three of them on a summer morning filling the blue light with their dark red rage! Her eyelids pressed against her eyeballs, wanting to shut the rage out.

The dining-room clock struck the half hour.

"Good Christ," Robert said. "I've got fifteen minutes to get to the station. With luck maybe a truck will hit me on the way, and you'll all be free to take the road to hell without my interference." He picked up his attaché case and, at the door, turned around. "You did say you wrote to Yale, didn't you?"

"Yes. I gave up my place."

"Well. Well, I'll tell you what. I'm not going to pay your bill anywhere but at Yale. Is that clear, young lady? You just write to them again and phone or go there and straighten the mess out with them, or you won't go anywhere. I'm not paying my good money so that you can go and shack up with that boy again."

"We won't. . . . I told you. . . . I promise. I've kept my promise, haven't I? If only you would listen . . ." Emily whimpered.

"And I told you: no tuition. I hope that's clear. Is it clear?"

Wordlessly, Emily nodded.

"Fine. So don't waste your energy or mine asking me again. No tuition. Not a penny. That's it. And it's your own doing. Now let me get out of here."

They stood, each behind her chair, as if frozen there, while the front door sounded its solid thud, and the car's engine raced, its tires spurted gravel on the drive and squealed around the curve.

Lynn sat down again, and Emily followed. A conference, it seemed, was called for, although Lynn was too distraught, too confused, to begin one. Emily, with her head down, fiddled with the silverware at her place. Its tiny clash and clink were unbearable, and Lynn scolded.

"Do stop that." Then more quietly, she said, "Well, you've managed to set the house on fire once again, haven't you?"

It was rotten of Emily. Rotten.

"It's Dad. He's unforgiving," Emily replied.

"No. He's crushed, that's what it is. And don't dodge the issue. Giving up Yale! After all your effort and our hopes. Why weren't you at least open about it? We could have talked it over. This is really—it's really unspeakable. I trusted you. Now you've put me in the position of a fool. No, what am I saying? I don't mean to talk about myself, about your father and me. Never mind us. What about you? What are you doing with your life, you foolish, foolish, capricious, thoughtless girl?"

"I don't think I'm foolish or thoughtless, Mom." The tone was earnest and reasoned, belying the tears that, unwiped, rolled over reddening eyelids. "We want to be married. Oh, not yet. We know it's much too soon. But we mean it, Mom. Why didn't I talk about this before I canceled Yale? Because you know as well as I do that Dad would have talked me out of doing what I want to do. He's so powerful, he gets his way. Oh, I wish our family was like Harris's family!"

How that hurt! What else had Lynn ever wanted but to build a life for her children that they would happily remember? And now this girl, across whose face and therefore in whose mind there passed the most delicate and subtle feelings, could wish that they were "like Harris's family."

"Yes? What are they like?" she asked in a dull monotone.

"Well, we told them how we feel. They aren't exactly thrilled about our being at college together, but they think we're old enough to make our own mistakes. His mother said we made one mistake, so probably that would be a warning not to make another. And she's right. Oh, you think—"

"You don't know what I think," Lynn said with bitterness. And it was a bitter thing to stand between this enmity, daughter against father.

"Well, Dad thinks—"

"Yes, try to imagine what he thinks. He works so hard for us all."

"He works for his own pleasure, Mom. The way you put it, anytime a person opposes Dad, you lay guilt on the person because Dad 'works hard.' Harris's father works hard too. Do you think a policeman's life is easy?" Emily's words came tumbling. "And you needn't think they're eager to have Harris marry me. They think too much of their son to have him marry into a family that doesn't want him. They're pleased that we're going to wait. But they do understand that we don't want to be separated. Is that so bad? Is it?"

Yes, it was pretty bad, a pretty bad trick this canny girl had played.

"This is all academic," Lynn said, "since without money you can't get to Tulane or any other place." At that her voice caught in a little sob. "So there go college and medical school. Both. Just like that."

"Won't you give it to me, Mom?"

"Money? I haven't got any."

"He would really do that," Emily said, asking a question and declaring a fact at the same time.

"You know he would."

"Then will you give me the money, Mom? Even though you don't approve?"

"I just told you, I have none. I haven't a cent of my own."

"Not a cent? None!" Emily repeated in astonishment.

"I never have had. Your father gives me everything I need or want."

The girl considered that. And Lynn, who knew so well the nuances of her daughter's expression, saw unmistakable distaste and was humiliated by it.

"Aunt Helen, maybe? For the first semester, at least!"

"Don't be silly. Aunt Helen can't afford it."

That was not true. Darwin had been doing well of late, well enough for them to buy a bigger house in a prettier suburb. But she wasn't going to exhibit her dirty linen to Helen.

"If I have enough for the first semester, I'm sure I could get a student loan. And I'd find work. I'd take any kind I could get."

"It's not so easy to get a loan. When they find out your father's position and income, you'll never get one."

"Oh, Mom, what am I going to do?"

"If I were you, I'd go back to Yale and be thankful."

"But you see—I can't! It's too late. They've already filled my place from the wait list."

Stupid, stupid girl . . . This crushing disappointment, this disaster, made Lynn hard.

"Then you've burned your bridges, so I guess that's the end of it."

Emily stood up. "Then there's nothing you can tell me."

"What can I tell you? Except," she added, knowing it was cruel to her, "that I'm on my way to visit a dying woman. You may come if you want to."

"No. I'm going upstairs."

Lynn sat with her face in her hands. She was furious with Emily, and yet felt her daughter's pain as if it were scarring her own flesh. I suppose, she thought, eventually I will have to go crawling to Helen. I will have to endure her sardonic questions: *What are you telling me? That Robert refuses?* But it was also likely that Helen would refuse. They had their own children to educate; one son was going to graduate school. The new house was certainly mortgaged; Darwin couldn't be doing *all* that well. . . . Her thoughts unraveled. Maybe as long as it wasn't where that boy was going, Robert would pay for some other place. But no, he wouldn't; he had had his heart set on Yale for this brilliant daughter. Robert never changed his mind.

She got up from the table and went to the window. Outside in the yard Eudora was singing while she hung clothes on the line. Eudora believed that white goods should dry in sunlight. Bobby was sitting up in the playpen. Falling backward, he would struggle up again, as if proud of his newfound ability to look at the world from a different angle. Eudora bent to talk to him. The scene was cheerful. It was wholesome. Wholesome. A good word.

The house inside was unwholesome. From the bottom of the stairs she could see the closed door to Emily's room and could well imagine that behind the door, Emily was lying facedown on her bed in despair. A part of her wanted to go up and give comfort, to stroke the poor, trembling shoulders. Meager comfort that would be! cried the part of Lynn in which anger was still stone hard.

She grabbed her car keys and started for the hospital. In the rearview mirror she practiced a noncommittal face, the only decent face to present to a sufferer, surely not tears, not even gravity.

And yet her resolution failed her. Josie, this day and for a brief hour, was wide awake. Bruce was telling her something about the new cat when Lynn came in.

"I'm so furious at myself," she began. "It's beastly hot, and I made a sherbet for you with fresh raspberries. It even looks cool, and I thought you'd love it, but then I went and forgot it. My mind—" And she clapped her hand to her forehead.

Josie looked quizzical. "So? What's your trouble? You never forget things, especially things for me. What is it?"

"Oh, nothing much, really."

But she was bursting; the trouble could scarcely be confined.

"Tell us," said Josie.

So Lynn did. When she had finished her account, Bruce and Josie were somber.

"She's tenacious, all right," Josie said. "You have to admire that much, anyway."

Lynn sighed. "Yes, like Robert."

"No." Josie corrected her. "Like herself."

It was clear that she didn't want Emily to resemble Robert. Now in some way, Lynn had to defend him.

"Emily tricked us into thinking she was finished with Harris. She lied to us."

"I don't remember," Bruce remarked calmly, "that she ever said she was 'finished.' She said she wouldn't see him all year, and she hasn't done so."

"A lie by omission, then, wasn't it?"

"When you were a year older than Emily is now, and someone had told you to stay away from Robert for another four years, and probably lose him in doing so, would you have obeyed?" asked Bruce.

Her glance fell under his chastisement. "No," she said, and then, recovering, protested, "but that was different. Robert was older. He was a man."

"Nonsense," said Josie. The voice was tired, but the word was crisp.

"Nonsense." She raised herself on the pillow. "If I've ever seen a real man, I've seen one in young Harris."

"But Yale," Lynn lamented. "To give that up! It has crushed Robert." She appealed, "Don't you understand that?"

"But Emily," said Josie. "It is a question of priorities."

Bruce's eyebrows drew together in his familiar expression of concern as he spoke.

"Yes, I can understand Robert. She should have told you, she should have been candid, but she wasn't. She was afraid to be candid, and that has to be understood too."

"You are leaving her alone with her mistake," Josie remonstrated. "Leaving her alone to pick up the pieces by herself."

In their quiet way they were scolding Lynn.

"She's an extraordinary girl," Josie said, making a little show of vigor. "Of all people Robert knows that. I must have heard him say so a thousand times at least. Does he want to take everything away, her chance at medical school, all that, so he can have the miserable satisfaction of saying later: 'I told you so. You transgressed, so you've paid for it, paid for it with the rest of your life'?"

How she hated Robert! Hatred had given her strength enough to speak out, and now having spoken, she lay back, exhausted.

And something happened to Lynn that had never happened before in her life: Thoughts that should not have been revealed took shape in speech, and she heard herself saying without any rancor at all, "You have always despised Robert."

"Yes," Josie said simply. "I have," and closed her eyes.

Lynn was feeling faint. It was the overpowering scent of gardenias, a little pot of them on the window ledge. Josie would not have said that if it were not for the medication and the pain. Bruce, shaking his head and with silent lips, spelled out the same: It is the medicine.

"Let her go," said Josie, faintly now.

They had to lean toward her, not sure they had heard correctly. Lynn stroked the hot forehead and pushed back the tousled hair.

"What did you say, darling?" Bruce asked.

"Let her go. She had highest honors. . . ." Josie's breathing was hard. "A good girl . . . woman. . . . Let her get away. . . . She needs . . . Take my money for her."

Lynn struggled against tears. "No, darling. We can't do that. You are an angel, but we can't do that."

"Yes, I said!" Josie's hands went frantic as pain struck again. "Bruce, listen to me."

"Dearest, I'm listening. We'll do what you say. I promise I'll give whatever Emily needs. She'll take it from me."

"No," Josie gasped. "Mine . . . Power of attorney . . . Not your name . . . Not you involved . . . at office. Not you."

Bruce turned helplessly to Lynn. "She means that my interference would complicate things between Robert and me. Yes, I see. And it would be terribly hard for you too. Lynn, will you let me take it for Emily out of Josie's account? Will you?"

Past reasoning about what was right, and yet feeling somehow that it probably was right, confused and troubled and in anguish for Josie, she bowed her head in assent.

As she went out and met the nurse who came hurrying in, she heard Josie's anguished cry repeated. "Let Emily go!"

Robert was beaten. Emily, swollen eyed and half sick, had taken a bowl of cereal to her room, so that Lynn sat alone with him at the dinner table. Unspeaking, they sat over the barely eaten food.

Only once he groaned, "Ruined her life. Ruined it."

"Would you consider another place, someplace where Harris wasn't?" Lynn asked.

"No. Maybe in a year or two. I'll see. She must learn a lesson. Parents cannot be defied. No."

Lynn's father had been full of old-time sayings: *The rigid tree breaks in the storm, but the soft one bends and bounces back.*

She would have liked to tell that to Robert out of compassion, to console and warn, but it would have been useless this night, so she said nothing and waited instead until he had fallen asleep before going in to Emily.

The girl wept when Lynn told her what Josie was going to do. She wept and was glad and grateful. Also, she was hesitant.

"Does Dad know?"

"I hadn't the heart to tell him tonight."

"The heart?"

"The strength, I should have said. He will be very, very angry."

The two looked at each other. And Lynn said honestly, "I was angry, too, you know that. It was Josie and Bruce who said, mostly Josie—" She could not go on.

"I know, Mom. I understand."

"Do you, Emily?"

"More than you have ever realized."

The morning began with dread. In the kitchen Lynn made the coffee and orange juice, moving on tiptoe, moving the utensils without a sound, to let Robert sleep another minute and to postpone the moment when he would appear and she would have to speak.

Perhaps with the same motive Emily came in on tiptoe, whispering.

"Uncle Bruce called on my phone. I have to rush over now with the college bill to get the check before he leaves for the hospital. They are so good to me, Mom! I don't understand why they want to do this for me."

"They love you, that's why." And she said also, "They trust you."

"And you? Do you trust me too?"

"You're old enough to be trusted, so I will have to."

"You won't be sorry, Mom. I promise. And I'm going to pay back every cent. I can't tell how long it will take me, but I'll do it."

So young and so sure of herself! Well, the world wouldn't survive for very long if people weren't sure of themselves at nineteen. And her heart ached over Emily's youth and courage.

"If I had money of my own I would do anything and everything for you. You know that, Emily. Oh, I wish I had money of my own! But—" She stopped before completing the sentence in her head. Your father never let me, he said it wasn't necessary because he gave me whatever I wanted, which was true, but it was being treated like a child, an imbecile, damn it—

She took a deep breath and spoke aloud.

"You'd better leave if Bruce is waiting."

"Was that Emily going out?" asked Robert as he entered the kitchen. "I heard her phone ring a while ago. That young bastard, I suppose."

"No, it was Bruce. Josie is going to pay for Emily at Tulane." And she waited for the explosion.

He sat down. "You can't really have said what I think you said. Maybe you should say it again."

She drew a deep breath. "When I was at the hospital, I told them about Emily. Josie can't bear"—she must be careful not to bring Bruce into this affair—"Josie can't bear to have Emily waste a year, and so she offered, she insisted on paying."

Robert's right hand made a fist. "That damnable woman! That damnable, interfering witch of a woman! I had her number the first time I saw her, and you know I did." The fist came down hard on the table, rattling the empty cups. "I'd like to smash this fist into her. I hope she rots. I'd like her to tell me to my face how I should deal with my own family."

"She's dying. She can hardly talk."

"Hardly talk? Then who masterminded this scheme? It must have been Bruce."

"No, it was Josie. She asked him, since he has power of attorney, to write a check, and he simply agreed. It was her idea, not his. She meant so well," Lynn pleaded.

"The hell it was only her idea! It was his too. And yours too. You could have put a stop to it. You're only the girl's mother, aren't you? You could have said, if you had any respect for your husband's judgment, for his wishes, you could have said no. Positively no. Well, say something. Why don't you?"

"Because I've been thinking, probably we were too harsh. It's Emily's life, after all," she said disconsolately. "Her life."

"God, I'm cursed! My wife, my daughter, the whole lot of you. The only one who hasn't disappointed me is the boy, and who knows how he'll turn against me when his time comes?" Robert sprang up so abruptly that he upset the coffeepot, which, as it smashed, sent a brown river meandering across the floor. And Juliet, who had been lying under the table, ran with her tail between her legs. "The humiliation! Think of it: that weakling, that excuse for a man, comes into my home and takes over. The next thing, he'll be sleeping with my wife."

"You're revolting, Robert. Let me tell you, I have no desire to sleep with Bruce. But if you had a few of his qualities, it might be better for us all."

"His qualities! You have the gall to say it would be better for the family if I were like him?"

"Yes, and better for you too."

Robert's eyes burned right through Lynn. He took a deep breath, a long step, and slapped her. Pressed as she was against the wall, she had no room to evade him, but could only twist helplessly. His open palm struck swiftly, stinging one cheek, then the other, and then the first, in succession; his ring, his marriage band, grazed her cheek as her head slammed against the wall, and she cried out. The dog came flying and yelping back into the kitchen. The backyard gate swung shut with a clang. Eudora's key turned in the lock at the kitchen door, and her face appeared in the upper half. Robert fled. Lynn fled. . . .

Panting and groping in the closet for his attaché case, he mumbled, "Fine condition for the commuter train. Smile the good-morning greeting, read the newspaper, act like all the other men, after a scene like this. Yes, fine condition," he repeated as the front door closed upon him.

On the sofa in the back den she sobbed. The attack had pained, but that was not the whole reason for her sobs. Not at all. A sudden light had flared in her head. It was so hot that it hurt.

For this attack was different from all the others. It had brought an end to the excuses and dodges, the concealment that had made the reality tolerable. There was no doubt that Eudora had seen, and now she knew. And it was this knowing that would take away Lynn's dignity. It had stripped her at last. It had damaged her very soul, or whatever you wanted to name the thing that, apart from blood or bone, was your self.

So she lay, and cried, and tried to think.

There came a knock at the door and a call. "Mrs. Ferguson? Are you all right? Is anything the matter?"

"Yes, thank you, I'm all right."

The door opened, and Lynn was revealed in her rumpled wet-eyed state. Now she had to sit up and make the best of it.

"I'm upset," she said. "I've been crying because of Mrs.—of my friend, Josie."

"Oh, sure, it's awful hard." Eudora's face was kind—she was a kind woman—but her eyes spoke, too, and they were saying plainly, "I know the truth, but I will pretend for your sake that I don't."

Kind as she was, she would talk at her other jobs. It was only human nature. The story was too juicy to be withheld. It would be all over the country club. It would be whispered behind Lynn's back. Whispered.

Up and down she walked now, past Robert's austere face framed in sterling silver, and past her own soft, childish face, her dreaming eyes beneath blond bangs and a bridal veil held by clustered lilies of the valley.

"I will leave him," she said aloud. And the sound of her voice, the sound of those daring, impossible words, those unthinkable words, stopped her in her walk, and the shock chilled her bones.

Eudora was singing as she carried Bobby down the stairs.

"Big fat boy. Beautiful, big fat boy, Eudora's boy. You beautiful—"

They went into the kitchen. And Lynn stood listening, asking herself, How much should I bear? How much can I bear? I shall have to keep my head. Am I to tear the roof down over his head?

"Beautiful big fat boy—"

Josie is dying. Emily is leaving. Let me take one day at a time. That's it. One day at a time.

She went into the kitchen, into the light near the window, and inquired anxiously, "Do I look all right, Eudora? I don't want Josie to see that I've been crying because of her."

Eudora considered. "You look all right. Put a little powder on, maybe. Up on your left cheek," she explained with tact.

In the hospital's corridors there are the smells of antiseptics and anxiety. So many large things are compressed in a narrow space, in a short time, as one walks: the night they came in their terror, rushing to see Emily, the gusty morning when Bobby came squalling into the world, and now, as the door opens off the corridor, there is Josie on the high bed with her wasted hands, on which the plain wedding band has been tied with a string.

Bruce got up from his chair in the corner.

"She went into a coma last night," he said, answering Lynn's unspoken question.

The sorrow in him was tangible. It made her chest ache to look at him. All the clichés were true; the heart does weigh heavily in the chest, heavy and sorely bruised.

"Why? Why?" she asked.

He shook his head, and they sat down together on either side of Josie's bed, where she lay as in peaceful sleep. As if a loving hand had passed across her face, the agony and torment were wiped away.

After a long time the noontime sun came glaring into the room. Someone pulled the shade, making a watered-green gloom on the walls. When later the room became too dark, the shades were raised again to let in a tawny summer afternoon.

A doctor came, murmuring something to Bruce, and then more audibly, he addressed them both.

"This can go on for days, or it may not. We can't tell. In any case, there's no point in staying here around the clock. I think you should go home, Bruce. You were here until three o'clock this morning, they tell me. Go home."

At the hospital's front steps they met the other world where cars passed, glittering in the light, and small girls played hopscotch and a couple strolled, thoughtfully eating double ice cream cones.

"Can you give me a lift?" Bruce asked. "My car's in the shop. I was lucky to get a taxi last night."

"Of course."

There was little to talk about until Lynn was compelled to say something about Emily.

"How can anyone say thank you? Thank you for saving a person when he was drowning, thank you for curing a person's blindness? How does one say such things?"

"How do I say thank you for being my support? We don't need words, Lynn."

Numbed by her dual sorrow, she drove without thinking, as if the car, like an obedient, well-trained horse, knew the route by itself.

"We go back a long time," Bruce said suddenly. "Eighteen years. Emily was a baby." He placed his hand over Lynn's. "Don't worry too much about her. I have a feeling that she will do very, very well."

"Perhaps. But do you know," she said sadly, "that I am glad she's leaving? I never thought I could say that, but I can." And a little sob escaped from her throat.

The car had stopped in front of his house, and he gave her a quick look, saying, "You don't want to go home like this. Come in and we'll talk."

"No, I'm not going to burden you with my troubles. You have enough and far more."

"Let's say I don't want to be alone."

"In that case, I will."

The house, though tidy, had the abandoned air that comes when there is no woman in it. The curtains that were usually drawn at night were still drawn, and the philodendron on the mantel were turning yellow. Lynn shuddered in the gloom and pulled the curtains back.

In the bay stood Josie's prize gardenias that she had nourished and brought all the way here when they moved.

"Gardenias need water," Lynn said. "It would be a pity to lose these."

That was a foolish remark. What could it matter to this man if the plant should die? But she was restless, and it soothed her at this moment to fuss with it.

"Bruce, I see a couple of mealybugs. I need cotton swabs and some alcohol. Where does Josie keep all that stuff?"

"I'll get it."

A nervous exchange of trivia came next.

"You can't ever seem to get rid of them," said Lynn as she rubbed each dark leaf.

"Josie told me."

"It's her pet plant. A miracle that it survived the move at all."

"So she says."

"I've never had any luck with gardenias. Josie has a green thumb."

"That's true."

In the bay, when Lynn had cleaned each leaf, topside and under, they stood looking out at the yard, where a flock of pigeons had taken possession of the bird feeder.

"See that one?" Bruce pointed. "The white one? It's her favorite. She claims it knows her."

He can barely see the bird, Lynn thought, with those blurred eyes.

"I want a brandy," he said, he who scarcely drank even wine. "What about you?"

She smiled wanly. "It wouldn't hurt."

They sat on either side of the fireplace, she on the sofa, he in his easy chair. He removed his glasses; she did not remember having ever seen him without them, and it seemed to her now that perhaps she had never really seen him before. The glasses had in some way given him a benevolent look; the simplicity of the man she had pictured in her head, striding on a hill alongside a bevy of large dogs, or else the one whom she had actually known, as he sanded old wood and looked up with that benevolent smile, was gone. This man was bitter.

He caught her studying him.

"What is it?" he asked.

She could say only, "I'm so sorry for you. My heart hurts."

"No, feel sorry for her. She gave so much to everybody. Everyone who really knew her . . . And now they're taking her short life away. Feel sorry for her."

"Oh, God, I do! But you, she worries about you, Bruce. She told me. About leaving you alone."

"She worries about you too."

"There's no need to," Lynn said, wanting to seem, and wanting to be, courageous.

He did not answer. Perhaps it was the positioning of the furniture and the fireplace and the same tension of immediate grief that restored abruptly the day when Bruce had brought Annie home. And she told him so, saying, "You have always been there when I needed you. I know that you talked to the girls when I was out of the room that day."

"I only tried to mend, to find a way for you all to survive together."

He swirled the brandy, tilting and tipping and studying the little amber puddle.

Then abruptly he inquired, "Has it worked?"

Lynn's courage left. She felt herself broken. She saw herself backed against the kitchen wall this morning, so small and weak, so insignificant in the face of Robert's anger. No one must ever know of that insignificance.

Bruce's eyes were studying her with a gravity almost severe. He asked again, "Has it?"

Faltering, she replied, "Yes, but now because of Emily, he—"

The cat came in, Josie's exquisite white cat; curling itself around Bruce's ankle, it made a diversion for which Lynn was grateful.

He smoothed the cat's fur and looked over again at her.

"What did he do?"

"He was quite—quite furious. He—" And now she was truly broken, unable to go on.

"He struck you, didn't he? This morning, before you came to the hospital."

She stared at him.

"Dear Lynn, dear Lynn, do you really think we don't know? And haven't known for I can't remember how long? That day in Chicago I knew, and even before that we both did. Oh, when first we suspected, we told ourselves we must be wrong. It's hard to think of Robert's using force; he's always so coldly polite when it's plain that he has a rage inside. One doesn't imagine him being common enough to be violent."

Bruce's laugh was sardonic. And Lynn could only keep staring at him.

"I remember when we first met. We were invited to your house. You had made a wonderful dinner, coq au vin. And we had never had it before, although it was a fashionable dish then. How trustful you were! It was what we both thought of you. The way you looked at Robert. How can I put it? I'm floundering. It's hard to make clear what I mean. Josie and I, we are—how shall I say it—more equal in our marriage. But you seemed so tender to him, and there's so much love in you, even for that plant over there."

"But there's love in him too," she said, choking. "You don't know. I've loved him so. You don't know—or maybe you do have some little idea how good he was when I let Caroline die. He never blamed me, although anybody else would—"

"Now, stop right there. Anybody else would say it was an accident. Accidents happen. A child pulls away from you and runs into the street. An adult stumbles and falls down the stairs in front of your eyes. Are we supposed to be infallible? And as for not blaming you—ah, Lynn, admit it, in a hundred subtle ways he lets you know it was your fault, but he— he the magnanimous—forgives you! Crap, Lynn. Crap. Stop the guilt. You did not kill Caroline!"

Bruce was on a talking jag. It was as if all the pent-up fear and grief and anger at the fates that were taking Josie away were storming within him, lashing to be released.

"Maybe I'll be sorry to have talked to you like this, but right now I'm sorry I didn't do it a long time ago. Only, if I had you wouldn't have listened and then you'd have ended up by hating me."

"No," she said truthfully, "no, I could never hate you. Not you."

For there was something about him that had always touched her heart: the candor, the simplicity, the vigorous bloom of a man who was healthy in body and in mind.

"That day you came over," he continued, "that morning when you told us you had fallen into the thorn hedge, don't you think we knew what had really happened? Tom Lawrence told us about the dinner at his house, and how he found you when he brought back your purse the next day. Oh, don't worry!" He flung up his hand. "Tom never talks. He's too decent for that. He was only concerned that you were in trouble."

Lynn put her face into her hands. And he went on relentlessly.

"The day when you came to tell us you were pregnant, we could hardly believe that you would tie yourself up again. Josie was sick over it."

"Why are you doing this to me, Bruce?" she burst out.

"I don't know. I suppose I hope you will start to think."

"Oh, my God, oh, my God!" she cried.

He jumped to his feet and, sitting down on the sofa, took both her hands in his.

"Oh, Lynn, I've hurt you. Forgive me, I'm clumsy, but I mean well. Don't you think I'm glad you had Bobby? That's not what I meant at all."

Her baby. Her little boy. She wanted to hide. And in her despair she turned and put her head on Bruce's shoulder.

"Yes, he struck me this morning. We had some words about Emily, and he was furious."

"I'm sorry, I'm sorry. Poor little Lynn."

"It wasn't—it wasn't so much that my face was hurt, it was that I felt, I feel, like nothing. Can you understand? Like nothing."

His big hands smoothed the back of her head softly, over and over.

"Yes," he murmured, "yes."

"Maybe you can't. It's so different with you and Josie."

"It is. It is."

His voice was bleak. Like an echo, it came from far off, detached from the warm, living shoulder to which she clung, detached from the warm hand that cradled her head.

"This morning I hated him," she whispered. "His filthy temper. And still there is love. Am I crazy? Why am I so confused? Why is living just so awfully hard?"

"Lynn, I don't know. I don't know why dying is so hard either. On this day, all of a sudden I don't know anything at all."

She raised her head and looked into his expressive face, on which, over the short season of this summer, deep lines had been written. And it seemed to her that they two, on this hollow, emptying day, must be among the most miserable people in the world.

He pushed her bangs aside and stroked her forehead, saying with a small rueful smile, "How good you are, how sweet. You mustn't give up, you mustn't despair."

"Please don't be kind to me. I can't bear it."

Yet, how clearly she needed the kindness of encircling arms, of human warmth! And so, impulsively, she raised her arms around his neck; he pulled her to him, and she lay against his heart. It was consolation. . . .

So they held to each other, each sunk in grief, not speaking. In unison they felt the rise and fall of breath, and in unison heard the beat of the other's heart.

The room was still. From the yard came pigeons' throaty gurgles, a peaceful sound of untroubled life. A clock somewhere else in the house struck the half hour with a musical ping, leaving a sweet, glittering chime in the air. Neither moved. In this quiet, one could simply float, assuaging against each other's limp and weary body the need for comfort.

Then, little by little, there began a response. Up and down her spine, perhaps unconsciously, his hand moved. It was so soft, this fluttering touch, this delicate caress, and yet from it a subtle pleasure began to travel through her nerves. After a time—how long a time she could not have said and never afterward remembered—there came from the deepest core of sensation a familiar fire. And she knew that he was feeling it as well.

It was as if, outside of the self that was Lynn Ferguson, she was observing ever so curiously a film in slow motion.

The film gathered speed. The actors moved inexorably, his lips on her neck, his fingers unfastening her blouse, her skirt falling into a yellow heap on the floor. Neither of them spoke. She lost all thought. He lost all thought. Desperate and famished, they hastened; it was a kind of collapse into each other, a total fusion. . . .

When she awoke, he was gently shaking her. Startled, disoriented in time and place, it was a moment before she understood where she was.

In that moment, as she later recalled it, she was free of care; the knot of tension at the nape of her neck had disappeared; she was *normal.*

That moment ended, and she knew what had happened, knew that after it had happened, she had dozed, resting in this man's arms as if she belonged there. Appalled, she met his eyes and saw in them a duplication of her own horror.

He had dressed himself, but she was naked, covered only by the plaid knit throw that he had put over her. Through long evenings and on rainy afternoons she had watched Josie knit that throw. Knit, cable, purl, rose and cream and green.

"I have to get to the hospital," he said dully.

"You have no car," she said.

"They've brought mine back."

This dialogue was absurd. It was surreal.

The afternoon had faded. From the window where Josie's beautiful white cat slept on the sill came an almost imperceptible movement of air and a creeping shade. The room became a place where, helplessly, one waited for some onrushing, unstoppable disaster.

"Oh, God," she groaned.

He turned away, saying only, "I'll let you get dressed," and left the room.

Shaking, with nausea rising to her throat, she put on her clothes. On the opposite wall there hung a mirror, one of Bruce's antiques, with a surface of wavy glass that distorted her face as she passed it. This ugly distortion seemed fitting to her, and she stopped in front of it. Ugly. Ugly. That's what I am. I, Lynn, have done this while she lies dying. I, Lynn.

And Robert said, "On the health and lives of our children, I swear that I have never been unfaithful to you." He would not have sworn it so if it were not true. Whatever else he was, he was not a liar.

She had expected Bruce to be in a hurry, but when he returned, he sat down on the chair across from the sofa. So she sat down, too, neat, proper Lynn Ferguson with the shaking stomach, the knot as tight as ever it had been at the nape of her neck, and her feet neatly placed on the floor. She waited for him to speak.

Several times he began, and as his voice broke, had to stop. Finally he said, "I think we must forget what happened, put it out of our minds forever. It was human. . . . We are both under terrible strain."

"Yes," she said, looking down at her feet, the suburban lady's nice brown-and-white summer pumps.

His voice broke again. "That this could happen—I don't know—my Josie—I love her so."

"I am so ashamed," she whispered, looking not at Bruce but at the white cat.

"We will have to forget it," he repeated. "To try to forget it. But before that, I must apologize."

She gave a little shrug and a painful frown as if to say, There is no need, the burden is just as much mine.

"And something else: I should never have told you what I did about Robert and forced your answer."

"It doesn't matter. What you said was true."

"All the same, you will be sorry you admitted it. I know you, Lynn. I know you very well."

"I have admitted it to no one but you, and I trust you."

He put on his glasses, restoring the old Bruce, the one she had known, the brotherly friend with whom such a thing as had just passed between them would have been an impossibility. And he said, "Perhaps that's your mistake."

"What? Trusting you?"

"Oh, God, no, Lynn. I meant your mistake in not admitting it to anyone else."

"Such as who?"

"Well, once I would have said—I did say—a counselor. But now I would say 'Tom Lawrence.'"

To ask for advice, for help, from Tom? And she remembered the scene at the club pool, remembered the humiliation and her own defiant invitation to the golden wedding.

"A lawyer? No."

"He's not only a lawyer, Lynn. He would care. He admires you. Believe me, I know."

He is also the man who thinks I belong in the nineteenth century, an anachronism, part charming, part absurd. That, no doubt, is what he finds interesting, only because it's different from what he sees around him, those blunt, independent women at his party that night. If he knew what I have done just now in this room, he would have to laugh through his amazement. "The joke's on me," he would say. She could hear him say it and see the crinkles forming around his light, bright eyes.

Her mind leapt: What if Robert knew! And terror seized her as if she were alone in a stalled car at midnight, or as if, alone in a house, she heard footsteps on the stairs at midnight.

She stood up, fighting it off. "I've been gone all day. The baby . . . And Emily, I must talk to Emily."

He saw her to the door and took her hand. "Go home. Drive carefully." The lines in his forehead deepened with anxiety. "Are you all right? Really?"

"I am. I really am."

Naked with a man who wasn't Robert. With Josie's husband . . .

"We've done no harm, Lynn. Remember that. It was just something that happened. We're both good people. Remember that too."

"Yes," she said, knowing that he hoped she would forget because, not believing it himself, he needed to have someone else believe it. But he himself would remember this betrayal of his darling Josie.

"I have to get to the hospital," he said.

"Yes, go."

"I'll call you if anything—"

"Yes, do."

So she left Josie's house.

It was Bobby who relieved the silence at the table, which Eudora had thoughtfully set before leaving, although it was not her job to do so. From the freezer she had taken one of Lynn's pot pies and heated it. Lynn thought, It is because she pities me.

Emily had eaten earlier by herself and gone to her room.

"Emily said to tell you she has a headache. But you're not to worry, it's nothing," Eudora said, while her eyes told Lynn, I pity you.

Eyes told everything. Eyes averted told of guilt or shame or fear. Robert's glance fell on Lynn's cheek, where the split skin showed a thin red thread. Lynn looked down at her plate. Robert fed soft pieces of potato to the baby.

The baby bounced in the infant seat. When he dropped his toy, Robert retrieved it; when he threw his toy, Robert had to get up and fetch it from under the table.

"Toughie," Robert said. "Little toughie."

Lynn said nothing. The boy was beautiful; the hair with which he had been born and that he had lost soon after birth was now growing back, silky and silver white.

She imagined herself saying to this child: Your father, whom I loved—love still, and God alone can explain that—I wish He would because I am incapable of understanding it myself—your father has struck me once too often.

Is it Josie who has made this time different from the other times? Or Eudora who has made it seem like the last straw? Or simply that it is, it truly is, the last straw for me, and me alone.

The telephone rang. "Shall I take it or will you?" asked Robert.

"You, please."

Any hour the phone could bring the news of Josie's death. Her legs were too weak to carry her to the telephone; her hand would not be able to hold it.

But it was only from the PTA. "A Mrs. Hargrove," Robert reported as he sat down again. "You're asked to be class mother for Annie. I said you'd call back."

He spoke without inflection or tone. Then he stretched his arm to reach the basket of bread, as if he could not bring himself to ask for the bread, he who was contemptuous of anyone who had poor table manners, of what he would call "the boardinghouse reach." So she handed the basket to him, their hands grazing, their eyes meeting blankly.

The evening light lay delicately on mahogany and turned the glittering pendants on the chandelier to ice. The baby, out of some secret bliss of his own, spread his adorable arms and crowed. And Emily was hiding in her room. And Annie, fragile Annie, would soon be coming home.

It was unbearable.

Emily looked up from the open suitcase on the bed when Lynn came in. The doorknobs were hung with clothes and the chairs were strewn with more; sweaters, shoes, skirts, and slacks were heaped together. On the floor along with Emily's Walkman were piles of books, and her tennis racket leaned against the wall.

"So soon?" asked Lynn.

"Mom, I wanted you to know beforehand, not shock you by having you walk in like this. The thing is, I delayed telling about Tulane, I delayed because I dreaded it, and now I'm at the last minute. Freshman indoctrination starts the day after tomorrow, and I'll have to leave tomorrow morning. Oh, Mom!"

"It's all right," Lynn said, swallowing the inevitable pain.

"I tried to call you at the hospital this afternoon, but you weren't there. I didn't know where else to try."

"It's all right."

"The nurse in Josie's room said you and Uncle Bruce had left."

"We didn't leave, we only went to the cafeteria for coffee and a doughnut." And Lynn, suddenly aware of exhaustion, shoved a shoe aside and sat down on the edge of a chair.

"I was hoping you'd get home early so we could talk."

"I went back to Josie's room and stayed late."

Emily's eyes filled. "Poor Josie! She was always so good to me, now more than ever. It's not fair for her to die."

Youth, youth, still astonished that life can be unfair.

"I wish I could see her again to tell her how much I love her and how much I thank her for what she's doing. But I did thank Uncle Bruce. I thanked him a thousand times."

"Josie wouldn't hear you if you did go. She's in a coma."

"Like a deep sleep."

"Like death."

On the pillow lay the face, the head so small now that the hair had fallen; under the blanket lay the body, so slight that it barely made a displacement. And while she lay there, where had her husband been, where her dearest friend?

With enormous effort Lynn pulled her mind back from the edge of the cliff. "Have you talked to your father at all?"

"I tried to, but he wouldn't answer me, wouldn't even look at me. I don't like to leave home this way, Mom," Emily said, now crying hard.

Lynn stood up to put her arms around her daughter. "Darling, this isn't the way I planned it either. Things will work out. They always do. Just have patience. Believe me."

How often, not knowing what else to say, you had to rely on platitudes!

"Patience isn't going to help you, Mom."

"I don't understand," Lynn said.

"I know he hit you this morning. Eudora told me."

"Oh, my God!"

A shiver passed along Lynn's spine and ran like cold fingers through her nerves. Her arms dropped; like bewildered rabbits or deer caught on the road at night by the sudden glare of headlights, unsure whether to stand or run, the two women paused.

"She said I mustn't let you know she told me."

"So why did she do it?" Lynn wailed.

"Well, somebody ought to know, and I'm your oldest child."

"How could she have done this? She had no right."

"Don't be angry at her, Mom. She feels so bad for you. She told me you're the nicest, kindest person she ever worked for."

Lynn was not mollified. What a terrible thing for Emily to be leaving home for the first time with this fresh information in her poor young head! This unnecessary information! It was mine to give when I was ready to give it, and not before, she thought.

"Promise you won't be angry at Eudora?"

Emily knelt at the chair onto which Lynn now fell and laid her head on her mother's knee, her wet cheeks dampening the thin silk skirt. Over and over, Lynn smoothed her daughter's hair, from the beating temples to the nape where the ribbon held the ponytail. A scent of perfume came from the hair, and she had to smile through her tears; Emily had been at her bottle of Joy again.

She stroked and stroked, thinking that this was to be another home broken in America. A statistic. This girl was a statistic, as were Annie and the baby in the crib across the hall. And her mind, as it went back to the beginning, asked almost reproachfully: Who would have believed it could end like this?

Her mind turned pages in an album, the pages rustling as they flashed disjointed pictures. Their first dinner, his wonderful face in candlelight, and she herself bewitched. People praising him, and she in a kind of awe that he belonged to her. The wedding music, the double ring, and the blaze of sunshine on the church steps when they came out together. The hotel room in Mexico and his dark rage. The death of Caroline and his arms around her. Slaps and shoves, falls and tears. The snowman on the lawn, hot chocolate afterward, and Robert at the piano with the girls. The bench in Chicago and the half-crazed beggar woman laughing at her. The rapture of the night when Bobby was conceived. This morning. Now.

Again Emily asked, "You won't be angry at Eudora?"

"No, I won't be."

What difference did it make, after all? When the end came, Emily would find out a whole lot more. And a great sigh came out of Lynn's heavy chest.

The unthinkable was happening, or was about to. Leaving Robert! Just yesterday she would have said, would have said in spite of everything, that there is always a way; there is so much good here too; there is always hope that the last time really was the last. But today was different. A great, unheralded, unexpected change had taken place within her. She was a good woman, deserving of a better life, and she was going to have it from now on.

Ah, yes! But how to do it? Ways and means. She calculated: In a short while, a few months, Robert would be sent abroad. It would be quite logical then for him to go ahead to prepare for their housing while she stayed behind to settle last-minute business here at home. Then, from a safe distance, she would let him know they were not going to follow him, and that she was through. Finished.

But where to go, with a baby still in arms and without a penny of her own? How to prepare? Bruce had said: Talk to Tom Lawrence. Well, perhaps she would. But she could see his bright, ironic face. He would be remembering, although surely he would never say, I told you so. Bruce had said: He admires you. Tom had said that brutal morning when Annie ran away: When you need help, I will be here for you. In a queer and subtle way, and in spite of the anguish of this day, she felt now a faint touch of self-esteem.

Emily got up, wiped her face, and began to fold sweaters.

"Let me help you," Lynn said. This movement, the physical action of emptying drawers and packing a suitcase, was a physical pain. It was too final for them both.

"Oh, Mom, I can't bear to leave you like this. Why do you put up with it? Why?" Emily cried, her tone high and piercing.

The tension had to be eased, the girl must get a night's sleep and leave in relative calmness to take the plane. So Lynn said softly, "Honey, don't worry about what Eudora told you. I'm sure she exaggerated."

"It isn't only what happened this morning. Before Bobby was born, something happened. I know the truth about that too."

Startled, Lynn stopped folding. "What do you mean?"

"The night you got into the thorn hedge and the people across the road, the Stevenses, called the police."

"Who told you that? Did Lieutenant Weber?" And a terrible anger rose in Lynn. Was the whole world conspiring to spread the news?

"No, no, he wouldn't do that, ever. Harris heard his father telling his mother. They didn't know he was sitting on the porch and could hear them in their living room. And when they found out that he'd overheard, his father asked him not to let me know. He said I mustn't be embarrassed or hurt in any way. But Harris did tell me. I suppose he shouldn't have, but he was worried, and he thought I ought to know. Not that I didn't already have my own ideas about it."

"I see," Lynn said.

She glanced at the wall where Emily's camp photo hung. Eight girls sat on a cabin's steps with Emily in the middle of the row, eight girls who perhaps knew more dreadful things than their naive expressions revealed. My girl, my Emily.

"I was sick. I was so ashamed before him when he told me. I was so ashamed for all of us, for the family that's supposed to be so respectable, with people all impressed by Dad's awards and his charities and this house and everything. I was so ashamed, I was sick. How could my father do that to you? But I'd been right the morning after when I didn't believe your explanation. Why didn't I believe it? Why ever did I suspect that there was something more? When I love Dad so? Then you denied it so strongly and I thought I mustn't think about my parents this way, it doesn't make sense. And when you came back from your trip and seemed so happy together, I thought surely that I'd been all wrong. I was even ashamed of myself because of the thoughts I'd had.

"You were already pregnant with Bobby when Harris told me. We were walking in the woods up at the lake. I guess I fell apart, and he took me in his arms to comfort me. He was so strong and kind! That's when it happened, when we made love. We'd planned not to do it until we were older, honestly we had. A lot of the kids start sex even in junior high, everybody knows that. But you never see things in the papers or on TV about all the kids who don't, even in high school." And Emily, giving a little sob, continued, "It's funny, Mom, when I go over it in my mind, how making love just seemed to grow out of the comfort and the kindness. It just seemed to be all one thing, do you know? And it happened just like that. I guess I'm not explaining it very well. I guess maybe you can't understand how it was."

Lynn was still looking at the photograph; that was the year Emily got braces on her teeth; there were elastic bands on the wires, and she'd gone around to show them off to her friends. She could not look at Emily when she answered.

"I understand," she said.

"It took so long for your hands and your arms to heal last summer, and every time I saw the scabs, I wanted to tell you that I knew. But I'd made so much trouble for you already, that I felt I had no right to make more. And that time Annie ran away, you remember that Uncle Bruce told us both to keep things peaceful for the baby's sake, for all our sakes?"

"You told me."

"And then," Emily said, "when Bobby came, he was so darling. You looked so beautiful holding him. And Dad was so nice, too, really himself. I thought, well, just forget what happened and keep your secret. It's the best you can do. Keep the peace, as Uncle Bruce said you should."

"And how well you have done it."

"I tried. But now that I'm going away, there's something I want to tell you. You were looking at that camp picture a minute ago. Now I have a picture I want to show you."

From a folder in her desk drawer she drew a photograph, evidently an enlarged snapshot, of a little boy not more than a year old. He was sitting on the floor; holding a striped ball three times the size of the tiny face under its full head of straight black hair.

"He looks like an Indian," Lynn said. "He's cute."

Emily turned the picture over.

"Read the name."

"Jeremy Ferguson, with love from Querida," Lynn read, and paused. It was a long pause. Then, "Where did you get this?" she asked.

"When Bobby was born and Aunt Jean came to visit, she brought me a box of pictures. There was Dad from birth to college, there were my grandparents and their grandparents, taken in the eighteen eighties, really interesting, and then I found this, which looks modern. When I asked who the boy was, she said very quickly, 'Oh, some distant cousin in your father's family, I'm not sure who. I cannot think how it ever came to me,' and changed the subject. But she was flustered and of course there has to be more to it. Who is he, Mom?"

Lynn was unnerved. There was too much happening all at once, too much to endure without adding a long, fruitless explanation and questions that she was in no mood to answer.

"I have no idea," she said.

"Mom dear, look me in the eye and tell me that's the truth."

Lynn closed her eyes, shook her head, and pleaded, "What difference does it make? Do we need any more trouble? Don't complicate things. You have no need to know."

Emily persisted. "Well, you're telling me in spite of yourself. You're telling me Dad has another child."

Lynn sighed and gave up. "Yes, all right. There was a boy born to his first marriage. I'm surprised Jean kept the picture. She must have been very fond of him."

"And Querida? Is she his mother?"

"Yes. Listen, Emily, if your father finds out that Jean gave this to you, he'll be wild."

"She didn't give it to me. I distracted her, and later when she looked for it, she couldn't find it."

"Emily! Why on earth do you do these things?" Lynn lamented.

"Because I want to understand. I have a half brother and I never even knew it. This secrecy makes no sense, unless there's a whole lot behind it, in which case it may make sense."

"You're looking for trouble. Your father's angry enough without your making things worse. Besides, he has a right to privacy, regardless of anything else. So do put that thing away. Please."

"All right, Mom, since it upsets you." With a swift tear Emily destroyed the photo. "There, that's over. But I have one more thing to tell you. Querida is in New York."

"How on earth do you know that?"

"I don't know it for a fact, but I'm making connections, Sherlock Holmes stuff. That time in New York before Bobby was born, when I met Aunt Jean there, we were in a taxi on my way to Grand Central to go home, and she got out first a few blocks before. We stopped at the corner for a red light, so I was able to see where she went. It was a store with the name 'Querida.' Mom, it's got to be the same person."

Lynn had a sudden picture of herself standing on the street with Tom on the day they had ridden home together on the train. In the window of the shop there had been a painting of sheep, and the name on the sign was QUERIDA. And she remembered the twinge of recognition, the stab of jealousy and curiosity, the wanting to know, the wanting not to know. But all that meant nothing, after this morning.

She said so now. "It means nothing, Emily. I don't care where she is or who she is. So please forget Sherlock Holmes, will you?"

"Okay."

Emily was packing a small stuffed polar bear among the sweaters. Her profile was grave, and her face when she turned back to Lynn was suddenly older than her years, so she questioned.

"May I ask you something, Mom?"

This child with the stuffed animal, this little woman . . .

"Anything, my darling. Ask."

"Why didn't you ever call the police?"

As if by an automatic reflex Lynn had to attempt a defense.

"Your father's not some drunkard who comes home and beats his wife every Saturday night," she said quietly, realizing in the instant that these had been Robert's very own words.

"But that night? That one night? The neighbors heard, and they called, so it must have been pretty bad."

"I couldn't, Emily. Don't ask for an answer I can't give. Please don't."

In a flood came the terrible sensation of the night when Weber had confronted Robert. Her one thought then had been that her children must be spared this hideous shame. Beyond her understanding were the women who could let their children watch their father being taken away by the police, unless of course they had been beaten most awfully. . . . This was not Lynn's case, and Emily knew it was not.

"I feel sorry for all of us," said Emily. "And in a queer way, for Dad too."

In a queer way, yes.

"Tell me, Mom, may I ask what you are going to do?"

"I am going to leave him," replied Lynn, and burst into tears.

The polar bear's black eyes looked astonished. The very stillness was astonished.

"When did you decide?"

"This morning. It came to me this morning. Why today and not the other times? I don't know. I don't know anything."

"It had to be sometime," said Emily with pity.

Lynn covered her face again, whispering as if to herself alone, "He was —he is—was—the love of my life."

The sentimental, melodramatic words were the purest truth.

"Sometimes I think I'm dreaming what's happened to us all," Emily said.

Lynn raised her head, pleading, "Don't commit yourself and your free will to any man. Don't."

"To no one? Ever? You can't mean that, Mom."

"I suppose not. Certainly don't do it yet. Don't let Harris disappoint you. Don't let him hurt you."

"He never will. Harris is steady. He's level. There are no extremes in him."

Yes, one could see that. There was no sparkle in him, either, thought Lynn, recalling the young Robert, who had lighted up her sky.

"If I tell you something, you won't laugh?" And before Lynn could promise not to laugh, Emily continued, "We made a list, each of us did, of all the qualities we'd need in the person we marry and whether the other one had those qualities. Then we read the list aloud to see how they matched. And they did, almost exactly. Now wasn't that very sensible of us? Harris said his parents did that, too, when they were young, so that's how he got the idea. They're really such good people, the Webers. You can feel the goodness in their house. I think a person's family is so important, don't you?"

"It's not everything."

"It helps, though," said Emily, as wisely as if she had had a lifetime's experience with humanity's woes.

The confident assertion was a childish one, and yet, perhaps . . . I knew really nothing about Robert, Lynn told herself. He came as a stranger. And comparing the wild, thoughtless passion she had felt for him with her daughter's "sensible" list, she felt only bafflement.

"I think Bobby's crying," said Emily, tilting her head listening.

"He's probably wet."

"I'll go, Mom. You're too upset."

"No, I'll go. You finish packing."

"I want to hold him. He might be asleep when I leave in the morning."

The night-light sent a pink glow into the corner where the crib stood. While Lynn watched, Emily soothed the baby, changed him, and cradled him in her arms.

"Look at his hair! I should have been the blonde," she complained with a make-believe pout.

"You'll do as you are."

So these were her children, this young woman in all her grace, and this treasure of a baby boy, the son of Robert, from whom she was about to part.

Emily whispered, swaying lightly while Bobby fell back to sleep on her shoulder, "When are you going to do what you said?"

"I have to think. I have to think of Annie and you and him."

"We'll be fine. We'll still be a family, Mom."

"Oh, my God!" Lynn exclaimed.

"It must be awful for you, but you have to do it. Eudora said it was terrible—"

Lynn raised her hand for silence. A sudden vision of the scene with Bruce that afternoon, a recurring shock, had produced the exclamation. If Emily knew *that*! If Robert knew it! And yet in a curious way, she wished he could be told and be wounded in the very heart of his pride, wounded and bloodied.

She steadied herself. "I'll drive you to Kennedy in the morning. Have you called Annie at camp to say good-bye?"

"No, I'll phone her when I get there. And I'll write often. I'll be so worried about you all, Mom."

"You mustn't be. I want you to concentrate on what you have to do. I want you to see yourself as Dr. Ferguson in your white coat with a stethoscope around your neck." And Lynn forced a smile. Then she thought of something else. "Will you talk to your father too? I'm sure his anger will fade if you give him a little time. And he is still your father, who loves you, no matter what else."

When they closed Bobby's door, the hall light shone on Emily's wet eyes.

"Just give me a little time first too," she said, "and then I will."

A familiar smoky scent drifted up the stairs. Robert must be smoking his pipe. Without looking Lynn knew that he was sitting in the corner chair by the window, brooding in the meager light of one lamp, in a room filled with shadows, and with a mind filled with shadows too. At the top of the stairs she hesitated; a part of her wanted to go down and tell him, in what is called a "civilized" fashion—as if anything as brutal as the termination of a marriage begun in passion and total trust could, no matter how many fine words were summoned, be anything but a devastation—that she was unable to continue this way. But another part of her knew that the attempt would lead to a horrified protest, to apologies and promises, then to tears—her own—and perhaps even more frantic blows. Who could be sure anymore? So she turned about and went to bed.

Every muscle, every nerve, was stretched. There was no sleep in her. Her ears picked up every sound, the swish of a passing car, the far high drone of a plane, and Emily's slippered steps from the bathroom back to her room. Clearly, she constructed tomorrow's departure, the final embrace, the giving of the boarding pass to the attendant, the ponytail and the red nylon carry-on disappearing down the jetway.

"I shall not cry," she said aloud. "I shall send her off with cheer."

And she reminded herself that Emily knew twice as much about the world as she had known at Emily's age. . . .

The screen door clicked shut as Robert brought Juliet inside. A moment later they came upstairs, the dog with tinkling collar tags and Robert with a heavy, dreary tread. Always, his footsteps had revealed his mood, and she knew what was to follow: He would sit down in the darkness and talk.

He began, "I'm sorry about this morning, Lynn. It was nasty, and I know it."

"That it was. Very nasty, and that hardly describes it."

He was probably waiting for her to say more, probably bracing himself for an attack of rage such as she had made in the past; he could not know that she was beyond such agonized rage, far beyond it, that she had reached a tragic conclusion.

Breathing hard, he began again. "It was Emily. I don't think my spirit has ever sunk so low in all my life. It crushed me, Lynn. And so I lashed out. I was beside myself. That's my only excuse."

Yes, she thought, it's your only and your usual excuse. When haven't you had a reason for being "beside yourself"? It's never been your fault, but always somebody else's, usually mine.

"Aren't you going to say something? Yell at me if you want to. But try to understand me too. Please, Lynn. Please."

"I don't feel like yelling. I've had a terrible day."

"I'm sorry." Sighing, he said, "I suppose we just have to tell ourselves that Emily will survive her mistake. What else can we do? What do you think?"

"I'm too tired to think."

Yes, but tomorrow she would weep storms. Weep for Emily, for the turmoil that had thrown her into the arms of Bruce, and for the collapse of this marriage that had been the focus of, the reason for, the central meaning of, her life.

"Maybe I can give you a piece of good news to make up for the rest," Robert said now, speaking almost humbly. "Monacco flew in today. He told me they'll be sending me back across the pond right around the start of the year."

And he waited again, this time no doubt for some enthusiasm or congratulations, but when she gave neither, he resumed, letting his own enthusiasms mount.

"I've been thinking that I should go a month or so ahead of you and get things ready. They have some very comfortable houses with gardens in back, very pleasant. We'd need a furnished place, naturally. I'll have it all cleaned up and ready by the time you arrive with Annie and Bobby. And maybe by that time Emily might—" He broke off.

"I'm tired," Lynn said again. "I really want to sleep."

"Okay."

He turned on the night-light and quietly began to undress. But he was too charged to be still for very long; he was a quivering high-tension wire.

"I've been thinking, too, that we could rent this house. We're not going to spend the rest of our lives in Europe, and we may want to come back right here. We can put everything in storage. What do you think?"

"Fine."

Emily's departure had "crushed him," and yet here he was, hale and strong enough to make his rosy plans. That's called "putting things into perspective," I suppose, thought Lynn. I am so bitter. I am so bitter.

"Did you know that our government sponsors a training program for bankers in Hungary so they can learn investment methods? They have no personnel. No accountants, for instance, a handful in the entire country. It's shocking to us how ignorant they are. Well, a whole generation lived under communism, after all, so all the more of a challenge, I say."

The bed creaked as Robert got in. He moved so near to Lynn that she could smell his shaving lotion. If he touches me, she thought, shuddering, if he touches my breasts, if he kisses me, I'll hit him. I will not be tricked into anything anymore. I will remember my head being slammed against the wall. I will remember Bruce this afternoon. No . . . no, I don't want to remember that.

"Sleeping?" murmured Robert.

"I would if you didn't keep waking me up."

"I'm sorry," he apologized, and turned over.

Yes, tomorrow she would weep storms, tomorrow she would weep for the waste, for the loss of the central meaning of her life. She would set free all the grief that was imploding within the little bony cage where her heart lay, and let it explode instead, to shatter the very walls of this house.

Then, somehow, she would pick herself up and keep going. If Josie could face death with quiet courage, surely she, Lynn, could face life.

On the third day Josie died. On the fourth day they saw her home to her grave. It was Josie's own kind of day; the air was soft after recent rain, pearl-gray clouds hung low, and the smell of wet grass rose among the tombstones. Lynn, almost blindly, read names that were meaningless to her and inscriptions that could only be ineffectual: BELOVED WIFE, DEAR FATHER. For how can a mere adjective describe wretched pain and endless loss?

And always, always, came the pictures: rain pelting the hearse when they followed her mother through the town and uphill to the burial ground; white flowers on Caroline's tiny coffin . . .

"Astonishing," Robert whispered as the crowd gathered. "The whole office staff is here. Half the country club, too, it seems, and they didn't even belong."

"Josie had friends," Lynn said. "Everybody liked her and Bruce."

Bruce's name caught on her tongue. She winced and feared to look at him. He looked like a man of seventy, like a man stricken and condemned.

"My heart, my right hand," she overheard him say to someone offering condolences.

"I know what this means to you," Robert whispered.

"How can you know? You never liked her. You were furious with her."

"Well, she loved you, and I can appreciate that, at least."

Up the small rise people streamed from the parking lot, all kinds and colors and ages of them, the fashionable, the workers and, too, the poor, who must have come to Josie in their need and been comforted, so that they remembered her.

The many voices were muted. All was muted: the spray of cream-colored roses on the coffin, and even the simple language of the prayers, giving thanks for the blessing of Josie's life and the memories she had left to those who loved her.

The brief service came, then, to an end. Too shaken to cry, Lynn looked up into the trees where a flock of crows were making a great stir. And turning her head, she met Tom Lawrence's somber gaze.

"If you need help," Bruce had advised, "ask Tom Lawrence."

"I know women inside out," Tom had told her once. "You'd eat yourself alive with guilt if you ever—"

And Robert took her arm, saying, "Come. It's over." They got into the car and he said, looking almost curious, "You really loved her, didn't you? Funny, I should still be mad at her because of Emily, but what's done is done, and why waste energy? Besides, you'd have to be heartless to look at Bruce's face just now and not feel something. Who knows what goes through a person's head at a time like this? I suppose people recall the times they fought and the things they said that now they wish they hadn't said. But that's only natural. Nobody's perfect. Anyway, he looks like a cadaver. He looks as if he'd been starving himself. He hasn't come to dinner these last few days, and maybe we should keep asking him over for a while until he can straighten himself out."

"That's kind of you," she said, somewhat surprised. And then, induced perhaps by this compassion that he now showed for a man whom he had never liked, she had a sudden insight into herself: If Eudora hadn't been a witness, if Bruce hadn't revealed that he and Josie had always known, might she not have gone on as before, burying the memory, denying it, as indeed she had been doing for years? Maybe she would even have gone on making love to Robert, as he had wanted her to the other night before Emily left, when she had by her silence and immobility rebuffed him. It was an odd, uncertain insight.

They drove on, while Robert ruminated: "I wonder what he'll do now. He's the kind who may never marry again. God forbid, if anything were to happen to you, I never would."

She had to say something. "You can't know that," she said.

"Yes, I can. I know myself. If I had to stand there in that awful cemetery the way he just did and watch you—I can't even say it."

She was thinking: He will suffer when I leave.

"I suppose he'll just go back to the office in a couple of days, back to his old plodding routine."

She thought then: But Robert will have his work. He will get the news, be stunned and furious, and suffer most awfully. She saw him now as clearly as if it had already happened; standing in some strange room on a strange street with a view, perhaps, of cobblestones and medieval towers, he would open her long, sad, careful letter; in expectation of loving words, he would start to read and, not believing his own senses, would read again. . . . And someday he would become the head of the company and have all the glory he so dearly wanted.

Her hands, faintly brown, lay on her lap. When she turned them over, the scars, smooth, white pinhead spots, were unmistakable. And on her cheek this morning, the thin red cut was just closing.

She turned her head to look at Robert, at the lean, fine face. He had scarcely changed. He was as fascinating as he had been when she first had seen him. For her there was something aphrodisiac about the white collar and the dark suit as, so many women admit, there is about a military uniform.

What you have done to me, to us! she thought. You had so much, we had so much, and could have kept it, but you have thrown it away. What you have done with your filthy rage!

The house was bleak. Almost it seemed a dangerous place with hazards and avoidances, as if one were walking through a minefield.

First there was Annie, who, fresh from scout camp, where unfortunately she had not lost a pound, had to be faced with two stupendous changes, the departure of Emily and the death of Josie. The matter of Emily was eased by some telephone calls, but the matter of Josie could only be eased, it seemed, by Bruce.

Lynn drove her to his house, where she spent the day and came out looking relatively cheerful in spite of her swollen eyelids.

"Uncle Bruce said it's all right to cry. He said after I've cried, I'll feel better, and I do. He said Aunt Josie wouldn't want me to be too sad. She'd want me to remember nice things about her, but she'd mainly want me to do good work in school and have friends and be happy. Why didn't you come inside, Mom?"

"I had a lot of errands, and Bobby's cutting a tooth. He's cranky."

"I think you should tell Uncle Bruce to come to dinner. There's nothing in his refrigerator."

"No? What did you have for lunch?"

"He opened a can of beans."

"He hasn't got his appetite back. It's much too soon."

"Aren't you going to tell him to have dinner with us?"

"He'll come when he's ready."

If Lynn knew anything at all about Bruce, she knew he would never be ready. The prospect of sitting down to dinner, the two of them facing Robert, would be as dismaying to him as it was to her.

"Do you suppose he'll get married now that Aunt Josie's dead?" asked Annie.

"How on earth should I know that?" And then, because she had shown such irritation at the question, Lynn made amends. "How about taking Bobby up the road in the stroller? He'd like that. He adores you."

The adoration was mutual, for Annie's reply was prompt. "Okay! You know I'm still the only person in my class who's got a new baby at home?"

"Oh? That makes you sort of special, doesn't it?"

That night Robert said, "I've been making inquiries about schools for Annie. We should really prepare her now and get her used to the idea. We don't want a too sudden disruption at midterm."

Lynn replied quickly, "Not now. She hasn't been back at school a week yet. Leave her alone for a while."

"I suppose you've heard from our other daughter?"

The tone had a knife edge, a serrated knife edge, she thought, saying calmly, "Yes. She likes the place. She's taking biology, of course, sociology, psychology—"

Robert stopped her, raising the newspaper like a fence in front of his face.

"I don't want the details of her curriculum, Lynn."

"Are you never going to relent?" she asked.

The newspaper crackled angrily as he shifted it. "Don't pin me down. 'Never' is a long time."

A bleak house indeed.

As she drove back from a PTA meeting, Lynn's mind was filled not with its agenda, the school fair and back-to-school night, but with her own uncertainties. Would she be staying in this house? Almost certainly not, for Robert would hardly support a place like this one after she had left him. So there would be a new home to prepare; should it be here where the family's roots had gradually been taking hold, or would it be better to turn to the older, deeper roots in the Midwest?

And then there loomed the larger, ominous problem: the severance itself. She had no experience at all with the law. How exactly did one go about this severance? Here on the road, dancing ahead of the car, she seemed to see a swirling cloud of doubt and menace, rising like some dark genie released from its jar.

The road curved. She was not often in this part of town, but she recognized a turreted Victorian house.

"It has two hideous stone lions at the foot of the driveway," Tom Lawrence had said. "Take the next left after you pass it. I'm a quarter of a mile from the turn."

The genie threatened to tower over the car, to descend and crush it. . . . Lynn broke into a chill and a sweat; she drove left beyond the lions and drew up in breathless fear before Tom's house.

It had not occurred to her, unthinking as she was just then, that he might not be home. But his car was there, and he answered her ring. She was taken aback at the sight of him. It had been crazy to come here, yet it would have been crazier to turn now and run.

"I was just passing," she said.

That was absurd, and she knew it as she was saying it.

"Well, then, come in. Or rather, come in and out again. It's too beautiful to be indoors. Shall we sit in the sun or the shade?"

"It doesn't matter." The chill wanted sun, while the sweat wanted shade.

He was wearing tennis whites, and a racket lay on a table alongside an open book. A bed of perennials, of delphinium, phlox, and cosmos, pink and blue and mauve, bordered the terrace; from a little pool lying in a grotto came the cool trickle of a tiny fountain. Upon this peace she had intruded, and she was too embarrassed to explain herself.

"An unexpected visit. An unexpected pleasure," Tom said, smiling.

"Now that I'm here, I feel a fool. I'm sorry. I don't really know why I came."

"I do. You're in trouble, and you need a friend. Isn't that so?"

Her eyes filled, and she blinked. Considerately, Tom gazed out toward the garden.

When she was able, she said in a low, tremulous voice, "I am going to leave Robert."

Tom turned quickly. "A mutual agreement, or are you adversaries?"

A lawyer's questions, Lynn thought, and said aloud, "He doesn't know yet. And he will not agree, you may be sure."

"Then you'll need a very good lawyer."

"You told me once that if I ever needed help, I should call you."

"I meant it. I don't take matrimonial cases anymore, but I'll get you somebody who does."

"You don't seem surprised. No, of course you aren't. You're thinking of my invitation to our golden wedding."

Mechanically, she twisted the straps of her handbag and, in the same low voice, continued, "He struck me. But this time something different happened. I knew I couldn't—I know I can't—I can't take it again."

He nodded.

"I know you think I'm stupid to have put up with what I did. One reads all those articles about battered women and thinks, 'You idiots! What are you waiting for?' "

"They're not idiots. There are a hundred different reasons why they stay as long as they do. Surely," Tom said gently, "you can think of some very cogent reasons yourself. In your own case—"

She interrupted. "In my own case I never thought of myself as a battered woman."

"You didn't want to. You thought of yourself as a romantic woman."

"Oh, yes! I loved him. . . ."

"From a woman's point of view I daresay he's a very attractive man. A powerful man. Admired."

"I wish I could understand it. He can be so loving and, sometimes, so hard. Poor Emily—" And briefly she related, without mention of the pregnancy, what had occurred.

Tom commented, "That sounds just like Bruce's generosity. You've seen him since the funeral, of course."

"No."

"Now I am surprised, close as you've been."

Close, she thought, wincing.

"I don't think he wants to see me," she said, and at once corrected this slip of the tongue. "To see anyone yet, I meant."

Tom inquired curiously whether Bruce knew of her plans.

"I haven't really made them yet," she evaded. "I've only been thinking about them. Robert will be sent abroad in a couple of months. He will go ahead of the rest of us, and I thought I would send him a letter with my decision."

"That gets complicated. Wouldn't it be better to have it all out now and have the wheels turning before he leaves?"

"No. He'll be crushed as it is—but if I do it now, he'll never leave, and his chance will be lost. This chance is all he talks about. I can't be that cruel. I can't destroy him utterly."

She was still twisting the strap of her purse. Tom reached over and put the purse on the table.

"Let me get you a drink. Liquor or no liquor? Personally, I think you could use a stiff drink."

"Nothing. Nothing, thank you."

They had sat on either side of the fireplace. The white cat had wound itself around his ankle. He had stirred his brandy. And after the brandy . . .

"So in spite of everything you don't want to hurt him. You still feel something," Tom said.

"Feel! Oh, yes. How can I not, after twenty years?" She had not expected to weep, to make a scene. Nevertheless, tears came now in a flood. "I can't believe this is happening. These last days have been a nightmare."

Tom got up and went into the house. When he returned, he held a damp washcloth, with which, most tenderly, he wiped Lynn's face. Like a child or a patient she submitted, talking all the while.

"I should be ashamed of myself to come here and bother you. I should solve my own problem. God knows I'm old enough. It's ridiculous, it's stupid to be talking like this. . . . But I'm miserable. Though why shouldn't I be? Millions of other people are miserable. Am I any different? Nobody ever said life is supposed to be all wine and roses."

She started to get up. "I'm all right, Tom. See, I've stopped crying. I'm not going to cry anymore. I'm going home. I apologize."

"No, you're too agitated." Tom pressed her shoulders back against the chair. "Stay here until you wind down. You don't have to talk unless you want to."

A cloud passed over the sun, dimming the garden's colors, quieting the nerves. And she said more calmly, "The truth is, I'm afraid, Tom. How is it that I'm determined to do this, and at the same time I'm so scared? I don't want to face life alone. I'm too young to live without love. And there may never be anyone else who will love me."

"What makes you think that?"

"I'm almost forty, and I have responsibilities, a baby, a teenager who can be troublesome, and Emily. And it's not as if I had a career or were free with an independent fortune and were a ravishing beauty besides."

Tom smiled. "I know one man who thinks you are. Bruce thinks so."
A flush tingled up Lynn's neck into her face. If Tom had told her this
two weeks ago, she would have shrugged. "Oh," she would have said,
"Bruce is as prejudiced in my favor as if I were his sister." But such a
reply would have stuck in her throat if she were to try it now.

"I just realized," Tom said, "that I've made a tactless remark. I've said
'one man'—although," he added with his usual mischievous twinkling
around the eyes, "I myself wouldn't really call you 'ravishing' either. It
sounds too rouged and curly, too flirtatious, to suit a lovely woman like
you."

"I'm not lovely," she protested, feeling stubborn. "My daughter Emily
is. You saw her. She looks like Robert."

"Oh, yes, oh, yes. Robert's your standard, I see that." The rebuke was
rough. "Get your mirror out."

She was puzzled. "Why?"

"Get it out. Here's your purse. Now look at yourself," he commanded,
"and tell me what you see."

"A woman's who's distraught and dreary. That's what I see."

"That will pass. When it does, you will be—well, almost beautiful. It's
true that your face is a shade too wide at the cheekbones, at least for
some tastes. And maybe your nose is too short." Tilting his head to study
her from another angle, he frowned slightly, as if he were criticizing a
work of art. "It's interesting, though, that you have dark lashes when
your hair's so light."

"Don't tease me, Tom. I'm too unhappy."

"All right, I was teasing. I thought I could tease you out of your mood,
but I was wrong. What I really want is to rejoice with you, Lynn. You're
finally going to end this phase of your life, get strong, and go on to
something better."

"I'm going to end this phase, that's true. But as to the rest, I just don't
know." She looked at her watch. "I have to go. I like to be home when
Annie gets out of school."

"How's Annie doing?"

"Well, I worry. I always feel uneasy. But at least there haven't been any
more episodes. No running away, thank God. She seems calm enough.
And Robert has been doing all right with her. As a matter of fact, he's so
tired and busy, so preoccupied these last few weeks with his big promotion, that he doesn't have much time for her or anything else."

Not even for sex, she thought wryly, and I don't know what I shall do
when he does make an attempt.

Sunk as she was in the deep lounge chair, she had to struggle upward. Tom pulled her and, not relinquishing her hands, admonished her.

"I want you to be everything you can be. Listen to me. You're too good a human being to be so unhappy." Then he took her face between his hands and kissed her gently on the forehead. "You're a lovely woman, very, very attractive. Robert knows it too. That's why he was so furious when he came here and saw you dancing that night."

"I can barely think. My head's whirling," she whispered.

"Of course it is. Go home, Lynn, and call me when you need me. But the sooner you leave him, the better, in my opinion. Don't wait too long."

In a state of increasing confusion she started for home. What did she feel for Tom? What did he feel for her? Twice now her need for comfort and support had led to a complication—in Bruce's case rather more than a "complication"!

But then, as she drove on through the leafy afternoon, she began to have some other thoughts, among them a memory that loosened her lips and even produced a wan little smile.

"I wish you would marry Tom," Annie had said once when she was at odds with Robert. "Of course, you could marry Uncle Bruce if he didn't already have Aunt Josie."

It was the babble of a child, and yet there was, for a woman in limbo, a certain sense of security in knowing that at least two men were out there in the great unknown world of strangers who found her attractive, and she would not be going totally unarmed into that world.

And she asked herself whether anyone, at the start of this short summer, could have imagined where they would all be at its waning. On graduation day Emily had been on a straight course to Yale, or so it had seemed; Josie had been smiling her congratulations, and now she was dead; Robert and Lynn, husband and wife, had sat together holding hands.

Robert, home early, explained, "I decided to call it a day at the office and shop for luggage. We haven't nearly enough. I was thinking, maybe we should buy a couple of trunks to send the bulk of our stuff on ahead. What do you think?"

It was strange that he could look at her and talk of normal things without seeing the change in her. "We have plenty of time," she said.

"Well, but there's no sense leaving things to the last minute either."

A while later Emily telephoned. "Mom, I just got back from my sociol-

ogy lecture, and what do you think the subject was? Abused women."
Her voice was urgent and agitated. "Oh, Mom! What are you waiting
for? The lesson is: They never change. This is *your life,* the only one you'll
ever have, for heaven's sake. And if you've been staying on because of us,
as I believe you have, you're wrong. I have nightmares now, I see your
scarred hands and the bruise on your face. Do you want Annie to find
out too?"

"I told you what I'm going to do," Lynn said. "And if you have any
feeling that you're responsible for my staying, you're mistaken. I've
stayed this long because I loved him, Emily."

Neither spoke until Emily, her voice barely breaking, said, so that
Lynn knew she was in tears, "My father, my father . . ."

There was another silence until Lynn responded, "Darling, if it's the
last thing I do, I'll take care of you all. I will."

"Not me. Don't worry about me, just Annie and Bobby."

"All right, darling, I won't worry about you."

Nineteen, and she really believes she doesn't need anybody anymore.

"Have you seen Uncle Bruce? How is he?"

She dreaded a face-to-face meeting with Bruce. It would be stiff and
strange. . . . It would be guilty. . . . "Not for the last few days. He's
doing as well as one might expect," she answered.

"Be sure to give him my love."

When she had hung up the phone, Lynn sat for a little while watching
darkness creep across the floor. From upstairs in Bobby's room came the
sound of Annie, singing. Bobby, delighted with this attention, would be
holding on to the crib's railing while he bounced. Annie's high voice was
still childish, so that its song at that moment was especially poignant.

A juggler must feel as I do now, Lynn told herself, when he steps out
onto the stage to start his act. One ball missed, and they would all come
tumbling. . . .

"But I shall not miss," she said aloud.

Eudora was waiting for her in the garage when Lynn came home with the
groceries.

"Mrs. Ferguson! Mrs. Ferguson," she called even before the engine
had been shut off. "They want you at the school, somebody telephoned
about Annie—no, no, she's not sick, they said don't be scared, they need
to talk to you, that's all."

Everything in the body from the head down sinks to the feet; so went
Lynn's thought. Yet she was able to speak with uncommon quietness.

"They said she's all right?"

"Oh, yes. They wouldn't lie, Mrs. Ferguson."

Perhaps, though, they would. They might well want to break bad news gently. . . .

But Annie was sitting in the principal's office when Lynn rushed in. The first thing she saw was a tear-smeared face and a blouse ripped open down the front.

Mr. Siropolous began, "We've had some trouble here today, Mrs. Ferguson, a fight in the schoolyard at recess, and I had to call you. For one thing, Annie refuses to ride home on the school bus."

Lynn, with her first fears relieved, sat down beside her child.

"Yes, you look as if you've been in a fight. Can you tell me about it?"

Annie shook her head, and Lynn sighed. "You don't want to ride home in the bus with the girl, is that it? I'm assuming it's a girl."

Annie folded her lips shut.

"Don't be stubborn," Lynn said, speaking still mildly. "Mr. Siropolous and I only want to help you. Tell us what happened."

The folded lips only tightened, while Annie stared at the floor. The principal, who looked tired, urged with slight impatience, "Do answer your mother."

Lynn stood up and grasped Annie firmly by the shoulders. "This is ridiculous, Annie. You're too old to be stubborn."

"It seems," Mr. Siropolous said now, "that some of the girls were taunting Annie about something. She punched one of them in the face, and there was a scuffle until Mr. Dawes managed to separate them."

In dismay Lynn repeated, "She punched a girl in the face!"

"Yes. The girl is all right, but of course we can't allow such behavior. Besides, it's not like Annie. Not like you at all, Annie," he said, kindly now.

Lynn was ashamed, and the shame made her stern.

"This is horrible, Annie," she chided. "To lose your temper like that, no matter what anyone said, is horrible."

At that the child, clenching her pathetic little fists, burst forth. "You don't know what they said! They were laughing at me. They were all laughing at me."

"About what, about what?" asked the two bewildered adults.

"They said—'Your father hits your mother all the time, and everybody knows it. Your father hits your mother.' " Annie wailed. "And they were laughing at me!"

Mr. Siropolous looked for an instant at Lynn and looked away.

"Of course it's not true," Lynn said firmly.

"I told them it was a lie, Mom, I told them, but they wouldn't listen. Susan said she heard her mother tell her father. They wouldn't let me talk, so I hit Susan because she was the worst, and I hate her anyway."

Lynn took a handkerchief from her purse, with a hand that shook wiped Annie's face, and said, still firmly, "Children—people—do sometimes say things that hurt most terribly and aren't true, Annie. And I can understand why you were angry. But still you shouldn't have hit Susan. What is to be done, do you think, Mr. Siropolous?"

For a moment he deliberated. "Perhaps tomorrow you and Susan, maybe some others, too, will meet in my office and apologize to each other, they for things they said, and you for punching. We'll talk together about peace, as they do at the United Nations. In this school we do not speak or act unkindly. How does that sound to you, Mrs. Ferguson?"

"A very good idea. Very fair." The main thing was to get out of there as quickly as possible. "And now we'd better get home. Come, Annie. Thank you, Mr. Siropolous. I'm awfully sorry this happened. But I suppose you must be used to these little—little upsets."

"Yes, yes, it's all part of growing up, I'm afraid," said the principal, who, also pleased to end the affair as quickly as possible, was politely holding the door open.

"She's such a good child," he murmured to Lynn as they went out. "Don't worry. This will pass over."

"Susan," Lynn reflected aloud when they were in the car. "Susan who? Perhaps I know her mother from PTA?"

"She's awful. She thinks she's beautiful, but she isn't. She's growing pimples. Her aunt lives across the road."

"Across our road?"

"Mrs. Stevens," Annie said impatiently. "Mrs. Stevens across the road."

Lynn, making the swift connection, frowned. But Lieutenant Weber had told the Stevenses that night that there was nothing wrong. . . .

"She's afraid of dogs, the stupid thing. I'm going to send Juliet over to scare her the next time she visits."

Needing some natural, light response, Lynn laughed. "I don't really think anybody would be afraid of our clumsy, flop-eared Juliet."

"You're wrong. She was scared to death the day Juliet followed Eudora to the Stevenses. She screamed, and Eudora had to hold Juliet by the collar."

"Oh? Eudora visits the Stevenses?"

"Not them. The lady who comes to clean their house is Eudora's best friend."

Was that then the connection, or had it been only Weber, or was it both? It surprised her that no hot resentment was rising now toward whomever it was who had spread the news. People would always spread news; it was quite natural; she had done it often enough herself.

Then came a sudden startling query. "But, Mom—did Dad ever?"

"Ever what?"

"Do what Susan said," Annie mumbled.

"Of course not. How can you ask?"

"Because he gets so angry sometimes."

"That has nothing to do with what Susan said. Nothing."

"Are you sure, Mom?"

"Quite sure, Annie."

An audible sigh came from the child. And Lynn had to ask herself how she would set about explaining the separation when it came, how she might explain it without telling the whole devastating truth; some of it, yes, but spare the very worst.

Well, when the time came, and it was approaching fast, some instinct would certainly show her the way, she assured herself now. But for the present she could feel only a deep and tired resignation.

6

THE baby was being dried after his evening bath when Robert, hours late, came home. Lynn, stooping beside the tub, was aware of his presence in the doorway behind her, but did not turn to greet him; the time for loving welcomes was past, and she waited for him to speak first, after which she would give her civil response.

"I'm home," he said.

Then some quality in his voice made her glance up, and she saw that he looked like death. He had opened his collar and loosened his tie; he, Robert Ferguson, to be disheveled like that in the commuter train!

"What's the matter?" she cried.

"You will not believe it," he said.

"I will believe it if you tell me."

"Ask Annie to put Bobby to bed. She won't mind. And come downstairs. I need a drink."

He's ill, she thought, that's what it is. They've told him he has cancer or is going blind. Pity, shuddering and chill, ran through her.

"Glenfiddich. Toss it down," he said, as if he were talking to himself. "And toss another."

The bottle made a little clink on the silver tray. He sat down.

"Well, Lynn, I've news. General American Appliance and I are finished. Parted. Through."

"Through?" she repeated, echoing the word that had, in the instant, no meaning.

"I didn't get the promotion, so I quit. That's why I'm late. I was cleaning out my desk."

"I don't understand," she said.

He stood up and walked to the long bow window that faced the road and the lighted lantern at the foot of the Stevenses' long drive. Like a sentry on duty he spun around, walked the length of the room to the opposite window, and stood there looking out into the dark lawn and the darker bulk of the hill beyond. When he turned again to face Lynn, she saw that his eyes were bright with tears. Then he sat down and began to talk in rapid, staccato bursts.

"Yes, cleaning out my desk. Twenty-three years of my life. And do you know how I got the news? In the elevator coming back to the office late in the afternoon. I hadn't been there all day. I'd gone straight from the train to an appointment. And a couple of kids were talking, clerks or mailroom kids; they didn't even recognize me. They were talking about Budapest, and Bruce Lehman going there to head the office. It sounded crazy. I didn't pay any attention to it, except to be amused. And then Warren called me in. He showed me a fax from Monacco, and I saw it was true. And still I couldn't believe it."

Robert put his hands over his face. His elbows rested on his knees, and his head sank. She was staring at a beaten man, as out of place in this rich room as any beggar sprawled upon marble stairs.

"I told him there had to be some ridiculous mistake, that everybody knew it had been promised to me. Why Lehman? It made no sense. I said I wanted to speak to Monacco then and there. So Warren phoned California, but we didn't reach Monacco. I demanded that Warren tell me what he knew. I wasn't going to spend a sleepless night trying to figure out what had gone wrong. Damn! It'll be a sleepless night anyway."

And again, Robert got up to pace the length of the room. At the mantel he paused to adjust the Herend figurines, which Eudora had moved when she dusted.

"I remember the day I bought these," he said. "I thought I had the world at my feet. I did have it too. Excuse me. These damn tears. I'm ashamed that you should see them."

"There's nothing to be ashamed of, Robert. A man has a right to show his grief too."

She spoke softly, not out of compassion alone, but also out of her own bewilderment in the face of this stunning complication.

"And Warren? Did he tell you why?"

"Oh, yes. Oh, yes. He was delicate about it, you know, very much the gentleman. But how he was enjoying it! He's home now, I'll bet on it, regaling his wife or maybe the crowd at the club, with the story. God, as hard as I've worked, brought marketing farther along than anyone else had ever done; and what has Lehman ever accomplished compared with me? A drudge, without imagination—"

"You haven't told me the reason," Lynn said patiently.

"The reason? Oh, yes. I said he was delicate about it. Very tactful. It seems that people—that someone has been saying things, personal things, exaggerations—God! Everybody, every marriage, has problems of one sort or another, problems that people overcome, put behind them. I told him the stuff bore no resemblance to reality, none at all. What right anyway do strangers have to draw conclusions about what goes on between a man and his wife? You'd think a man like Monacco would have more sense than to listen to idle gossip."

"Idle," Lynn murmured, so faintly that he did not hear her.

All the whispering had united into one tearing shout, loud enough to reach to California. It was a confirmation of sorts, but useless to her, for to what end would it lead? And her path that had seemed so clear, though painful, had brought her into a blind alley.

"Would you believe a man like Monacco could stoop so low? What have I done that's so terrible, after all?" When she was silent, a note of faint suspicion came into his voice. "I wonder who could have spread this dirty stuff. You couldn't—you didn't ever run to the Lehmans with anything, did you?"

She interrupted. "Don't dare say such a thing to me!"

"Ah, well, I believe you. But then, how and who?"

The question hung between them, and he was expecting an answer, but she was numb and could give none. In all this horror there was the kind of fascination that draws a person unwillingly to look at an accident, to stare at bloody wreckage.

Robert resumed, "Warren said—and he was speaking for Monacco 'according to instructions,' he said, that of course I was free to stay on in my present position. 'Of course,' " Robert mocked.

"And you're not going to," she said, recognizing the mockery.

"Good God, Lynn! I wrote out my resignation then and there. What do you take me for? After a slap in the face like that, do you think I could stay on? While Bruce Lehman enjoys the reward that belongs to me?"

"Bruce never wanted it," she said.

"He's damn well accepted it now."

The world is spinning around me, and I make no sense of it, Lynn thought. Then, for want of something to say, she inquired, "Are you sure you're doing the right thing by leaving?"

"No doubt of it. Anyhow, they want me to go, don't you see that? They'd find a way to ease me out. They'd make it so miserable that I'd want to leave." Robert's face contorted itself into the mask of tragedy, with cheeks puffed, brows upward drawn, and mouth gaping. "I'm ruined, Lynn! Destroyed. Disgraced. Thrown out like trash, a piece of trash."

It was all true. He had done it to himself, but it was still true. What could she, what should she, say? She could think of nothing but some trivial creature comfort.

"Shall I fix you something? You've had no dinner."

"I can't eat." He looked at the clock. "It's half past eight. Not too late to see Bruce. Come on."

"See Bruce? But why?"

"To offer congratulations, naturally."

Dismayed, she sought a sensible objection. "He won't want us to visit. We'll be intruding, Robert."

"Nonsense. He'll appreciate congratulations. We'll bring a bottle of champagne."

"No, no. He's in mourning. It's not fitting," she protested.

"This has nothing to do with Bruce's mourning. It's a question of Robert Ferguson's honor and good taste, of his sportsmanship. I want him to see that I can take this like a man."

"Why torture yourself to make a point, Robert? A phone call will do as well."

"No. Get the champagne. He can chill it in his freezer for half an hour."

Silently she asked: Whom are you fooling with this show of bravado? By your own admission you're dying inside.

"If it's a celebration you want," she said, not unkindly, "button your collar and change your tie. It's stained."

Bruce wouldn't care, but Robert would see himself in a mirror and be appalled.

She had not been in Bruce's house since that day. He had been reading when they arrived; the book was in his hand when he opened the door. The evening was cold and windy, a harbinger of winter, and apparently he had been using Josie's knitted afghan on the very sofa where they had lain together, where he had covered her nakedness with that afghan.

And she wondered whether the same thought was in his mind, too, and could not look at him or at the sofa, but made instead a show of greeting the white cat.

Bruce asked whether they would mind if he saved the wine for another time together, explaining, "I am not quite up to it. It's been a rather bad day for me, Robert."

"Now, why should that be?"

"It's very simple. The post was yours. You earned it, and it should have gone to you."

Robert shrugged. "That's generous of you, Bruce, but it wasn't in the cards, that's all."

The remark was almost flippant; it could have aroused compassion for its attempt at bravery, or, given the fact that the others present knew why "it wasn't in the cards," it could arouse anger.

Bruce, though, was compassionate. "I have to tell you that I'm overwhelmed. It won't be easy to follow in your footsteps, Robert. I only hope I can do the job."

"I'll be available for advice if you need it anytime. It might be a good idea for you to come over one night soon and let me give you some background on what's already been done over there."

"Well, thanks, but not just yet. This has come down on me like a ton of bricks, while I'm still buried under a mountain of bricks. I'm not thinking very clearly."

"I understand," Robert said sympathetically.

"At least, though, this will force me to get away. I'd been wishing there was someplace where I could get away from myself, Outer Mongolia, maybe, or the South Pole. So now it's to be Hungary. Not that it makes any difference where. I'll still be taking myself with myself, and myself's pretty broken down."

Bruce had not given Lynn a glance, but now he turned fully toward her and made a request.

"I'm worried about Barney." The cat, lying curled in front of the fireplace, looked like a heap of snow. At hearing his name he raised his head. "I can't take him with me, and Josie would haunt me for the rest of my days if I didn't get a good home for him. So do you suppose you could take him, Lynn? I don't want to give you any more work or any problem, but I'm stumped."

"You don't know Lynn if you can say that," Robert declared. "She'd take in any four-legged creature you can name."

"Of course I will," Lynn said quickly.

"No, you don't know Lynn," repeated Robert.

But he does know Lynn, and very well too. The words, on the tip of her tongue, came so close to slipping out that she was shocked.

"What's your schedule?" Robert asked.

"Sometime in December, I think." And Bruce said again, "It's all so sudden. . . . I'll keep Barney till I go. . . . It's good of you. . . . I'm grateful. . . . Josie would be grateful."

"He's in a fog. He'll never measure up. Doesn't know what he's in for," Robert said when they left.

At home he resumed his agitated pacing, saying, "He'll never measure up."

Annie came quietly into the room, so quietly that they were startled by her voice.

"What's wrong? Has something awful happened? Is Emily sick again?"

Robert made a choking sound. "Oh, Annie. Oh, my little girl, no, Emily's well, thank God. Thank God, we're all well." And pulling Annie to him, he kissed the top of her head and held her, saying tenderly, "I'll find a way to take care of you. They think they've ruined me, but they can't crush my spirit, no—" He began to weep.

"You're terrifying her!" Lynn cried. "Daddy's upset, Annie, because of some trouble at work. He's leaving the firm. He's upset."

The child wriggled free of Robert and stared at him as if she had never seen him before. A variety of expressions moved across her face, ranging through curiosity and distaste to fear.

"I need to talk to Emily," Robert said. "Get me her number, Lynn."

"You'll scare her to death too. Wait till you calm down."

"I'm calm," he said through his tears. "I'm calm. I need to talk to her, to tell her I'm sorry. We're a family, we make mistakes, we have to stand together now. What's the number, Annie?"

If I hadn't seen how little he drank of it, I would have said it's the Scotch, Lynn thought.

"Emily, Emily," Robert was saying into the telephone. "No, don't be frightened, we're all right here, it's just that I quit GAA. It's a long story, too long to explain over the phone, but—excuse me, I'm very emotional at the moment, I feel that the stars have fallen—But I'm going to pull myself together and I—well, I want to apologize, to straighten things out between you and me. I've been heartsick over the situation. I want to apologize for not understanding you, not trying to understand. I just want to say, don't worry about the tuition, I'll pay it, I'm not broke yet. You just stay there and do your work and God bless you, darling. I love you, Emily. I'm so proud of you. Tell me, how's Harris?"

Later, in their bedroom, he became subdued, sighing and questioning, "Tell me, do I—do we—deserve this? I wanted everything for you, and now—now what?"

In bed he turned and, pulling her gently from where she had been lying with her back toward him, drew her close. And she knew it was assurance that he wanted, a bodily relief from tension, some sweet recompense for loss. He wanted proof that he was still a man, her man. Had he asked this of her even a few hours ago, before disaster had befallen him, she would, she knew, have scratched and fought him. Now, though, she hadn't the heart to inflict another hurt; what did it matter, after all? A woman could lie like a stone and feel nothing. In a few minutes it would be over, anyway.

So often during these past weeks she had imagined the humbling of Robert Ferguson, and yet now that he had been humbled beyond imagining, the sight was almost too dreadful to be borne. And she felt his pain as if she were herself inside his skin.

In the tight little world of the company, many of whose officers lived in the town, news spread. On Saturday in the supermarket a group of women had obviously been talking about the Fergusons, because when they saw Lynn, they stopped and abruptly gave an unusually cordial greeting.

Not that it makes any difference, she thought, and it's probably absurd of me to ask, yet I have to know how this happened. And going to a pay phone, she telephoned Tom. Perhaps he would know; if he did not, he would find out.

"It's about Robert. Have you heard that he's left the firm? They found out that . . ." Her voice quavered.

"Yes, I know. Come over, Lynn. I'm home all morning."

In the large room where the table had glittered on that night from which the present trouble had stemmed, she felt suddenly very small. She felt like a petitioner.

"How did you hear?" she asked.

"Monacco phoned me. He's always had the impression, for some unfathomable reason, that Robert and I are close friends."

"But why did he phone you? To ask or to tell?"

"Both. He told me that a letter had come to him, and he asked me whether the accusations in it were true, whether I knew anything about them."

"A letter," Lynn echoed.

"I don't know who sent it. It was a woman's letter, anonymous. But it sounded authentic, Monacco said, as if the wife of one of the firm's officers had written it. It had a good deal of corroborating evidence, one thing being a report from some neighbors."

Tom lowered his eyes to study his shoes before saying anything further. Then, looking directly at Lynn, as if he had had to consider the decision to say more, he continued, "It was about what happened the night you came here to make dinner."

"An anonymous letter. How dirty!"

She was thinking rapidly: Who, except the Stevenses, could have known what happened that night? And they were related to that child Susan's family. And Eudora, who had seen too much, was a friend of the woman who worked for the Stevenses.

"And since the letter said there'd been a call to the police, Monacco had a check made."

Weber. He hadn't "buried" it, after all. Weber had wanted to get back at Robert for the things Robert had said.

"So they made the check and found that there had indeed been a complaint, and that somebody in the police department had tried to hide it, had actually hidden it, as a matter of fact."

Then she had misjudged Weber. At once guilty and pitying, she asked Tom, "Did he get into trouble, the man who had hidden it?"

"No. The police chief is a friend of mine, and we had a talk."

"Then you know about Emily and his son," she said softly.

"Nothing except that they've been going together." Tom smiled. "Do they still say 'going steady'? My teenage vocabulary is definitely out of date."

"I don't really know. It's all a tangle," lamented Lynn.

Tom nodded. "*Tangled* is the word. Even the cop at the club knew all about it. He used to be my gardener before he joined the police force, and he tells me things. You'd be surprised how many people know about Robert, things true and untrue. That's what happens in these towns; you find your way into the stream of gossip, and soon everybody knows what kind of breakfast cereal you eat."

"The meanness of it!"

It seemed to her as if, in exposing Robert, the slack-tongued mob, inquisitive and gloating, had exposed them all, herself and the girls and even the baby boy. Anger exploded, and she protested, "You would think people might find better things to do than to probe into other people's trouble!"

"You would think, but that's not the way it is." And Tom added, "Monacco won't tolerate scandal, you see, not even the slightest."

"It isn't fair! The thing's all blown out of proportion. It's between Robert and me, anyway, isn't it? Not GAA, or the town. Why should any wrong done to me affect his job? Why?" she ended, demanding.

Tom's expression, as he raised his eyebrows and shook his head, seemed to be saying, I give up!

"Oh, you think I'm naive?"

"Yes, very. Corporations have an image, Lynn. There's morale to maintain. How can you get respect from a subordinate when your own behavior is—shall we say 'shady'?"

"All right, it was a silly question. All right."

Then, following Tom's glance, she became aware that she had been twisting her rings, working her nervous fingers on her lap. And she planted her hands firmly on the arms of the chair. But she ought to go home; having heard what she had, there was nothing more to wait for.

"Monacco was really distressed," Tom said gently. "This isn't anything a man likes to do to someone he admires. And of course he said what you might expect, that this was the last thing he would have believed of Robert, as brilliant as he is, with such a future ahead."

"Like seeing a murderer's picture in the paper, I suppose. 'Oh, my, he's got such a nice face!' Is that it?" And Lynn's fingers went back to the rings, twirling and twisting.

Tom reached over and held one of her hands quietly. "It's the devil for you, I know."

"One has to ache for Robert, regardless of everything. He can't sleep, just walks around the house all night, upstairs and down. He barely eats. He looks older by ten years. The rejection . . . The humiliation . . ."

"Especially because Bruce is the one who got his place?"

"Well, naturally. He certainly never thought that Bruce, of all people, could be his competition."

"Why do you say 'of all people'?"

"I didn't say it, Robert did. He always said Bruce was not competitive."

"He was dead wrong. When the Hungarian project was first conceived, Bruce was right up among the top prospects."

"How do you know all this? Even if you're connected with Monacco, you still don't work for GAA. So how do you know?"

"I never did know or care about GAA. But this one time I made it my business to. I wanted Robert to get a promotion. I did it for you."

At that Lynn slipped her hand out of his so quickly that he, too, spoke quickly.

"I knew, it didn't take much to see, in spite of your protests, Lynn, that the marriage wouldn't last. And then you'd be needing a decent settlement. Courts aren't giving much to wives these days."

The room was absolutely quiet. A phone rang somewhere in the house and stopped when Tom did not answer it. A man passing on the walk outside gave a rumbling laugh, and a woman laughed in return. Then the sound faded. So people were still finding humor in the world! The thought came to her that she might never again have anything to laugh about. And another thought came, a questioning: If I were free now, unencumbered by events, would I accept this humorous, quirky, kindly man who's sitting here carefully looking at his shoes again and not at me? Surely his last words meant something: *I did it for you.*

"How good you are!" she exclaimed, and would have said more, but was fearful of tears.

"Well," he said. "Well, I like to set things straight. Lawyers, you know. They're orderly. So tell me, where do we go from here? Or I should say first, where do you go?"

"Where can I go, Tom? The man is ill. He begs forgiveness—oh, not only for the bad things, but for his failure. There's been very little money put aside. I was surprised how little. He needs a position, he'll need one soon, but first he'll have to get back some pride and courage. He wants to move away from here, to start fresh. I don't know. I don't know anything. I'm sick at heart myself, Tom. It's a whole strange, sad new page. He's so humble, so changed."

"No, Lynn. He's not changed."

"You can't say that. You haven't seen him. On the telephone, talking to Emily, he sobbed."

"I don't need to see him. You're too good," Tom said. "That's the trouble."

"Does one step on a person when he's already fallen down?"

Tom did not answer, and she hid her face in her hands, thinking that Tom, after all, couldn't know what was churning inside her. Twenty years together, with so much good! Oh, yes, bad too, bad too. And yet grown together, one flesh even when he hurt her, so that now she could feel his suffering as no outsider, no matter how sensitive or how subtle, could ever feel.

She raised her face, appealing for understanding. "I can't leave a sinking ship, Tom. I can't leave."

He nodded. "But you will eventually," he said.

It was a time of waiting, an uneasy suspension of customary life. The days went slowly, and although it was autumn, they were long. From this house, surrounded by heavy foliage, Lynn looked out into a haze of faded colors, of greens gentled into gray and reds turned rusty, mournful yet lovely in their melancholy. It seemed to her that the earth was reflecting the mood of the house, for the fall should be bright and blazing. But it is all in the mind, she told herself; one sees what one needs to see.

On the far lawn under a maple Annie was doing her English assignment, reading *Huckleberry Finn*. Robert, kneeling on the grass, extended his arms toward Bobby, who, now going on ten months old, had already taken a few independent steps. Robert was proud; the boy would be athletic; the boy would be a strong tennis player, a swimmer, a track star.

If that gives him comfort, Lynn thought, let him have comfort. It was strange to see him here at home in the middle of the afternoon. Eudora, as she passed now between the garage and the grape arbor, must think so too.

Poor woman, only a week ago she had come, hesitant and shy, to make a confession.

"There's something I have to tell you, Mrs. Ferguson. All Mr. Ferguson's trouble, I heard about it from my friend, she shouldn't have talked, but I shouldn't have talked, either, I know I shouldn't. It was just that we were all having lunch at church, and you know when people work in other people's houses, they hear things, and they talk. I didn't mean to hurt you all, honestly I didn't. Even Mr. Ferguson, he's a gentleman, and I really liked him until he—"

Lynn had stopped her. "Dear Eudora, I understand. And it wasn't just you or your friend at the Stevenses'. Even the policeman at the country club knew, it seems that a great many people did. Oh, don't cry, please. Don't make it harder for me."

There had been no stopping the contrition. "I wouldn't hurt you for the world, you've been so good to me, all those clothes, and not just your old ones, but the new things for my birthday and last Christmas. You've been my *friend*. I couldn't stand it that morning when I came in and saw what he was doing to you, such a little thing you are, can't be more than a hundred pounds. Such a little thing."

The mild, anxious eyes had been asking a question that Eudora dared not ask aloud: "Are you staying, Mrs. Ferguson? Are you really?"

Lynn, raising her chin ever so slightly to show determination, had replied to the unspoken question. "We always need to look ahead in life, not back. What's past is past, isn't it?"

And in the saying she was conscious of maturity and strength.

"It's between Robert and me, our affair alone," she had told Tom Lawrence.

But of course, it was not. It was the proverbial stone thrown into a pond, with the widening ripples. It was Emily and Annie. . . .

Annie had been the surprise. The resilience of this so-often-troubled child was always a surprise. Unless she was holding it all in . . .

"Uncle Bruce told me not to believe what the kids said. He told me not even to answer them. 'They want you to cry and get angry,' he told me. 'But if you don't do either, you'll spoil their fun, and they'll stop.' We talk on the phone a lot." And she had finished with assurance, "Uncle Bruce gives me good advice." Then abruptly switching, she had demanded, "Why doesn't he come here anymore?"

"He's been busy getting ready to go away," Lynn had explained.

It was a question whether Bruce was more concerned to avoid Robert or to avoid her.

She wished Bruce would talk to Emily, but then was almost positive that his remarks to her would be quite different from his advice to Annie. Anyway, Emily was determined not to be moved.

Speaking to her sometime after the day of Robert's first frantic telephoned appeal, Lynn had come up against a wall of resistance.

"Mom, you're making a dreadful mistake," she had said in a sorry tone of disapproval. "Dreadful. I've done a lot of reading about marriages like yours."

"I know. I saw a book in your room. Those statistics don't fit every case. Emily. *People* aren't statistics."

"But there's a pattern, no matter how different each case may seem. We're still discussing wife abuse in my sociology course and I tell you, I've felt cold chills. You've got to take care of yourself, Mom. You can't depend on Dad anymore. You need to leave, and soon, Mom."

"No. If you could see your father, you'd know what I'm seeing. He's a different man. This has done something drastic to him, something terrible."

"You may be looking at him, but you're not seeing him."

"Have you no mercy or forgiveness, Emily? No pity?"

"Yes. Pity for you." And at the end Emily had said, "Well, Mom, you have to do what you think best."

Offended and defeated, Lynn had replied rather coolly, "Of course I must. Don't we all?" Then, softening, she had tried again. "In spite of his worries Dad's looking forward to Christmas, to the family being together. Would you like to bring Harris to dinner too? I'll make a feast, a *bûche de Noël* and everything."

"Harris has his own family dinner," Emily had replied, in the dry tone she seemed lately to have acquired.

"Well, one other day during vacation, then."

"We'll see," said Emily.

Stubborn! When Robert was really trying so hard to make amends!

"Don't tell Emily I'm worried about what I'm going to do," he kept saying. "I don't want her work to be affected. She needs a clear mind."

"But what are you really going to do?" Lynn had asked again only last night.

"I don't know yet. I need more time to think. In the meantime we can manage with my severance pay." The tone was dispirited, and the words were certainly vague. "Something, I'll find something."

On her birthday he had laid a long-stemmed rose at her plate.

"It's the best I can afford right now. I won't buy jewelry unless it's flawless, you know that. So, a flawless rose instead." Straightening his shoulders, and with a smile intended to be brave, he had said, "But next year at this time there'll be a shiny box tied with ribbon."

Something within Lynn had been displeased with this image; she had picked up the rose, so alive in its perfect simplicity, and held it against her cheek, saying only, "This is perfect, Robert. Thank you."

She could have said, "I don't measure things by shine and ribbon, don't you know that?"

But it would have come out prissy and righteous-sounding, which was not her intent at all, so she had just let him go to the piano, where, while she ate her breakfast, he played a birthday song.

Yesterday when it rained, she thought now, watching the baby stagger across the grass and fall into Robert's arms, he had spent the whole afternoon at the piano playing dreamy nocturnes. How long could the man go on this way? He went nowhere, not even on simple errands to the shopping center, where he feared to meet anybody he knew.

"You have to go out and hold your head up," she kept saying. "After all, you're not a murderer out on bail, are you? This is a seven-day wonder, anyhow. There's something new every week for people to chew over. Already, I'll take a bet on it, your departure from GAA is old stuff, forgotten."

But that was not true. At the supermarket there were no more curious glances and conversations broken off at her approach, but the telephone at home, an instrument that had once rung steadily, was now silent. And she recalled the conversation at Monacco's dinner table, the caretaker's light in the vacant house across the lake where had lived that couple about whom "you'd never guess it was possible."

Now Robert, seeing her at the window, waved, and she opened the casement.

"Bruce phoned while you were out," he called. "He's cleaning the house out and has some stuff he wants to give us, though I can't imagine what. Will you go over in the station wagon? He'd bring it himself, but his car's too small. Can you go now?"

"Can't you do it?"

"I'd rather not get into conversation with him in the circumstances," Robert pleaded.

Dismay was her instant reaction. Clothed though she was, she knew that she would feel naked in that room with Bruce, with no third person there to draw attention away from her. And yet, as she closed the casement, another thought came: I have neglected him, and he was, he is, or he and Josie were, our dearest friends. Shameful to have been so engrossed in her own trouble when his loss was so much greater! Yes, on one hand, came the argument: You have to remember that afternoon; how can you face each other, Lynn, tell me how? But on the other hand . . . So she stood, fearing to go, not wanting to, then in a queer, shamefaced fashion, wanting to.

Some time ago, before Josie's death, she had meant to give her a collection of pictures that they had taken together over the years. In the hall chest lay this folder, this record of the radiant hours that people want to save, the picnic on the Fourth of July, the birthdays, the company outing, and the silly hats on New Year's Eve. Surely Bruce would want this treasure. He would want every scrap and crumb of memory. Yes.

He was standing in a house half stripped when Lynn arrived. The first thing she noticed was that the living-room sofa was gone. A pair of early American matching chests were all that remained in the room.

"The new owners bought the best stuff," Bruce said. "The tall clock under the stairs, the stretcher table—stuff. The rest I gave away to the homeless project. Come, I'll show you what I thought might look nice in your garden. The new people don't want it."

Through the garden door, which stood open, he pointed to the birdbath that had been bought during his and Josie's only trip abroad. It was a large marble basin, on the rim of which there stood a pair of marble doves, drinking. Bruce laughed about it.

"Damn thing cost more to ship home from Italy than I paid for it! But Josie fell in love with the doves. And it is rather nice, I have to admit."

Now he added, "Would you like to have it? If you do, I can ask my neighbor's boy to help me load it into your car."

"It's beautiful, Bruce. But are you sure—?" she began.

"That I won't ever use it? Yes, Lynn. Quite sure. I've had my time for a home, and my time's passed."

What a pity, she thought, to feel so old at his age. He was beginning to look himself, though; the haggard desperation that had marked his face during these hard months had lessened; the body tries to heal even when the spirit cannot. Rest healed, and so did the sun that was now glinting on his curly, summer-bleached hair. Funny, she thought, I never noticed his lashes are golden.

They were standing in the doorway. A white butterfly fluttered and poised itself on a clump of dead, still-yellow marigolds.

"Butterflies," murmured Lynn, "and it's almost Thanksgiving."

He, apparently not inclined to speak anymore, stood there with his hands in the pockets of his jeans, his glasses thrust up into his curly hair, and eyes that seemed to be seeing, not the quiet surrounding afternoon, but something different, something far away.

And she, feeling superfluous, made a move to leave, asking hesitantly, "Did you say your neighbor will help carry?"

"Yes, his son. They're across the street. I'll go out the front door and get him."

The kitchen cabinets had been almost all cleaned out, Lynn saw as she followed him. The floor was littered, a broom stood in a corner with a new trunk next to it, and a pile of books stood waiting to be packed into stout crates.

"I'm taking my books and Josie's, the only things I want to save."

"Oh," Lynn said, "I almost forgot, I've got a collection of pictures that you'll want. I left them in my car. They go all the way back to when you first came to St. Louis. Oh, my head's a sieve."

"You've had a few other things to fill your head with," Bruce said. "How is Robert these days?"

"Subdued. You wouldn't know him. Subdued and worried, but nothing like what he was in the first days, thank God. I'll never forget how he cried on the telephone to Emily. I'd never seen a man show grief that way, although there's no reason why men shouldn't. But still, my father, even after my mother's funeral—" Abruptly, shocked at her own tactlessness in mentioning funerals, she stopped.

"I take it that you're staying, Lynn." And when she nodded, he said quite gently, "I thought you probably would."

"He's changed," she told him, aware as she spoke it that she had used the same word, *changed,* both to Emily and to Tom.

Unlike either of those two he made no protest but looked at her with an expression of utmost sweetness. Leaning against a kitchen counter, he faced her as she leaned against the counter opposite, the two of them standing among the disarray of an abandoned home. Neither one would venture to speak of what surely must have been in each of their minds; she was thinking, as she regarded him, that it had always been a total impossibility for her to have sex with any man but Robert, and yet it had happened with this man.

"It is your loyalty," Bruce said suddenly, as if he were thinking aloud. "You feel his pain as if it were your own."

"Yes," she said, surprised that he had expressed her feelings so exactly. "I suppose it makes no sense to you. You can't understand it. And Josie would be furious with me if she could know."

"You're mistaken. Josie would try to talk you out of it, but she would understand. There are very few things that Josie failed to understand or forgive."

He meant what had happened between the two of them, on that day when she lay in such pain that even morphine could not assuage it. That's what he meant.

"Oh, she was no saint," Bruce said. "I don't want to draw false pictures. She deserves to be remembered as she really was."

Indeed, not saintly, with that sharp scrutiny of hers and that peppery tongue! Only good, purely good, to the very last day.

Bruce made a little gesture with both hands, a movement implying emptiness.

"They say an amputated limb still aches. So I suppose it doesn't really do any good to go away, since the ache will only go along with me. Still,

I'm relieved to be given this chance, although not at Robert's expense, it's true."

"When are you going?"

"Next week. Tuesday."

"And how long will you be gone?"

"Years, I hope. They tell me I'm climbing up the ladder. I don't know. If I do well in Budapest, there'll be more places, they say. Moscow, maybe. I don't care, Lynn. But the communists have left a lot of ecological cleaning up to be done, and I care about that." He smiled. "For the Emilies and the Annies and the Bobbies of the world, I care."

The cat roused itself from where it had been sleeping in an empty box, crossed the room, and rubbed against Lynn's ankle. Extremely moved by the words and the memories that had just passed, she stooped to stroke its back, and the cat, to acknowledge the soft stroke, raised its small face, its pink mouth, and its astounding periwinkle eyes.

"You did ask us to take him, didn't you, Bruce?"

"If you still want to."

"He can come with me now," she said, wanting a reason not to have to see Bruce again, only to leave quietly now, to say the last good-bye and have it over with. "I'll take good care of him. Don't worry."

"Do you remember how she used to say she married me because I liked cats?"

"I remember." And she thought, but did not say, It was because your eyes smiled too. She said instead, "Are there—do you have instructions about Barney's food and things?"

"I'll write them out. Where's a pencil?" He went rummaging and, in an obvious attempt at cheer, kept talking. "Let's see: litter box, carrier, collar and leash, almost never used but good to have, some canned food, his favorite kind. Of course, he likes scraps whenever you have fish for dinner."

"Dover sole?" she asked, forcing a laugh, needing to seem lighthearted.

He responded in kind. "Oh, naturally. Only the best. And you might let him have a couple of spoons of ice cream now and then, any flavor but coffee. He doesn't like coffee."

Standing on the walk, she watched while Bruce and the neighbor's son put the birdbath and the unprotesting cat with his belongings into the station wagon. Then the moment of departure came, and suddenly there was nothing to say. Uncomfortable with this vacuum, she remarked that the neighbor's son seemed to be a fine boy, rather mature for fifteen.

"That's what you have to look forward to with Bobby," he replied.

"I hope so. I'll do my best."

"I know you will."

"So, I guess it's good-bye," she said, and, absurdly, held out her hand.

"A handshake, Lynn?" Holding her face, he softly touched her lips with his own. Then he put his arms around her, held her close, and kissed her again.

"Take care of yourself, Lynn. Take good care."

"And you. You do the same."

"I worry so about you. I have for a long time."

"There's no need. I'm fine. I'm strong."

"Well, but if you ever need anything, call Tom Lawrence, will you?"

"I won't need anything. Honestly. Believe me."

"Tom cares about you, Lynn."

Tom, she thought, says the same about you. It would be comical if things weren't all so mixed up. And, turning from him so that he might not see her wet, blinking eyes, she climbed into the driver's seat.

"Be sure to write to us now and then, especially to Annie."

"My special Annie. I'll always be there for her."

"You are the best, the kindest," she said, and, able to say no more, started the engine.

The last she saw of Bruce as the car moved off was the sunlight striking his glasses and his arm upraised in farewell. The last she saw of the little house was the kitchen window, where Josie's red gingham curtains still hung. Her eyes were so wet that she could barely see to drive.

Robert is probably right about him, she thought. He's the kind who really may never marry again. He's lost. And the word echoed: lost. It was a tolling bell, grave and sorrowful and final. She would probably never see him again. He would drift and she would drift, and they would not meet.

At home there was hustle and bustle. Annie at once took over the care of the cat.

"Barney knows me best," she insisted. "He should be my cat. I'll be responsible for his food and his vet appointments and everything."

"And will you clean the litter box too?" Lynn asked.

"Absolutely. Now I have to introduce him to Juliet. I really don't think there'll be any trouble, do you?"

"I don't think so. If there is, we'll learn how to handle it."

Robert was still in the yard with Bobby. At the moment the little boy was stretched on the grass with Juliet, and both were watching Robert hammer a playhouse into shape. He does everything well, Lynn thought, observing the swift competence and the masculine grace.

Seeing her, he called, "Like it? He'll be able to use it before you know it."

"It's time for his bath." She walked out and picked up the baby. "Oh, my, wet through. You do need a bath."

The boy laughed and caught hold of her hair. Robert gave them a look of such intensity that she had to ask curiously, "What is it?"

"You. Both of you together. Your lovely, tranquil spirit. I don't deserve you."

She did not want her heart to be touched or moved. She wanted just peace, calm and practical and friendly.

"Dinner will be heating while I bathe Bobby. Then I have Annie's scout meeting tonight. It's for mothers and daughters, so will you put him to bed?"

"Of course I will."

"Come see when you're finished there," she called back from the kitchen door. "I've brought Bruce's cat."

Then she closed the door and carried Bobby upstairs. *"I worry about you," Bruce had said, with the implication that she was somehow in peril. But it was not so, for she was going to be in control. I can run this house and this family like clockwork, she told herself, holding her child. I can keep a happy order here, and I can cope with anything.*

She was strong, and she was proud.

A few days later she went to New York for the pre-Christmas sales. Now that their financial future was uncertain, she had to shop with a particular care, to which for a long time she had been unaccustomed. Hurrying homeward past Salvation Army Santa Clauses and shop windows festooned with glass balls and tinsel arabesques, she worried whether the coat and skirts would fit Annie properly.

But there was something else on her mind, something that, because of her preoccupation with Josie's death and Robert's depression, she had locked away in the dark. However, it did not accept the darkness, but struggled out again and again, as if to force her to examine it.

There was something odd about Aunt Jean's connection to Querida. Or there would be, provided that Emily's report was correct. Or provided that the name over the shop's door belonged to *the* Querida—which it might well not, she thought now, summoning common sense and probabilities.

She was passing through the neighborhood, and it gave her immediate recall, such as follows a chord, a flavor, or a scent; it brought back the day when events had crashed upon each other like cars on a foggy highway; there had been Robert's attack in the kitchen, her flight into Bruce's arms, and Emily's sorrowful leavetaking. And it seemed to her that all these were somehow linked in ways that she could not fathom, that these things had their origin in one place, one time.

I have to know, she thought, as she came to the street, to the shop, and, with a thumping of the heart like a pounding on a door, stood there looking in the window.

A row of dog paintings was on display. They were all the fashion these days; the English-country-house look was the right look, casual elegance among rural acres for the homes of people who had never owned either an acre or a dog and possibly would never want to, she thought, surveying the haughty pugs, Queen Victoria's favorites, and the sporting setters, flaunting their proud tails. But there among them hung an unfamiliar creature, a strange beast, looking so much like Juliet that it could have been Juliet.

Abruptly her feet made the decision to enter and she found herself inside.

A small, dark woman limped across the room and took Juliet out of the window.

"It's not old," she said in reply to Lynn's query. "I've put it with the old ones because it has a nineteenth-century look. Actually, it's the work of a man who simply likes to paint dogs, any kind."

"It's charming."

The dog, sitting on a doorstep, had the same alert, faintly concerned expression that Juliet wore whenever the family drove away without her.

"Yes, I see by your face how much you like it," the woman said.

"It's the image of our dog."

Lynn's heart was pounding, and while she was seeing the painting, she was also seeing the woman. Had Robert not spoken about "a job in a gallery," and "a dabbler"? Still, his "beauty" could certainly not be this person, whose angular face with its flat black eyes was topped by a dome of coarse black hair. Relief and disappointment met and mingled. In one way she "had to know," she wanted to behold the woman who had first occupied her place; but in another way there was dread.

She returned to the picture. It would be a fine surprise for Robert, something to enliven him. They might hang it in his den at home or better still in his office. For an instant she forgot that at present he did not have an office.

"It's not expensive. The price is on the tag."

The price was most fair. Since the painting was small enough, she could carry it home right now. And she handed over her credit card.

The woman looked hard at the card and slowly turned her eyes up toward Lynn.

"Robert V. W. Ferguson. So now you've come too," she said. "I was wondering whether you would."

Lynn's knees went so weak that she had to perch on the stool that stood beside the counter, and she stammered.

"I don't understand."

"Your daughter Emily was here a while back, the day after Thanksgiving."

Emily in New York? But Emily was in New Orleans! We talked on the phone on Thanksgiving day. She must have flown in to see this woman, and gone back to college without telling us. . . .

The woman was staring at Lynn in open curiosity.

"She had a lot of questions, but I didn't answer them. She's too young, sweet and young. Besides, it's up to you to tell her whatever you want her to know."

Lynn's voice came in a whisper. "I know nothing."

"Nothing?"

"Not much. Only that you didn't get along."

"Didn't get along! There's a bit more to it than that, you can be sure."

The black eyes bored into Lynn. "You're a pretty woman. He liked blondes, I remember."

Lynn was in panic. She had come here wanting to find out—what? To find out something about Robert that other people—Aunt Jean—knew and had kept hidden. And now that she was here she was in panic.

"He must have told you something about me."

"That there was a child, a boy," Lynn whispered again.

"Yes. He's a man now, living in England. He's had a good life: I saw to that. And you? Do you have other children?"

"Another girl, and a boy ten months old."

"A nice family."

The air in the confined and cluttered space held bad vibrations; there was an impending intimacy from which Lynn now shrank. What she must do was to stand up and leave the place, picture and all. But she was unable to move.

Querida's eyes roved over her, coming to rest on the fur coat and the fine leather bag. "I see that he has accomplished what he wanted to."

And Lynn, mesmerized, submitted to inspection. The brusque remark, that could have been offensive, was somehow not. It was merely odd. Whatever could Robert have seen in this woman? Two more ill-matched people one could hardly imagine.

As if she had read Lynn's mind, Querida said, "I don't know how we ever got mixed up. It was just one of those things, I guess. He was brilliant, won all the scholarships, and God knows he was good looking. I was Phi Beta Kappa, and I suppose he was impressed by that. I was no beauty, although somewhat better looking than I am now, that's for sure. We were together only three or four times and I got pregnant. I didn't want an abortion, and I'll say this much for him, he did the right thing for those days, anyway. He married me."

Had she no inhibitions? Why was she telling these things to a person who had not asked to hear them?

"We were dirt poor, both of us. Hadn't anything, never had had anything."

Poor? The trips to Europe and Querida's prominent family? What of them?

"Why do you look surprised? Are you surprised?"

"Yes," Lynn murmured.

"I suppose he told you I was beautiful. He always liked to tell me about his former lovers, how exceptional they were. And I suppose he drew you a picture of his distinguished patrician background. Poor Robert. He did it so often that he really believed it. Anyway, by your time they were dead, so what difference? But I knew. I knew the mother with the doilies and the tea wagon. The genteel poor. Pretense, all pretense. She was pathetic, a decent little woman, half the size of her husband, and helpless under his fists."

"I don't want to hear this!" cried Lynn, shuddering.

"But maybe you should."

You could feel the anger burning in this queer woman, as if her very skin would be hot to the touch. She was eccentric, neurotic, or even perhaps a trifle mad . . . And still you had to listen.

"Jean worries about you. Oh, yes, she's kept in touch with me over the years. She's a good soul, like her sister, and she's never been sure about you and Robert."

This was too much, this infringement of the decent privacy that Lynn had guarded all her life.

"People have no right—" she blurted, but the other, ignoring her indignation, continued.

"Do you know how Robert's mother died? They were in their car on the turnpike, the two of them. A man at a tollbooth notified the police when he saw what was wrong, but by the time the police caught up with them it was too late. She had been trying to jump out of the moving car, away from him. The people in the car behind had seen it. The car swerved and hit a tree. They were both killed. Good for him, and none too soon. And those," Querida said, "are the distinguished Fergusons."

Oh, the horror! And the woman would not stop the gush of words. Perhaps she could not.

"Do you see this leg? My hip was broken. Yes, the story repeats itself, although not all the way, because I knew enough to get free. Yes, Robert did this to me."

Now Lynn recognized that she herself was in a state of physical shock; her mouth went dry, her palms wet, and her heart was audibly drumming in her ears. She sat quite still, not having moved from the support of the counter at her back, sat and stared as the nervous voice resumed.

"It wasn't the first time, although it was the worst. We were ice skating. He asked me what there was for dinner, and I said we'd pick up some fast food on the way home. I wasn't a good housekeeper. I'm still not, and that infuriated him. But he infuriated me with his compulsive ways, so neat, so prompt, so goddamn perfect. So he went absolutely mad about the dinner. A thing like that could trigger him."

Lynn's dry lips formed a statement: *I told you I don't want to hear any more.* Yet no sound came out.

"It was almost dark, and we were the last ones on the lake. So he slapped my face, and his gloves had buckles on the wrists. He shoved me, and I fell on the ice. He kicked me, and I couldn't get up. Then he was scared, and he ran to a public phone to call an ambulance. When they came, I was almost fainting with the pain. I heard him say, 'She fell.'"

If she would just stop and let me get out of here, Lynn thought, and then rebuked herself: You know you have to stay to the end, to hear it all.

"A neighbor woman cared for the baby while I was in the hospital. When he came and started talking about the 'accident,' I told him I never wanted to see him again. So I took my child and left. I had a friend in Florida who gave me a job, and I let him get the divorce on the grounds of desertion. I didn't care, I wanted no part of him. I said if he ever came near me or the child, I would expose him and ruin him forever." Again there came that forced, grim laugh. "I must say he has supported the boy generously—not me, because I wouldn't take a penny of his anyway. Now my son is twenty-four and independent.

"My hip wasn't set right. They tell me it should be broken again and reset. But I don't want to go through all that. I keep it this way as a remembrance of Robert."

Why was she revealing this terrible story after all these years? It was to take revenge for her suffering. It was to destroy Robert's marriage, especially if it should be a good one.

"And do you think it does any good to go to the police? Do you? Well, I'll tell you. It doesn't. I went once. They didn't even take me seriously. I came in a nice car. We both had jobs then, and we had pooled our money for it. We had a neat apartment in a decent neighborhood. 'What are you complaining about?' they asked me. 'The guy can't be all bad. You should see the things we see. Straighten it out. Don't make him angry. Of course, if you want to swear out a complaint, we can arrest him and make a big stink. Then maybe he'll lose his job, and where'll you be? Nah, think it over. You women don't know when you're well off.' That's what they told me. I see I've upset you."

"What did you expect?" Lynn's pity and horror collided. Her head reeled, and her voice filled with tears. "You had no right to dump all this stuff on me. I came in to buy a picture, and—"

The other woman's tight face softened. "I suppose I shouldn't have talked," she said. "I shouldn't be involved in this at all. But when your daughter came I suspected—never mind. Do you still want the picture? I'll let you have it for nothing. My way of apologizing."

Lynn slid off the stool. "Yes, I want it. And I want to pay for it."

"As you wish. I'll wrap it."

Although her heart was still pounding, she was beginning to recover and take command of herself. With a show of casual dignity she walked around the walls as if to examine the paintings hung there, yet, in her agitation, scarcely seeing them at all.

After a moment the voice pursued her. "You don't believe me."

Lynn turned and went back to the counter. "Whether I do or not," she said quietly, "doesn't matter. Just give me the picture, please, so I can go."

In the silence, now throbbing with the words that had been spoken there, she waited while the package was being wrapped. Querida's fingers delicately handled paper, cardboard, and twine; she had oval nails and a strong profile as she bent over the work. An intelligent face, thought Lynn.

The silence broke abruptly. "He made her life a hell. I'm talking about Robert's father and mother. Her people hated him. They begged her to leave him, but she wouldn't. A little bit proud, a little too ashamed. I know. I've seen them, the soft ones who listen to the sweet apology and believe it won't happen again. You, too, I'm thinking."

Now words came, choking in Lynn's throat. "You don't know anything about me!"

"But I do. I know that lovely girl of yours wouldn't have sought me out unless she had a great trouble on her mind. She knows plenty, but she wants to know more. I saw. Pull yourself together, my dear; take care of yourself and your children. I know you think I'm queer and maybe I am, but I mean well."

The door slammed and cold air struck Lynn's face. A blast of wind from Canada rounded the stone corner and almost knocked her over as she ran toward Grand Central. Her legs barely held her.

The soft ones—the sweet apology . . .

A strange woman, with those wild eyes. How they must have hated each other! Not like Robert and me because we—in spite of all, we—

But he lied to me. All those lies. And yet she—is everything she said true?

Faintly dizzy, she struggled through the wind and the crowds. Within the vast cavern of the terminal "Good King Wenceslaus" reverberated heartily. People returning to their suburban homes were normal; there was reassurance in the cheerful sound of greetings; a fat man clapped another on the back and two matrons squealed with delight at seeing one another. These were common, everyday noises. These were ordinary, everyday people.

The train clicked over the tracks. It's true, it's not, it's true, it's not, said the wheels. This had been the worst day . . . Lynn laid her head back against the seat. And the woman next to her, young and fashionable with no troubles on her face, asked anxiously, "Are you not feeling well?"

"It's only a headache, thank you. I'm all right." Embarrassed, Lynn smiled.

The car was parked at the station. When she got in and drove through the town, which looked the same as it had that morning, it seemed astonishing that everything should be the same. Station wagons were parked in the supermarket lot, the yellow school buses were returning to the garage, and the windows were prepared here, too, for the holiday as if nothing of any importance had happened since the morning.

It seemed too early to go home. Actually, it was early, for she had wanted to make another stop in the city on the way to the train. But after what had happened, she had needed only to rush away. So she stopped the car at a dingy luncheonette on the fringe of the center and sat down to order a pot of tea with a bun. Tea was soothing.

He kicked me while I lay on the ice with my hip broken. Now, that, that's hard to believe. Yes, he had bursts of rotten temper—how well I know! But sadism like that, never. No, that's hard to accept. Out of a kernel of truth, a large kernel, she has developed this sickly growth, this enormous exaggeration.

She's odd, filled with rage and, in some way that I can't diagnose, disturbed. But if she were more, let's say for want of more accurate words, more reasonable, temperate, sweeter, *acceptable,* then would I be more apt to believe her?

Yet even if only some of it is true, how terrible and sad it is that he has needed to conceal it all these years! Why, when I would have tried to help him? Didn't he know that I would have tried?

But weigh the sin of his concealment against all our years together, all the good, all the good. . . .

The warm cup, held between Lynn's hands, brought remembrance of her parents, sitting at the kitchen table on other winter afternoons. They had used to hold their cups just so, and the cups had had daisies around the rims. It had been a simple time. . . . Her eyes flooded, and she thrust the tea away.

Someone put money in a jukebox left over, probably, from the fifties, and canned voices, moaning over love lost or remembered or found, swelled out into the gray, depressing room. Lynn got up and paid her bill. It was time to pull herself together and go home. It was time, Josie would say, to face reality. Go home and, making no fuss, ask him what you want to know, and tell him what you have found out.

Robert had put a candle bulb in each window, so that the house appeared to float through the early darkness like a ship with lighted portholes. Through the bow window, where the curtains were still open, she could see him sitting in his big leather chair with Bobby on one knee; they were looking at a book spread on the other knee.

The little boy adored the man: His dark blue eyes were rounder than Emily's and Robert's; they were round like his dear head and his little fat hands. She felt a twinge of pain, like a tender wound, a soft something that was both merciful and sorrowful. For a moment she was almost within their skins, that of the vulnerable baby, and that of the man who perhaps had once known such grievous hurt that he was unable to admit its existence.

Opening the door, she heard Annie practicing her piano lesson at the other end of the hall, and she paused a moment to listen. Annie was really doing better, doing better at everything. It might be that the new quietness in Robert, the slowing of the house's rhythm, had affected the child too. It was a strange irony that the father's most cruel defeat should have brought about a subtle kind of peace that had not been there before, whose absence she had not even been aware of until it occurred.

The dog jumped to announce her presence and Robert looked up in surprise.

"Hello! We didn't hear you come in."

"I've been watching you. You're so cozy, you two."

"We're halfway through Mother Goose, up to Little Jack Horner." He got up, set the baby in the playpen, and kissed Lynn. "You've been shopping, I see. Did you buy anything nice?"

"I hope you'll think so. It's your Christmas present."

"Didn't we promise each other just books this year? And now you've gone and broken your promise," he said with a rueful smile.

"This wasn't horribly expensive, honestly. It's a picture. Open it."

"Why not wait till Christmas?"

"Because I don't want to wait."

Bobby, attracted by the crackle of paper as Robert cut the string, stretched out his arms as if he could reach the bright redness and the crackle. And something caught again in Lynn's chest, in her heart and throat, at the sight of the merry child and the father's dark head bent over the package.

Surely this family's path would straighten and all the past evil be forgotten! This was only a sharp turning in the path, a crooked obstacle to be got over, and she would get over it. There was so much else to be thankful for; no one had cancer, no one was blind. . . .

"Wherever did you find this?" Robert cried. "It's Juliet to the life. Fantastic!"

"I thought you would love it."

"It's wonderful. Dog portraits are always the same, spaniels or hounds or faithful collies. Thanks a million, Lynn."

"You'll never believe where I found it. Quite by accident, I saw it in a window on the way to the train, in a tiny gallery called 'Querida.' "

Robert's face changed. As if a hand had passed over it, the eyes' lively shine, the smile crinkles at their corners, the smile pouches of the cheeks, and the happy lift of the lips were wiped away. And she saw that he was waiting for the words that would come next, saw that, quite understandably, she had stunned him.

"The odd thing is that it really was she. I couldn't believe it. It was when I showed the American Express card and she recognized the name."

Say nothing about Emily having been there. Be careful. Nothing.

"Very interesting." He clipped the words like a stage Englishman. "Interesting, too, that you didn't turn right around and walk out."

"But I wanted the painting," she protested, and was aware, even as she spoke them, that the words were too innocent. Then she added, "Besides, it would have been awkward just to turn on my heel and leave."

"Oh, awkward, of course. Much easier to stay and have a cozy chat with the lady."

Robert's eyes narrowed, and he straightened his posture. As always, it seemed that he grew taller when he was angry. And in dismay she knew that he was very, very angry.

This was not what she had expected; perhaps she'd been foolish to think he would defend himself. Instead he was on the attack.

"There was no chat. I was only there for the time it took to pay and have this wrapped. It was only a minute. A couple of minutes," she said, stumbling over the defense.

"So you didn't open your mouths, either of you." He nodded. "After that astonishing revelation there was total silence, I'm sure."

"Well, not exactly."

"I suppose you got quite an earful about me."

It was he who was to have been on the defensive, he who was to have been scared. How had the tables been turned like this? And she murmured, almost coaxing now, "Why no, Robert, not at all."

"I don't believe it. Your curiosity would have kept you listening, with your ears open and your mouth hanging open, while your husband was smeared with filth. Don't tell me not, Lynn, because I know better." He was trembling. "Talk about loyalty! If you had any, you wouldn't have entered there in the first place."

"How would I know? How could I have known?"

"You knew damn well that that—creature—played around with art and worked in a gallery. You didn't forget that, Lynn. And the name— you didn't forget that either. You could have thought, when you saw that name—it wasn't Susan, it wasn't Mary; do you see it on every street corner? You could have thought, Well, maybe it's possible, I won't take a chance. But your curiosity got the better of you, didn't it?"

The iota of accuracy in what he said brought a flush of heat that ran up her neck and scorched her cheeks.

"Well, didn't it?"

His voice rose and filled the room so that Bobby, hearing the unfamiliar tone, turned a puzzled face to his father.

Now Lynn had to go over to the attack. "You're impossible! How can you have so little understanding, when my only thought was to bring you something that might make you a little bit happy in these hard days? And I did cut her short. I didn't want to hear anything, so I walked out when she—"

"You cut her short? But you just told me nothing was said. You'd better get your story straight."

"You get me all mixed up. You tie my tongue. When you're like this, I can't even think straight. I get so muddled, I don't know what I'm saying."

"You're muddled, all right. Now, listen to me—I want to know exactly what was said, and you had better tell me exactly."

Like a whip he sprang and grasped her arms at the place where he had always grasped before, in the soft flesh above the elbow. His hard fingers pressed his thumbs against the very bone.

In the playpen the baby now pulled himself up and stood swaying against the railing. His wide eyes stared at them.

"Let go," Lynn said, keeping her voice low for Bobby's sake.

"I want an answer, I said."

The pain was horrible, but she still spoke evenly. "Keep your voice down, Robert. The baby's terrified. And do you want Annie to hear this too?"

"I want to know what that crazy woman said, that's what I want. Answer me!"

He shook her. There was a fierceness in his expression that she had never seen there before, something desperate and grim, something fanatical. And, more frightened than she had ever been, she began to cry.

"Ah, the tear machine. Don't answer a simple question. Just turn on the tear machine."

He shook her so violently that her neck jerked.

"Robert, let go! I'll have to scream, and everybody will know. This is insane. Look at the baby!"

Bobby's wet pink mouth hung open and his round cheeks were puckering toward tears. "Look what you're doing to the baby!"

"Then talk."

"All you do is find fault with me! I can't stand it!"

In a nasal whine he mocked her. "All I do is find fault with you. You can't stand it."

The baby rattled the playpen, fell on his back, and wailed. And Lynn, frantic now with fright and pain and concern over Bobby, screamed out, "Let go of me, Robert! Damn you—"

"Talk, and I will."

There was a tumult within her, the desperation of a captive who has been wrongly accused, a victim of terror. And this desperation exploded.

"All right, I'll talk! Enough of lies! Let the truth blare! Why have you hidden yourself from me all these years? I had thought to talk to you in a civil way and ask you why you never trusted me enough to be open with me. Why did you hide what your father did to your mother? Oh, I see now why Aunt Jean was never welcome! It's you! You didn't want her around for fear she would say too much. And why? Did you think so little of me as to believe I wouldn't understand about your family? Did you think so little of yourself that you had to invent a family? Why do you feel that you have to be without flaw, descended from saints or something?"

She saw the pulses throbbing in his temples, where suddenly on each a crooked blue vein had swelled. And now that she had begun, now that the pressure of Robert's hands was unbearable, she, too, screamed, not caring or able to care who heard.

"Why did you tell me Querida was beautiful and rich? To make me jealous? Why didn't you tell me about her broken hip? Why have you lived with all these lies, so that I've had to live with them too? Now I see, I see it all. My life, my whole life . . . What's the matter with you? What have you done?"

Her words tumbled and raced and would not cease.

"A sham, a cover-up, all the excuses I made because I wanted not to admit anything. I needed to keep the dream. She told me everything you did to her, Robert, everything. She said—"

He let her go. He picked up the painting, raised it high, and brought it down hard, splintering the frame and ripping the canvas from top to bottom over the back of a chair. The baby screamed; in a distant room the piano sounded a smashing discord and stopped. The vandalism was atrocious. He was panting like an animal.

"You disgust me!" she cried. "People should know this, should see what you can do! Yes, you disgust me."

He struck her. A violent blow landed on her neck, and she fell back, crashing into the playpen. When she picked herself up, he struck her again, grazing her eye as she turned, gasped, and tried to flee. With his left hand he seized her collar; his right fist smashed her nose so hard that the crack was audible, as bone met bone. Blood gushed; she reached for support, but there was only empty air. The room slowly circled and tilted around her as she fell, and was still.

She had fallen or been laid upon the sofa. Vomit and blood had smeared her white silk shirt, and for some reason that later she was to find incredible, this damage to the shirt was the first thing she saw. It was a terrible humiliation. She heard herself wail, "Oh, look!" She sobbed. In a confusion of sound and sight she seemed to see Eudora clutching Robert's coat and screaming at him, "What the hell have you done?" At the same time she seemed to see Eudora holding Bobby on one arm while Annie, somewhere at her side, was crying.

Next came the pain in a wave of fire, so that, as if to cool it, she pressed her hands to her face, then drew them away in revulsion over her own sticky blood.

The room was filled with a swelling crowd of many people, many voices making a vast, low roar. But after a while she knew that the roar was only in her head. When she opened her eyes again, she began to distinguish among the faces. Eudora was still holding Bobby. Annie was at the foot of the sofa. Somebody was wiping her face with a cold towel; the hands were gentle and very careful. She focused her eyes. The room had stopped circling, and things had righted themselves so that she began to see quite clearly. It was Bruce who stood over her holding the towel.

"What are you doing here?" she whispered.

"Annie called me." He took his glasses off and wiped them. His eyes were moist, as though they might have held tears; yet at the same time they were fierce. His mouth, his full-lipped, easy mouth, was a hard line. "You fainted," he said.

Annie knelt and laid her face on Lynn's shoulder, whimpering, "Mommy. Oh, Mommy."

"Careful, dear. Her face is sore," said Bruce.

Now came Robert's voice. "I've got the ice bag. Move away a little, Annie."

"Don't you touch her," Bruce commanded. "The ice bag can wait a minute."

"I have a first-aid certificate," protested Robert.

"You know what you can do with your goddamn certificate! She'll see a doctor after she's pulled herself together. You keep away from her, hear?"

Now Robert moved into view, his eyes and his voice making joint appeal.

"Oh, God, Lynn, I don't know how to say what I feel. I never intended . . . But things just got out of hand. . . . We were both angry. . . ."

Bruce shouted, "Oh, why don't you shut up!"

"Yes, why don't you?" Annie repeated. Her head was buried in her mother's shoulder while her mother's arm held her.

"Annie dear," Bruce said, "your mother will be happier, I think, if you go upstairs. I know this is awfully hard for you, but if you'll just try to be a little patient, we'll talk about it in the morning, I promise."

Robert coaxed. "Don't worry about Mom. It looks worse than it is. I'll see that she's taken care of. Do go up, darling."

When he moved toward her, as if to take her away from the sofa, Annie scrambled up out of his reach and, with her hands on her chubby hips and her eyes streaming tears, defied him.

"I'm not your darling. You're an awful father, and Susan was right. You do hit Mom. I saw you just now, I saw you. And, and—I never told anybody, but sometimes I have a dream about you, and I hate it because it wakes me up and I feel so bad, and I tell myself it's only a dream, but now, now," she sputtered, "look what you did! It's as horrible as the dream!"

"What dream, Annie? Can you remember it?" asked Bruce.

"Oh, yes. I see Mom in a long white dress, wearing a crown on her head and he—he is hitting her."

This blow, this other kind of blow, struck Lynn again between the eyes. And it had struck Robert hard, too, for, dazed as she was, she was able to see how clearly he was recalling that night of the New Year's Eve costume party, so long ago. Annie had been no more than three. . . .

And she gave Robert a terrible look. She wanted to say, So, this explains a good deal about Annie, doesn't it?

But instead she whispered, summoning the top of her strength, "You're *my* darling. So will you do something for me and go up with Eudora? Tomorrow I'll tell you about the dream, about everything."

"Come, Annie," said Eudora, "come up and help give Bobby his bottle. I'm going to sleep on a cot in your room with you. I'm staying here tonight."

Annie raised her head, and Lynn, too miserable to speak, gave the child a look of appeal.

"Juliet has to sleep in my room too."

"Of course she will," said Eudora.

And the little group shuffled out, the woman holding the baby and the girl, for comfort, holding on to the dog.

And we were sure, thought Lynn, silent in bitter grief, that we had kept the children from knowing.

The doorbell rang just as Eudora started up the stairs.

"That's Tom Lawrence," Bruce said. "I called him."

"What? He has no business here. Don't open the door, Eudora," commanded Robert.

Bruce countermanded the order. "Yes, please open it, Eudora. I'd do it myself, only I don't want to step away from Mrs. Ferguson."

"What in blazes—" said Tom. Stunned, he stood in the doorway and stared at the scene. "What in blazes—"

He walked over and looked down at Lynn, grimaced, shut his eyes for an instant from the sight, and turned to Robert.

"So, you bastard, it's finally happened. It took a while coming, but I knew it would. You ought to be strung up."

"You don't know what you're talking about! We had some upset here, an argument, and I only meant—"

The words diminished and faded. As shocked and foggy as Lynn's brain was then, still there came a lucid thought: He is considering that Tom is a lawyer, and he's scared.

"You 'only' nothing, Ferguson." Tom walked toward Robert, who drew back. It was strange to see him drawing back from a man whose head barely reached past his shoulder. "I'm calling the police."

Lynn struggled up against the pillows. Her eye throbbed. When her tongue touched her front teeth, one moved. She tried again. Definitely, it had been loosened. And she spoke through swollen lips.

"No. No police. Please, Tom." She wanted him to understand that Annie had already seen horror enough. "All I want is for—him," she said, motioning toward Robert, "for him to get out." She lay back again. "I'm so dizzy."

"Ah, you see? Even Lynn doesn't want the police," said Robert.

"I'd like to overrule you, Lynn," Tom said gravely. "This is a public matter now. A man can't be allowed to get away with this kind of thing."

"Stay out of it, Lawrence," Robert said. "Nobody invited you here."

Bruce jumped to the attack. "I invited him. Lynn needs friends, and she needs legal advice, which I can't give."

"My advice again is to call the police," Tom urged. "They need only to take one look at her, and it'll be worth a thousand words for future use."

Robert pounced. "Future use?"

"It would be in the newspapers," Lynn murmured. "My children have been hurt badly enough without that too."

"You're not thinking," Bruce said quietly. "Everyone knows about it, anyway. In the office now—"

At that Robert shouted out. "In the office? Yes, yes, do you think I don't know about the lies you've spread? You wanted to tear me down, you wanted to take my place."

Bruce pointed to Lynn. "Lies? Look at your wife's face. If I had talked, and I never did, which you know quite well, there would have been no lies. No. Robert, if I had ever wanted to talk, I could have done it long ago, that morning in Chicago, or maybe even before that, and you would never have gotten as far as New York. Let alone Europe," he shouted. His rage and contempt had set him on fire. "You aren't fit to live, after what you've done here tonight. You ought to be taken out and shot."

I'm not here, Lynn was saying to herself. All this has nothing to do with me. It's not happening to me.

Tom took her hand, which was cold, as one chill after another began to shake her.

"What do you want us to do, Lynn? Tell us. There's no point in arguing who said or did not say what. You're too exhausted."

She answered him softly, as if she feared Robert's wrath if he should overhear. "Just make him go. I don't want to see him ever, ever, ever."

But Robert had heard. "You don't mean that, Lynn," he cried. "You know you don't."

Tom gave an order. He was a small, active terrier badgering a Great Dane. "You heard what she said. Go! Get your coat and get out."

Robert, clasping his hands, beseeched her. "Lynn, hear me. These people, these strangers, are egging you on. I'll spend the rest of my days making up to you for this, I swear I will. And telling me to go is no solution. These people—it's no business of theirs."

"Tom and Bruce, whom you call 'these people,' are my friends," she answered, finding voice. "I wanted them here. I need them. And I want you to go. It's I who want it. I."

He beat his clenched hands on his breast. "You and I have lived a life together. Can any third person know what we have had, you and I? The things that have been between us? I'll change. I'll go anywhere you want, talk to anyone you want, take any counsel. I promise, I swear."

"Too late," she cried. "Too late."

"I beg you, Lynn."

His shame and his agony were contagious; absurd as it was, as her intelligence told her it was, he could still elicit pity. It was odd that when he was angry, he could seem so tall; now between the other two men, pleading, he shrank.

Bruce held out his hand, commanding, "Give me your house keys, Robert. Does he have duplicates?" he asked Lynn.

Still overcome with the shame of this, she told him, "In the drawer of the table behind you."

"I'll take them." Bruce put them in his pocket. "I'll throw them out when I get home. You'll change your locks tomorrow. Now get out of here, Robert. Now. This minute."

"You may come back tomorrow morning at nine o'clock for your clothes," Tom said. "But you heard Bruce, so go, and hurry up about it. Lynn needs rest and attention."

"I want to hear that from Lynn," Robert answered.

His face had gone gray. She thought: He knows I pity him, even now. But I am not wavering. If I had any tendency to do it, and I do not, the thought of Annie alone would stop me.

And drawing herself upright, she said sternly, "I will tell you, Robert. Leave now, or weak as I am, I shall take Annie and Bobby and sit at the airport until the first plane leaves for my sister's in St. Louis, and you'll have the damned house to yourself."

Tom cried, "Oh, no! This house is yours as much as his. You'll stay in it until your lawyer says you may leave it. I'm getting a fine Connecticut lawyer for you tomorrow. And you had better get going, Ferguson," he threatened. "Otherwise, no matter what Lynn says, I'll have the police here in ten minutes."

The two men stood side by side in front of Robert. He looked them up and down, then looked at Lynn for so long that she had to shut her eyes. His face was like that of a man who has come upon a ghastly slaughter and is helpless. She supposed that her expression might be the same. Then he turned on his heel and went rapidly from the house.

The door closed. There was the sound of wheels on the gravel drive, and then nothing.

*   *   *

The two men took charge. First came a doctor, a friend of Tom's who, in a situation like this one, was willing to make a house call.

Bruce explained. "Mrs. Ferguson doesn't want to press charges, and if she goes to the hospital—"

The doctor understood. "There would be questions. As long as there's no damage to the retina, I think we'll be able to manage here at home." Plainly shocked, he bent over Lynn and flashed a light into her eye. "No, there's not. You're lucky. It almost—" And he shook his head.

When he had gone, Tom and Bruce made decisions for the morning. New door locks must be installed. Appointments with a dentist and an attorney must immediately be made. Bruce would talk to Annie and assess the damage to her.

"I'm staying all night," he said. "I can stretch out on the sofa in the den."

He would certainly not stretch out on this one. Lynn's blood had ruined the moss-green damask, ruined it forever. And Robert had always worried about their guests' palms on the armrests.

"Your flight's tomorrow night. You need some sleep," she protested.

"It doesn't matter. There's no sleep in me now, anyhow. I'll make up for it on the plane."

Until long past midnight they talked. Bruce wanted to know what had led to such horror, and she told him everything, starting with the painting, which still, in its innocence, lay wrecked on the floor.

His comment, when she had finished, was thoughtful and sorrowful. "He was afraid that, after what you had heard, you would leave him. He was terrified. Don't you see?"

"I see that he went into an insane rage. It was unimaginable," she said, shivering again. "He could have killed me."

Bruce said grimly, "He might well have if Eudora hadn't been here."

"Such rage! I can't comprehend such rage."

Bruce shook his head. "You have to look deeper. Robert has always been filled with fear. He's one of the most fearful people I've ever known."

"Robert?"

"Oh, yes. He doesn't think much of himself. That's why he has always had to be the dominant one."

She thought. Doesn't think much of himself? But it was I who looked to him! I who always felt, so secretly that I could hardly acknowledge it even to myself except in a pensive moment now and then, that I was never quite good enough, neither accomplished nor beautiful enough for him.

"Have you just thought of this now, Bruce? Tell me."

"No, it was clear a long time ago, almost at the beginning."

She raised her swollen, tired eyes to Bruce and asked him quietly, "So that's what you saw in Robert. What did you see in me?"

"That you were always too terribly anxious to please. That you deferred to him. It was plain to see, if one looked only a little beneath the surface."

"And you looked."

"No, strictly speaking it was Josie who looked and saw. I learned from her. I learned a great many things from Josie."

"Did she think it would ever come to what happened here tonight?"

"We both feared it very much, Lynn."

"And yet you must have seen so many of our happy times, our good times."

Lamplight struck her ring when she moved her hand, so that the diamond came to life; absently, nervously, she twirled it around and around her finger, playing, as was her habit, with needles and sparks of light. Good times and undercurrents . . . Annie playing duets with Robert and Annie having nightmares, concealing her nightmares . . .

"What is to become of Annie?" she asked, lifting her eyes from the ring. "I am so afraid, so worried about her."

"I think now you really must take her for counseling. I have always thought so, anyway. You know that."

"Yes, but will you talk to her too?"

"In the morning, I told you."

"We shall all miss you so, Bruce."

"I'll miss you too." And in a familiar gesture he pushed his glasses up into his hair. "But I'm ready to go, Lynn. I couldn't even wait to get the furniture out of the house. The chairs she sat in, the address book in her handwriting, everything—I can't look at the things."

It would be years before he got over Josie, if ever. But I, too, Lynn thought, in my very different way I, too, face loss. I am opening a door and stepping into darkness, to a flight of stairs and a fall into darkness.

"I have lost my courage," she said suddenly. "This morning I still had it, and now it's gone."

"And no wonder. But you haven't really lost it. You've been under attack. Your good mind will recover and pull you through. I know it will."

He stood up. "Go on to bed, Lynn. It's late. Do you need help up the stairs?"

"Thanks, I'll manage." Stretching her sore cheeks, she tried to smile. "I must look awful. I'm afraid to look in the mirror."

"Well, you certainly don't look your best. But you'll mend. By the way, you should sleep in some other room, in Emily's. He'll be coming for his clothes, and they're probably in your room, aren't they? I want to keep him out of your way. And, oh, yes, you should take a sleeping pill. Are there any in the house?"

"Robert kept them for the times when he felt keyed up. But I've never taken one."

"Well, take one tonight."

Painfully, she pulled herself upstairs and got into bed. It crossed her mind, as some hours later she fell into the mercy of sleep, that she had quite forgotten to be ashamed before Bruce.

A stream of sunlight had already crossed the room at a noontime angle when Lynn awoke. Groggy and unwashed, she had fallen into bed, and now, still groggy and unwashed, she got up to go to the mirror.

The sight stunned her. She could hardly bear to look, and yet she had to keep on looking. That a human being could do this to another human face! One's identity, one's face that is like no other among all the billions on the earth! This violation of the most intimate property—it's rape in a dark alley, it's a sleeping household entered through a broken window, it's a freight car filled with half-crazed refugees, a prisoner led to a torture cell, it's every hideous thing that men do to one another.

She sobbed: Oh, my life . . . I wanted to make everything so beautiful for all of us. I did. I tried. I did. . . .

And then, a terrible fury took over. If he had been in the room and she had had a knife, she would have plunged it into his heart. Thank God, then, that he wasn't there, for she must preserve herself, get well, and be strong. She had brought three dependent lives into the world. *She* had. Not *he*. She, alone now. He had forfeited those lives, whether he knew it or not, had given them up forever. And Lynn gritted her teeth on that.

Then she ran the shower. Gingerly she cleansed her swollen, livid face of the blood that had dried black around her lips and nostrils. Carefully she pried open the eye that was half shut and bathed it. Then she powdered herself all over, put on scent, and fastidiously cleaned her nails. Let the body, at least, be presentable, even if the face was not. This was a question of self-respect.

When she came out into the bedroom, Eudora was straightening the bed. Most tactfully, she did not focus upon Lynn, but reported instead the events of the household.

"Mr. Lehman said to tell you good-bye. He had a long talk with Annie before he left, I didn't hear it, but Annie was willing to go to school, I didn't think she would be, but she was, and he drove her himself. Mr. Lawrence phoned, the doctor's coming again this afternoon, unless you need him sooner, then Mr. Lawrence will send a cab to take you to the office. Bobby's fine, he's already had his lunch, and I put him down for his nap. And Emily's on the way, she phoned from the airport, Annie called her last night, I couldn't stop her. So I guess that's about all."

"Oh, dear. She's in the middle of exams."

"Well, they'll wait. You're her mother," Eudora said firmly.

The house trembled when Emily arrived. The front door banged, and feet clattered up the stairs; she plunged into the room and, halfway toward Lynn, stopped.

"Oh, my God," she whispered, and began to cry.

"Oh, don't," said Lynn.

Poor child. She shouldn't have come, shouldn't see this.

"Emily darling, don't cry so. It looks worse than it is. Honestly."

"You would say that! I don't believe you. What are you doing, protecting him again?"

"No, no. That's over."

"Oh, my God, this is a nightmare! But it was only to be expected. It was only a question of time."

"Was it? I suppose so."

"Oh, Mom, what are you going to do?"

Emily sat down on the edge of the bed. There was such anguish in her question that for an instant Lynn had to turn away without answering.

"Do? Many things. My head's swimming with all I have to do."

"How did it happen? What led to it this time?" Emily asked, emphasizing *this time.*

"I'll tell you the whole thing, but first tell me how you came to that place. I was there too. I bought a picture, and she told me about you. You were in New York without letting me know. What happened? Why?"

So many secrets. So much going on behind each other's back.

"You knew what my thoughts have been, Mom. Suddenly I wasn't able to rest any longer while they were whirling in my head. So I took a plane to New York, spent a couple of hours, and flew right back."

"Whatever was in your mind when you went there? What did you expect to learn?"

"Maybe I felt there was some dark secret, I don't know. I was curious about Jeremy, though, and there wasn't any other way to find out about him."

"Well, did you find out anything?"

"He lives in England, and in a nice enough way, terse but still nice, she made it clear that he should be let alone. Obviously she doesn't want Dad to learn where he is. But who knows? Maybe someday—or maybe never—he'll want to know Annie and Bobby and me."

The winter afternoon was closing in and Lynn pulled the lamp cord to lighten the gloom.

"You're wondering what brought me there," she said, conscious that each of them had avoided saying the name "Querida." "When I considered what you had learned through Aunt Jean—it took me a while—I knew I had to reach back into the past. I had deliberately closed my mind. I realize that. And so I had to open it. Perhaps," Lynn said ruefully, "perhaps in a way I hoped, when I went in, that the woman would turn out not to be—to be Querida, and then I would not have to face facts. If there were any facts. And of course there were."

Now, having made herself say the name, Lynn made herself continue to the end of the horrifying story.

There was a long silence when she'd finished. Emily wiped her eyes, got up, walked to the window, and stood there looking out into the oncoming night. Lynn's heart ached at sight of the girl's bowed head; revelations like these are not what you want your nineteen-year-old daughter to hear.

"Poor Aunt Jean," Emily said. "She must have struggled all these years with herself: to tell or not to tell?"

"She couldn't possibly have told. There are some things too awful to let loose. It would be like opening a cage and letting a lion out."

"The lion got out anyway last night."

And again there was a silence; it was as if there were no words for the enormity of events.

Lamplight made a pale circle on the dark rug, laying soft, contrasting shadows in the far corners of the flowery room, with its well-waxed chests, its photographs and books.

And almost absently, Emily remarked, "You love this house."

"I don't know. I love the garden." The roof had caved in. Everything was shattered. "It will be sold."

"What's going to happen to Dad, do you think?"

"It's a big world. He'll find a place, I'm sure," Lynn said bitterly.

"I meant—will he go to jail for this?"

"No. He could, but I don't want that."

"I'm glad. It's true that he deserves it. Still, I should hate to see it."

"I know. I guess we're just that kind of people."

There was a tiredness in the room. They were both infected with it. They were people who had come, breathless after a steep climb, to the top of a hill, only to find another hill ahead.

"I had to come and see you." Emily spoke abruptly. "I thought I would lose my mind when I heard last night."

"But you have exams this week."

"I'll take a makeup on the one I missed today. Once I've seen the doctor, if he says you're all right, I'll go back. Harris came with me," she added.

Lynn was surprised. "Harris?"

"He insisted. He wouldn't let me go alone."

Lynn considered that. "I always liked him, you know."

"I do know, and he knows it too."

"So then, how are things with you both?"

"The same. But we're not rushing."

"That's good. Where is he?"

"Downstairs. He didn't think he ought to come into the house, but I made him."

"What, freezing as it is? Of course he should have come in. I'll put on some decent clothes and go down."

"Downstairs?" Emily repeated.

"It's just my face that's awful, not my legs."

"I meant—I thought, knowing how you are about yourself, that you wouldn't want anyone to see you like this."

Go down, put out your hand, and don't cringe. Don't hide. That time's over, and all the burden of pride is over too.

"No," Lynn said. "I don't mind. It's out in the open now."

7

S HE had spent so many hours in this chair across from this man Kane, whose ruddy cheeks, gray-dappled hair, and powerful shoulders were framed by a wall of texts and law reviews, that she was able to feel almost, if not entirely, comfortable.

"It's funny," she said, "although I know perfectly well that it's not true, I still, after all these months, have the feeling that something like this only happens among the miserable, helpless poor. How can it have happened to me? I ask myself. Ridiculous of me, isn't it?"

Kane shrugged. "I guess it is, although most people like you would be surprised to learn that twenty percent of the American people, when polled, believe it's quite all right to strike one's spouse on occasion. Do you know that every fifteen seconds another woman is being battered by her husband or her boyfriend in this country? There's nothing new about it either. Have you ever heard of the 'rule of thumb'? It's from the English common law, and it says that a man may beat his wife as long as the stick is no thicker than his thumb."

"What a fool I was! A weakling and a fool," she said softly, as if to herself.

"I keep telling you, stop the blame. It's easy enough for the world to see you as having been weak, for staying on so long. You saw yourself, though, as strong, keeping the home intact for your children. You wanted a house with two parents in it. In that sense you really were strong, Lynn."

Her mind was racing backward into a blur of years, as in an express train, seated in reverse direction, one sees in one swift glimpse after the other where one has just been. At the same time her passive gaze out of the window at her side fell upon a street where a cold, late April rain was sliding across a stationer's window, still filled with paper eggs and chicks, although Easter was long past. Holiday decorations were inexpressibly depressing when the holiday was over. . . . Robert had used to dye the eggs and hide them in the garden.

"And besides, in your case," Kane was saying, "one could say you had plausible reason for hope. One could, that is, if one hadn't the benefit of knowledge and experience with these cases."

His fingers formed a steeple; the pose was pontifical. Men in authority liked to make it, she thought, observing him.

"He is an extraordinarily intelligent man, according to Tom Lawrence and to his own counsel. And of course, there was his status. I don't mean that status was anything you sought, but he was admirable in the public's eyes, and that had to have had its effect on you."

"I guess so. But how unhappy he must have been in his youth!"

"Yes, but that's no excuse for making other people—a wife—pay for it. *If* that's the explanation at all."

"When he lost that promotion, he lost everything. I had an idea that he might even kill himself."

"More likely to kill you, it seems."

Kane shrugged again. It was an annoying habit, and yet she liked the man. He was sensible and plain spoken.

"I understand he has the offer of a job with some firm that's opening an office in Mexico. He's probably glad enough to go, even with a deal less money. But he's lucky, and his counsel knows it. You've let him off easily. No criminal charges and no publicity."

"I did it for my children. They have a terrible memory of this as it is. Annie's still having bad dreams, even with therapy."

"Well, he's out of their lives, even without Mexico. His attorney says he's satisfied about custody—he damn well better be! Your children are all yours. He said he thinks it will be better for them and for himself not to see them."

"My daughters don't want to see him. But it's a terrible thing for a man to lose his children, so if they should ever want to see him, I would not stand in the way. Right now, though, they refuse."

"He knows that. I believe he meant the little boy."

The little boy, now surefooted, could run all over the house. The first week or so after Robert's disappearance he had called "Daddy," but now whenever Tom came, he seemed to be just as comfortable playing on the floor with him as he had been with Robert.

"Bobby will not remember," she said, thinking, This is the second time that Robert has lost a son.

"So there being no contest, this will move along easily. You'll be free before you know it, Lynn." He regarded her with a kindly, almost fatherly smile. "How's the baking going? That cake you sent for my twins' birthday was fabulous. They're still talking about it."

"I've been doing some. One friend tells another and I get orders. But my mind's been too disturbed to do much of anything."

"And no wonder. Is there anything else you want to ask today?"

"Yes, I have something." And from the floor beside her chair she picked up a cardboard box and, handing it over to Kane, said only, "Will you please give this to Robert's lawyer for me? It belongs to Robert."

"What is it? I need to know."

"Just jewelry, some things I no longer want."

"All your jewelry?"

"All."

"Come, Lynn. That's foolish. Let me look at it."

"Open it if you want."

Each in its original velvet container lay the diamond wedding band, the solitaire, pearls, bracelets, and earrings, twenty years' worth of shimmering accumulation.

"Heavy. The best," he said as he spread the array on the desk.

"Robert never bought anything cheap," she said dryly.

Kane shook his head. "I don't understand you. What are you doing? These things are yours."

"They were mine, but I don't want them anymore."

"Don't be foolish. You'll have a pittance when this is over, you know that. There must be over one hundred thousand dollars' worth of stuff here."

"I couldn't wear any of it. Every time I'd touch them, I'd think"—and she put her finger on the bracelet, on the smooth, deep-toned cabochons in a row, emerald, ruby, sapphire, emerald, ruby—"I'd remember too much."

She would remember the diamond band on the white wedding day: flowers, taffeta, and racing clouds. She would remember the earrings bought that week when Bobby was conceived, when the night wind rustled the palms. She would remember the bench by the lake in Chicago, the cold windy night, the despair, and the crazy woman laughing. And she withdrew her finger as if the jewels were poisonous.

"Then sell the lot and keep the cash. You won't have anything to remind you of anything." Kane laughed. "Cash is neutral."

"No. I want to make a clear, clean break. Just get all you can for my children from the man who fathered them. For myself, I will take nothing except the house, or what's left of the sale after the mortgage is paid off."

Kane shook his head again. "Do you know you're incredible? I can't decide what to think about you."

He looked at Lynn so long and hard that she wondered whether he was seeing her with admiration or writing her off as some sort of pitiable eccentric.

"I've never had a client like you. But then, Tom Lawrence told me you were unique."

She smiled. "Tom exaggerates."

"He's always concerned about you."

"He has been a true friend in all this trouble. To me and to my children. Annie adores him."

Annie asks: "Will you every marry Tom, Mom? I hope you do."

And Emily, even Eudora, too, put on such curious expressions whenever his name is mentioned, just as Kane is doing now.

Well, it's wonderful to be wanted, she thought, and I daresay I can have him when I'm free, but right at the moment I am not ready.

"By the way, his lawyer mentioned something about Robert's books. He'll want to come for them. I'll let you know when. Perhaps you can have them packed so he can remove them quickly. And you should certainly have someone in the house when he comes."

"I'll do that."

"The house should sell fast. Even in this market the best places are snapped up. It's a pity that the mortgage company is going to get most of it."

"A pity and a surprise to me."

She stood up and gave him her hand. When he took it, he held it a moment, saying kindly, "You've had more surprises in your young life than you bargained for, I'm afraid."

"Yes. And the mystery is the most surprising."

"The mystery?"

"That when all is said and done, all the explanations asked for and given, I still don't really know why."

"Why what, Lynn?"

"Why I loved him so with all my heart."

"You need to get married again," said Eudora some months later. "You're the marrying kind."

"Do you think so?"

Eudora had gradually become a mother hen, free with advice and worries. She had taken to sleeping several nights a week at the house, ostensibly because she "missed Bobby," but more probably because she feared that somehow, regardless of new locks and burglar alarms, Robert might find his way in.

It was natural, then, that a pair of women in a house without a man should develop the kind of intimacy that enabled Eudora to say what she had just said.

"I was thinking maybe you shouldn't sign any papers to sell the house just yet." She spoke with her back turned, while polishing Lynn's best copper-bottomed pots. "You might want to stay here, you never know," she said, and discreetly said no more.

Of course they all knew what she meant. Tom Lawrence was in all their minds, as in Lynn's own. The two girls, Annie and Emily, home for Thanksgiving, were having lunch at the kitchen table and giving each other a sparkling, mischievous look.

"I shall never stay in this house," Lynn said firmly. She was breaking eggs for a sponge cake. "Eight, nine—no, eight. You've made me lose count. I have only stayed here this long because I've been instructed to until everything becomes final."

Divorce was a cold, ugly word, and she avoided it. *Everything* said it all just as well.

"And when will that be?" asked Emily.

"Soon."

"Soon," shouted Bobby, who was pushing a wooden automobile under people's feet.

"He repeats everything. And he knows dozens of words. Do you suppose he always understands what he says?" asked Annie.

Eudora's reply came promptly. "He certainly does. That's one smart little boy. One smart little boy, aren't you, sweetheart?"

"He's crazy about Tom," Annie informed Emily. "You haven't seen them together as much as I have. Tom spends half an hour on the floor with him every time he comes to take Mom out."

They were pressing her for information, and Lynn knew it. What they

wanted was some certainty: along with the relief of knowing that the
shock, the plural shocks, they had undergone were never to be repeated,
they were feeling a certain looseness. There was neither anchor nor des-
tination; the family was merely floating. So they were really asking her
what was to come next, and she was not prepared to answer the question.

"I'm trying out a new recipe with the leftover turkey," she told them
instead. "It's a sauce with black Mission figs. Sounds good, doesn't it?"

"Why, what's the celebration?" Emily wanted to know. "Who's coming?"

"Nobody but us. It's celebration enough to have you home. Do you
want to invite Harris for leftover turkey?"

"Oh, thanks, Mom, I'll call him."

"Is Tom coming?"

"No, but he's coming tomorrow afternoon. It's the day your father will
be here for his books."

In spite of herself Lynn felt a tremor of fear. She had not seen Robert
since that horrendous night. And dread mounted now even as she stood
stirring the yellow dough. Still, Tom would be there. . . .

"Eudora's going to put Bobby in his room while he's here, and I'd like
you two to be out of the house. Go visit friends, or maybe there's a
decent movie someplace."

Emily said cheerfully, "Okay." She got up and laid her cheek against
Lynn's. "I know you worry about us. But we're both, Annie and I, pretty
solid by now. As solid as we'll ever be, I guess, and that seems to be good
enough."

"Thank you, darling, thank you."

As solid as they'd ever be. No, one never "got over" what they had
seen. It would be with them for the rest of their lives, and they would just
have to work around it. That was what they were doing; now in her
second year, Emily had a 3.6 average, and Annie—well, Annie was trudg-
ing along in her fashion.

Alone in the kitchen a short while later, Lynn's thoughts found a center: Tom. No man could be more attentive. All through this troubled time
he had been there, solid as a rock, for her to lean on. And as the trouble
began, ever so gradually, to recede into the past, during these last few
months especially, she had begun to feel again the stirrings of pure fun.
They had danced and laughed and drunk champagne to commemorate
the day when her last scar faded away. He had brought her again the
brightness that had surrounded him on the fateful night of the dinner in
his house.

He never made love to her, and that puzzled her, for how many times since they met had he not told her that she was lovely? It was not that she wanted him to attempt it; indeed, she would have stopped him, for something had died in her. Perhaps it was that that he sensed, and he was simply being patient. But it troubled her to think that she might never again be the passionate woman she once had been.

And Robert had always said, "Funny, but to look at you, no man would guess."

Yet she felt sure that ultimately Tom would ask her what the girls were hoping he would ask. Sometimes it seemed that when that moment came, she would have to say no to him, for what was lacking, she supposed, was the painful, wonderful yearning that says: *You and no other for the rest of our lives.* Yet, why not he, with his intelligence, his humor, charm, and kindness? A woman ought to have a man, a good man. It was a terrible thing to be alone, to face long years going downhill alone.

She would have to make up her mind, and soon. For only this morning on the telephone, he had answered her invitation to stay for lunch after Robert's coming: "Yes, I'll stay. I've been wanting to have a talk with you."

The day was bright. She had carefully considered what she was to wear, dark red if it should be raining, or else, in the sun, the softest blue that she owned. When she was finished dressing, she examined herself from the pale tips of her matching blue flats to the pale cap of her shining hair, and was more pleased with herself than she had been in a long time. Simplicity could be alluring without any jewels at all.

Eudora appraised her when she came downstairs.

"You look beautiful, Mrs. Ferguson." And she nodded as if there was complicity between the two women.

Eudora thought the dress was for Tom's benefit, which it was, but in a queer way, it was also to be for Robert's; let him see, especially with Tom in the house, that Lynn was still desired and desirable.

The books had been packed, and the cartons put in the front hall. Tom was already there when the car stopped in the driveway.

"He's got a driver with him to help him carry," he reported to Lynn, who stood half hidden in the living room. "Are you afraid? Why don't you go back into the den?"

"No." She could not have explained why she wanted to look at Robert, other than to say it was just morbid curiosity.

He wore a dark blue business suit out of the proverbial bandbox. She

did not know whether it was surprising or not that he should be as
perfect in his handsome dignity as he had ever been.

No greeting passed between him and Tom. It took several trips from
the house to the car before the books were removed, and they were all
accomplished in silence. She had thought and feared that perhaps he
might try to talk to her and to plead, but he did not even seem to notice
where she was standing.

On the last trip Eudora came out of the kitchen to give him a vindic-
tive smile as she passed.

Ah, don't, Eudora! It is so sad. So very sad. You don't understand.
How can you, how can anyone, except Robert and me?

At the doorstep Juliet came from the back of the house, wagging her
tail at the sight of the man who had been her favorite in the family.
When Lynn saw him stoop to caress the dog, she ran to the door. Something compelled her, and Tom's wavering touch did not restrain her.

"Robert," she said, "I'm sorry, so sorry that our life ended like this."

He looked up. The blue eyes, his greatest beauty, had turned to ice;
without replying he gave her a look of such chilling fury, of such ominous, unforgiving power, that involuntarily, she stepped back out of his
reach.

Tom closed the door. She went to the window to watch Robert walk
down the path; it was as if she wanted to make sure that he had really
gone away.

When Tom put a comforting hand on her shoulder, she was whispering, "To think he was my entire world. I can't believe it."

With his other hand on her other shoulder he turned her about to face
him.

"Listen to me. It's over," he said quietly. "Let it be over. And now, I
believe you promised me some lunch."

On a little table in front of the long window, she had set two places
with a bowl of pink miniature chrysanthemums between them.

"If I can't eat outdoors when cold weather comes, I can at least look at
the outdoors," she said, to start conversation.

And she followed his gaze across the grass, which was still dark emerald, although the birches, spreading their black fretwork against the sky,
were quite bare.

They talked, and Lynn knew it was prattle, that, comfortable as they
appeared to be, there was an underlying nervousness in each of them.
The moment was approaching. At some time before they were to leave
this room, she was certain, a momentous question would have been put.

It was incredible that even now, she could be still uncertain of her answer, although it seemed more and more as the minutes passed that her answer ought to be yes.

Thoughtfully, Tom peeled a pear, took a bite, pushed it aside, and began.

"We've had a rather special understanding, a feel for each other, haven't we?" And he paused as if waiting for confirmation, which she gave.

"That's true."

"There are things I want to say, things I've thought about for quite a time. What's brought it all to a head is that you've reached a turning point. Kane told me the other day that you're about to be free." He picked up the pear and then put it back on the plate. "I'm being really awkward. . . ."

Lynn said lightly, "That's not usual for you."

"No, it's not. I'm usually pretty sure of myself. Blunt, like a sledge-hammer."

"Oh, yes," she said, still lightly, "I found that out one day at the club pool."

He laughed, and she thought, He's acting like a boy, a kid scared to be turned down.

"Well," Tom resumed, "perhaps I should organize my thoughts, begin from the beginning. You remember, I think I've told you about that night at my house when we were dancing and I confessed I'd had the intention of dancing you right into bed—you were so blithe, so sweet, so fresh-from-the-farm, and I had always been rather successful with women. That's an awful thing to say in 1990, so forgive me for saying it, will you? I hope you're not going to take it too badly."

"No, go on."

"Well, aside from that, I was mistaken in being so sure of you that night. I knew that later and was ashamed of myself, too, especially when on the very next morning I saw what trouble you were in. I surely wasn't going to add any other complications to your life. I suppose you're wondering what the point of all this rambling talk can possibly be."

"That you want to be honest about your feelings. Isn't that the point?"

"Precisely. Honest and open, which brings me to the present."

He stopped to take a drink of water that she knew he must not really want; it was only a means of delay. His forehead had creased itself into three deep, painful lines.

"So what I want to say is—oh, hell, it's difficult—I think we've come to the time we should stop seeing each other."

"Stop?" she echoed.

"Oh, Lynn, if you could know how I have anguished over this! I've thought and thought. Probably I should have ended this months ago but I couldn't bring myself to do it because I didn't *want* to end it, and I still don't *want* to now. But I know I must. It wouldn't be fair to you—or to myself—to go on misleading us both."

Tom took another drink of water and, to cover his agitation, adjusted his watch strap. Lynn was tingling and hot with shame; the blood beat in her neck.

"You haven't misled me, not at all," she cried. "I can't imagine how you ever got such an idea!"

Suddenly he reached and grasped both her hands. She tried to wrench them away, but he held them fast.

"You wouldn't want an affair, Lynn, while I would. But I don't want to get married again. I'm not the man to start another life rearing an adolescent girl and a toddler. Playing with Bobby for an hour is something very different. It wouldn't be right for any of us."

The irony of this, she was thinking. How foolish of me to have been so sure, to have misread—

He was tightening his hold on her hands; his voice was urgent and sad.

"Lynn, if I were starting life again now without all these experiences I've had, I would look for a wife like you. There's no one with whom I'd rather have spent my life. If I had met you in the beginning, I would have learned things about myself. . . . I've had two divorces, as you know, and other involvements besides. I live a certain way now, without obligations. It's a long story. No, don't pull your hands away, please don't. I know you haven't asked me to psychoanalyze myself, but I have to tell you. . . . I wouldn't do for you, Lynn, not in the long run. In the kind of life I lead, with the people I know, we are wary with each other. We don't expect things to last."

"I don't expect anything either. Not anymore. And you don't have to tell me all this."

"I wanted to. I did have to, because someday, I hope you'll find someone steady and permanent, not like me. I could have been that, I know that much about myself. But now—well, now I'm not the faithful type, and I know that too."

"Robert was faithful," she said for no reason at all, and her lips twisted.

"Yes. Confusing, isn't it?"

She pulled her hands away, and this time he released them.

"I've hurt you. I've hurt your pride, and that's not at all what I intended to do."

"Pride!" she said derisively.

"Yes, why not? You have every reason for it. Oh, I knew I'd be too damned clumsy to make this clear! But I couldn't simply stop calling or seeing you, could I? Without any explanation? It would have been far worse to leave you wondering what was wrong."

She said nothing, because that much was true.

"I only want you to move on now, Lynn, and you can't very well do that with me or any one man hanging around."

Still she said nothing, thinking, I have been rejected, and the thought stung hard. *A woman scorned.*

Yet he had not scorned her.

"Lynn? Listen to me. I only wanted not to mislead you, even though you say you expected nothing."

"That's so," she said with her head high.

"Then I'm glad. You've had betrayals enough."

When he stood up from the table, she rose, too, asking with dignity whether he was leaving now.

"No. Let's sit down somewhere else if you will let me. I have more things to say."

He took a chair near the unlit fire and sighed. She had never seen him so troubled.

"I told you once, didn't I, that I used to do matrimonial work? I quit because it wore me down. Too many tears, too much rage and suffering. The price was too high. But one thing it did was to teach me to see people, and that includes myself, far more clearly than I ever had."

"So you've told me I must find a man to marry me who will be faithful and permanent, ready to cope with my children. But that's not what I want. Right now I don't ever want to depend on a man again."

"Right!" The syllable exploded into the room. "Right! What I was going to tell you is that you shouldn't look for any man at all. Not now. You should look to yourself only. Put yourself in order. You don't *need* anyone. That's been your trouble, Lynn."

"What are you doing, scolding me?" The day was awful, first seeing Robert and now undergoing this humiliation, for say what one would, it was humiliation. "If you are scolding, it's inhuman of you."

"I'm sorry. I don't mean it that way. It's only that I know what you are and what you can be. I want you to be your best, Lynn." He finished quietly. "Robert didn't. He wanted you to be dependent on him."

Her right hand, reaching for her left, tried to twirl the rings that were no longer there. Remembering, she put her hands on the arms of the chair. And, meeting Tom's look of concern, admitted, "Until he left, I had never balanced a bank statement. I had hardly ever written a check."

"But now you do both."

"Of course. I've had to."

"Tell me, whatever happened to Delicious Dinners?"

"You know what happened. I had Bobby instead."

"Why can't you have both?" he asked gently.

Lynn shook her head. "The very thought is staggering. Money and child care, a place and time—I don't know how to begin."

"This very minute you don't, but you can learn. There are people who can tell you how to start a business, where to get the right child care, everything you'd need to know. Step out into the world, Lynn. It's not as unfriendly as it often seems."

For an instant the crinkles smiled around his eyes, until the look of concern replaced them again, and he asked, almost as if he were asking a favor, "Don't you think you can try? Look squarely at the reality of things?"

She smiled faintly. "Yes, that's what Josie used to say."

"And she was right."

The cat plodded in from the kitchen, switched its tail, and lay down comfortably at Tom's feet.

"He's made himself at home here, hasn't he? What do you hear from Bruce?"

The change of subject relieved Lynn. "Postcards with picturesque scenery. He writes to Annie and me, he tells about his work, which seems to be going well, but doesn't really say much, if you know what I mean."

"I had a card from him, too, just a few lines, rather melancholy, I thought."

"He'll never get over Josie."

"I don't think I ever felt anything that intense," Tom said soberly. "I suppose I've missed something."

"No. I'd say you're fortunate."

"You don't really mean that."

"Well, maybe I don't."

"Will you think seriously about what I've just said? Will you, Lynn?"

It was his look, affectionate and troubled, that finally touched her and lessened her chagrin. Aware that he was making ready to leave, she got up then and went over to take his hand.

"You are, when all is said and done, one of the best friends a person could ever want. And yes, I will think seriously about what you said."

So it ended, and for the second time that day she stood at the window to watch a man walk out of her life.

He had told her some rough truths. *Put yourself in order. Be your best.*

In a certain way these admonitions were frightening. Indeed, she could, she wanted, and would need to be an earner again. She had already been thinking about refreshing her secretarial skills, renting an apartment, and squirreling away for the inevitable emergencies whatever might remain to her after the mortgage company got its share.

It would be a meager livelihood for a woman with a family, yet it would be manageable; the hours would be regular, which meant that good day care for Bobby would not be too hard to find. But this was not at all what Tom had meant by "be your best."

She walked into the kitchen and stood there looking around. Everything sparkled, everything was polished, from the pots to the flowered tile, from the wet leaves of the African violets to the slick covers of the cookbooks on their shelves. Peaches displayed their creamy cheeks in a glass bowl on the countertop, and fresh, red-tipped lettuce drained from a colander into the sink. It came to her that this place was the one room in the house that had been completely her own; here she had worked hour upon hour, contented and singing.

For no particular reason she took a cookbook from a shelf; it fell open to the almond tart that she had made for that fateful dinner at Tom Lawrence's. And she kept standing there with the book in hand, thinking, thinking. . . .

Le Cirque, they'd said, applauding. The finest restaurants in Paris . . . Well, that's a bit of an exaggeration, a bit absurd, isn't it?

She walked back into the hall and through the rooms and back to where Tom had sat. "Put yourself in order," he said. So possibilities were there. You started simply, took courses, studied, learned. People did it, didn't they? You took what you might call a cautious chance. . . .

And after a while she knew what she must do. The thing was to move quickly. Hesitation would only produce too many reasons not to move. She went to the telephone and dialed her sister Helen's number.

"I have a surprise for you," she said.

Helen's voice had the upward lilt of eager curiosity. "I'll bet I know what it is."

"I'm sure you don't."

"It's about a man named Tom. Emily and Annie have both told me things. Isn't he the one who sent the needlepoint chair for Bobby?"

"You have a memory like an elephant. No, it's not about him or any other man. It's about me and what I'm to do with my life. I'm going into business for myself."

And a kind of excitement bubbled up into Lynn's throat. It was astonishing how an idea, taking shape in spoken words, could become all at once so plausible, so inevitable, so alive.

She could almost feel Helen's reaction, as though the wire were able to transmit an intake of breath, an open mouth, and wide eyes, as Helen shrieked.

"Business! What kind, for goodness' sake?"

"Catering, naturally. Cooking's what I do best, after all. I've been baking cakes to order, but we can't live on that."

"When did you decide on this?"

"Just an hour or two ago."

"What next? Out of the blue, just like that?"

"Well, not exactly. You know it's been in and out of my mind for ages. I've toyed with it. And now things have come together, that's all. Opportunity and necessity."

"And courage," Helen said, rather soberly. "It takes money to open a business. Is your lawyer getting any more out of Robert or something?"

"Nothing more than you already know."

"It's not much, Lynn."

"I wouldn't want more from him even if he had it."

"Well, I would. You are the limit, you are. Where's this business going to be, anyway?"

"Somewhere in Connecticut. Not this town, though. I want to get away."

There was a silence.

"Helen? Are you there?"

"I'm here. I'm thinking. Since you want to get away from where you are, why not make a big move while you're at it?"

"Such as?"

"Such as coming back here. You've been away only four years, and everybody knows you. People will give you a start here. Doesn't that make sense?"

Lynn considered it for a long minute. It did seem to make practical sense. She had perhaps not thought of going "home" because it might seem like going back for the refuge of family and a familiar place. But then, what was wrong with that?

"Doesn't it make sense?" Helen repeated.

"Yes. Yes, I believe it does."

"It will be wonderful to have you here again! Darwin," Lynn heard her call. "Come hear the news. Lynn's coming home."

The house, with its furnishings, was sold overnight. A formal couple, impressed by Robert's formal rooms, walked through it once and made an acceptable offer the next day.

Except for the kitchen's contents and the family's books, there was little to take with them. There were Emily's desk and Annie's ten-speed bicycle; to Lynn's surprise she also asked to keep the piano, although she had not touched it since the night when that final dissonant chord had crashed. Carefully, in a carton lined with tissue paper, Lynn packed pictures and photographs, treasured remembrances of her parents on their wedding day, of her grandparents, and her children from birth to graduation. When these were done, she stood uncertainly, holding the portrait of Robert in its ornate silver frame. As if they were alive, his eyes looked back at her. She had an impulse on the one hand to throw it, silver and all, into the trash, while on the other hand she reflected that posterity, perhaps at the end of the twenty-first century, might be curious to behold a great-grandfather. By that time probably no one alive would know what Robert Ferguson had really been, and his descendants would be free to praise and be pleased by his distinguished face. So she would let the thing lie wrapped up in an attic until then.

Two unexpected events occurred just before moving day. The first was a Sunday-afternoon visit from Lieutenant Weber and his wife.

"We weren't sure you would welcome us," said the lieutenant when Lynn opened the door. "But Harris said you would. He wanted us to come over and say good-bye."

"I'm glad you did," Lynn answered, meaning the words, meaning that it was good to depart from a place without leaving any vague resentments behind.

When they sat down, Mrs. Weber explained, "Harris thought, well, since you are moving away, he thought we ought to be, well, not strangers," she concluded, emphasizing *strangers* almost desperately. And then she resumed, "I guess he meant in case he and Emily—" and stopped again.

Lynn rescued her. "In case they get married, he wants us to be friends.

Of course we will. Why wouldn't we? We've never done each other any harm."

"I'm thankful you feel that way," Weber said. "I know I tried to do my best, but I'm sorry it didn't work."

"All of that is beginning to seem long ago and far away." Lynn smiled. "Can you believe they're already halfway through their sophomore year?"

"And doing so well with their A's," said Weber. "They seem to kind of run a race with each other, don't they? On the last exam Emily beat, but Harris doesn't seem to mind. It's different these days. When I was a kid, I'd've been sore if my girlfriend ever came out ahead of me."

"Oh, it's different, all right," Lynn agreed.

Talking to this man and this woman was easy, once the woman had recovered from her first unease. Soon Lynn found herself telling them about her plans, about the store she had rented and the house that Darwin had found for them.

"My brother-in-law's aunt and uncle have moved to Florida, but they don't want to sell their house in St. Louis because the market is so bad. So they'll let me stay there for almost nothing, just to take care of it. We'll be house-sitters."

Almost unconsciously, Mrs. Weber glanced around the living room, which was as elegant as it had ever been except for the slipcover on the blood-stained sofa. The glance spoke to Lynn, and she answered it.

"I shan't miss this at all, not even the kitchen."

"Yes, Emily told us about your kitchen."

"I'll show it to you before you leave. Yes, it's gorgeous. I'm taking my last money, my only money, to fix one like it in the shop. It's a gamble, and I'm taking the gamble."

So the conversation went; they talked a little more about Emily and Harris, talked with some pride and some natural parental worry. They admired the kitchen and left.

"No false airs there," Lynn said to herself after the couple had gone. "If anything should come of it, Emily will be in honest company. Good stock."

The second unexpected event concerned Eudora. She wept.

"I never thought you'd go away from here. I was sure that you and Mr. Lawrence—"

"Well, you were wrong. You all were."

"I'll miss my little man. And Annie too. And you, Mrs. Ferguson. I'll think of you every time I make the crepes you taught me to make. You taught me so much. I'll miss you."

"We'll miss you, too, don't you know we will? But I can't afford you. And the house isn't at all like this one. It's a little place that any woman can keep with one hand tied behind her back."

For a moment Eudora considered that. Then her face seemed to brighten with an idea.

"You'll need somebody in the shop, won't you? How can you do all the cooking and baking and serving by yourself?"

"I can't, of course. I'll need to find a helper, or even two, if I should be lucky enough to see the business grow that much."

"They wouldn't have to be an expert like you, would they? I mean, they would be people to do easy things and people you could teach."

There was a silence. And suddenly Lynn's face brightened too. Why not? Eudora learned fast, and she was so eager, waiting there with hope and a plea in her eyes.

"Eudora, are you telling me that you would—"

"I'm telling you that I wish you would take me with you."

The day arrived when the van that was to take the piano and the sundries rumbled up the drive. It was a colorless day under a motionless sky. The little group, almost as forlorn as the gray air, stood at the front door watching their few possessions being loaded into the van.

"Wait!" Lynn cried to the driver. "There's something in the yard in back of the house. It's a birdbath, a great big thing. Do you think you can make room?"

The man gave a comical grin. "A birdbath, lady?"

"Yes, it's very valuable, it's marble, with doves on it, and it mustn't be cracked or chipped."

"Okay. We'll fit it in."

"Mom, what do you want with it?" asked Annie.

"I don't know. I just want it, that's all."

"Because Uncle Bruce gave it to you?"

That canny child was trying to read her mind.

"Maybe. Now bring out Barney in the carrier and put on Juliet's leash. Don't forget their food and a bowl for water. We've a long way to travel."

So the final moment came. The van rumbled away, leaving the station wagon alone in the drive. For a moment they all took a last look at the house. Aloof as ever, it stood between the long lawns and the rising hill, waiting for new occupants as once it had waited for those who were now leaving it.

"The house doesn't care about us," Lynn said, "and we won't care about it. Get in, everybody."

The station wagon was full. Annie sat in the front, Eudora and Bobby had the second row, and in the third, alongside Barney in his carrier, sat Juliet, so proud in her height that her head almost touched the roof.

"We're off!" cried Lynn. And not able, really, to comprehend the tumult of regret and hope and courage that whirled through her veins, she could only repeat the cry, sending it bravely through the quiet air: "We're off!"

The car rolled down the drive, turned at the end, and headed west.

PART FIVE

---◇---

Winter 1992–1993

EMILY, who was home for spring break, propped her chin in her hands and leaned on the kitchen table as she watched Lynn put another pink icing rosebud on a long sheet cake.

"It seems so strange to have it still cold in March," she remarked. "Right now in New Orleans the tourists are sitting in the French Market having a late breakfast, beignets and strong, dark coffee. Do you know how to make beignets, Mom?"

"I've never made any, but I can easily find out how."

"That cake's absolutely gorgeous. Where and when did you ever learn to be so professional?"

"At that three-week pastry course I took last year."

"I'm so in awe of what you've done in just two years."

"Two years and five months. But talk about awe! Harvard Medical School! I'm so proud of you, Emily, that I want to walk around with a sign on my back."

"Wait till next September when I'll actually be there."

Cautiously, Lynn inquired, "How is Harris taking it?"

"What? My going to Harvard? He wasn't admitted there, so I'll go to Harvard and he'll be at P & S, which is mighty good too. I don't feel happy about it, but I certainly wasn't going to turn down an opportunity like this one."

You turned Yale down, Lynn thought, but said instead, "I wouldn't expect you to. And if you still keep on loving each other, the separation won't alter things."

"Exactly," agreed Emily.

She had come a long way. Yet she still looked like a high school girl with her jeans and sneakers and the red ribbon holding her hair back from her radiant face. From her father she had received some intellectual gifts and the handsome bone structure, but thank God, nothing more. She would do well with or without Harris or anyone else.

Never tell a daughter, Lynn thought now, that she'll find a wonderful man who will love and take perfect care of her forever. That's what my mother told me, but then it was in another time, another age.

With the last rose firmly affixed she stepped back to appraise her work.

"Well, that's finished. I like to do jobs like this one here in my own kitchen. There's too much going on at the shop for me to concentrate on fancy work."

The kitchen smelled of warm sugar and morning peace. It was quiet time while Annie was in school and Bobby in nursery school, time for a second cup of coffee. And she sat down to enjoy one.

In their big basket five puppies squealed and tumbled, digging at their mother in their fight for milk.

"They're so darling," Emily said. "Are you going to keep them all?"

"Heavens, no. Annie wants to, of course, but we'll have to find homes for four of them. I've consented to keep one. Then we'll have Juliet spayed."

Emily was amused. "How on earth did such a thing happen to our pure-bred Bergamasco lady?"

"She got out somewhere, maybe before I had this yard fenced in. Or maybe somebody got in. I have my suspicions about a standard poodle who lives near here, because a couple of pups have long poodle noses. They're going to be enormous."

One of them fell out of the basket just then and made a small puddle on the floor. Lynn jumped, replaced the pup, and cleaned the puddle, while Emily laughed.

"Mom, I was thinking, wouldn't Dad be furious that Juliet had mongrel puppies?"

"He wouldn't approve, that's sure. He wouldn't approve of this whole house, anyway."

She looked out into the hall, where Bobby's three-wheeler was parked and a row of raincoats hung on an old-fashioned clothes tree. How relaxing it was not to be picture perfect all the time, neat to the last speck of dust, prompt to the last split second. . . .

Emily remarked, "I rather like old Victorians with the wooden gingerbread on the front porch and all the nooks. Of course, this furniture's pretty awful."

"If I buy the house, I'll certainly not buy the furniture. And I might buy it. They've decided to sell, and since they're Uncle Darwin's relatives, they've offered easy terms. Maybe I shouldn't do it, but the neighborhood's nice, the yard's wonderful for Bobby, and I am finally meeting expenses with a little bit left over. So maybe I should." Lynn smiled. "Live dangerously! Have I told you that I've given Eudora a ten percent interest in the business, plus a salary? She's my partner now, and she's thrilled. She learns fast when I teach her. And, of course, she has her own Jamaican dishes that people love, her rice-and-peas, her banana pies, all good stuff. She can oversee the shop while I'm home baking or, if I'm busy at the shop, she'll come back here to let Annie and Bobby in after school. So it's been working out well for all of us."

Emily, absorbed in this account, marveled at the way the business had just "leapt off the ground" and "taken flight."

"There's a big demand," responded Lynn. "With so many women working now, it's not just a question of dinners and parties, it's also all the food we freeze and cook daily to sell over the counter. Besides, it was a good idea to come back here where dozens of people remembered me."

Emily asked, "Does Uncle Bruce write often?"

"Well, I wouldn't say often, but he certainly writes."

His friendly chatty letters. His work, his travels. And nothing more.

"The latest news is that they want him to open a new office in Moscow. He's been taking lessons in Russian."

Emily opened her mouth, made a sound, and closed her mouth.

"What is it? What is it you want to say?"

"I wanted to ask—to ask whether you ever heard from Dad."

"The only contact I have or will ever want to have is with the bank, when they forward his remittances for all of you. Apparently he has a very good job." Lynn hesitated over whether to say anything more, and then, deciding to, went ahead. "Have you heard from Dad?"

"A birthday present, a check, and a book of modern poetry. He didn't say anything much about himself, just hoped I was happy."

His girls, his Emily, Lynn thought, and, in a moment of painful empathy, felt Robert's loss. But it was done, there was no undoing it. . . .

She stood up and removed her apron, saying briskly, "I have to go to the shop now. Oh, Aunt Helen's going to come by to pick up the cake."

"Twenty-five years married!"

"Yes, and happily."

"Dad always thought Uncle Darwin was an idiot, didn't he?"

"He thought a lot of people were, and he was wrong."

It was uncomfortable to be reminded of Robert's scorn, the twist of his mouth, the sardonic wit at other people's expense, the subtle digs about the Lehmans' being Jewish or even about Monaco's being Italian. And it was obvious that Emily, too, had been uncomfortable asking.

On sudden impulse Lynn bent to stroke her daughter's forehead. "What are you going to do while I'm gone, honey?"

"Nothing. Just be lazy. It's vacation."

"Good. You need to be lazy. Enjoy it."

Let life be sweet, let it be tranquil, Lynn thought as she drove through the quiet suburban streets. As best we can, we must plaster over the taint and the stain. Bobby would not remember that night, and Annie always would; but her intelligence, which Robert had so disparaged, would help her. It had already helped her. And therapy had helped, but chiefly she had improved because Robert was gone. It was as simple as that. She had lost twenty pounds, so that her face, no longer pillowed in fat, had developed a kind of piquant appeal. Her hair had been straightened, and now, for the first time, she was pleased with herself. She had even gone back, entirely unbidden, to the piano!

They had come far since the day the station wagon had crossed the Mississippi and they had spent their first night in the strange house. It had been after midnight, raining and very cold. Darwin had started the furnace, and Helen had made up the beds into which they had all collapsed.

The rain had beaten at the window of the strange room where Lynn lay. From time to time she had raised her head to the bedside alarm clock. Three o'clock . . . Her heart had jumped in a surge of pure panic. Here she was, responsible for all these people, for her children and even for Eudora, so hopeful, so faithful, and so far from home. Panic spoke: You can't go it alone. It's too much and too hard. You don't know anything. All right, you can cook, but you're no five-star genius. What makes you think you can do this? How dare you think you can? Fool, fool, you can't. And the rain kept beating. Even the rain, as it told of the relentless world outside, was hostile. Then dawn came, a dirty gray dawn, to spill its dreary light upon the ugly furniture in the strange room.

What are you thinking of? You can't do it alone.

But she had done so. She had admonished herself: Head over heart. You won't accomplish anything lying here in bed and shivering with fear. So she had gotten up, and in that same dreary dawn, had taken pen and paper to make a list.

First there was school registration and continued counseling for Annie. Then a visit to the store that was, she had thought wryly, to make her fortune, to see there what needed to be done. Next, a visit to one of those volunteer businessmen's groups where someone would show her how to go about starting a business; she had read that these groups could be very helpful.

"The world is not as unfriendly as it often seems to be," Tom had assured her. Maybe, she had thought in that gray dawn, maybe it's true. I shall find out soon enough.

And now Lynn had to smile, remembering how very friendly it could be. For the man who had helped her the most, a fairly young man, retired in his mid-forties, had been sufficiently admiring of what he called her "enterprise," to become very serious, serious enough to propose marriage.

"I like you," she had told him, "and I thank you. I like you very much, but I am not interested in getting married."

It was one thing and very natural to desire the joy of having a man in the bed; it was one thing to welcome the trust and commitment of a man as friend; but to be *possessed* in marriage, to be *devoured* in marriage as she had been, even discounting Robert's violence, was another thing. He had *devoured* her. It was this that she feared. The day might come when equality in marriage might seem a possibility and she would have lost her fear, but not yet. Not yet. At least not with any of the men she had been seeing.

There had been men to whom Helen and their old friends had introduced her, men decent, intelligent, and acceptable. Some of them had been fun in many ways. Yet that was all. She was not ready.

She liked to say, laughing a little at the excuse, although it was obviously a true one, that she simply hadn't the time! When people, usually women, inquired and urged, "Why don't you? George or Fred or Whoever is really so nice, so right for you," she would protest that she had Annie and an active little boy, she had the business, she hadn't an hour; couldn't everyone see that?

Sometimes—often—she thought of Bruce. She relived the day, the only day, they had made love. Time had faded the guilt and left her with the memory of a singular joy. She thought about it long and deeply now, wanting to relive it and to understand it. And, ultimately, she came to understand the subtle difference between sex that was giving and sex that was all taking, sex that was ownership. Robert had *owned* her, while Bruce had not. And she knew in her heart that Bruce would never want to own a woman; he would want her to be free and equal.

But it was useless to be thinking at all about him. Except for those brief letters and postcards with pictured castles from Denmark or Greece, he had disappeared into another life, vanished from the stage on which Lynn's life was being played.

Once, a month ago, she had been surprised by the appearance of Tom Lawrence. He had been in St. Louis to take a deposition and had telephoned the shop.

"I took a chance on 'Delicious Dinners' and looked it up in the phone book," he said. "Will you have dinner with me?"

And she had gone, feeling both gratitude and pride in being able to show him how well she had carried out his advice. Gratitude and pride, but nothing more.

She had been completely honest with him.

"I would have married you if you had asked me that day. I was prepared to," she said. "Now I thank you for telling me it would have been a mistake."

He answered seriously, "As I told you then, it would have been different if I had met you when I was twenty years younger and maybe wiser."

She laughed. "You would have spared me a ton of trouble if you had."

"Why? Would you have taken me then instead of Robert?"

Considering that with equal seriousness, she shook her head.

"No. At that time the Prince of Wales probably couldn't have gotten me away from him."

"Lynn, it's so good to see you! And you're looking so lovely, younger; all the tension seems to have been wiped away."

She said playfully, "You don't think running a business is tension?"

"Yes, but it's a very different kind." He smiled at her with the old brightness, not mischievous now, but affectionate. "I like your suit. I like your pearls. I thought you had given back all the jewelry."

"I did. I bought these myself."

"They're handsome. Pure white, European taste. Americans prefer creamy ones. You see how much I know?"

She had been passing a jeweler's on the day that her bank loan, obtained through Darwin's willingness to cosign the note, had been paid off. She was then in the black. And she had stood for a minute staring at the marvelous blue-white pearls, struggling with herself. She didn't need them. But she loved them. She wanted them. So she went in and walked out with the pearls in hand, *her* pearls, for which there was no reason to thank anyone but herself.

"What do you hear from Bruce?" Tom had inquired.

It had seemed that everyone in town who had ever known Bruce was always asking that, and now she replied as always, "Not very much. He seems to be frightfully busy."

"He is. I happened to mention him the last time I saw Monacco and he told me. Actually he said Bruce is a 'brilliant guy. Quiet, with no brag about him.' "

"I'm glad for him. At that rate I don't suppose we'll ever see him again."

Tom had looked at her keenly. "What makes you say that?"

"The paths life takes. You meet, you stay for a while, and you part."

"He was very fond of you."

"And I of him."

"I understand you went back a long time together."

"That's true."

A long time. Back and back into the dimmest corners of the mind and memory. Young days in the sun, easy and familiar as brother and sister. Snatches of memory popping like switchboard lights. The morning Robert bought the bracelet and Bruce said, "Take it, you deserve it." She had not known then what he meant. The day he phoned from the hospital where he had taken Emily. The day he fetched Annie after she had run away. The day they had made love in Josie's house; wrong as it had been, it had been comforting, it had been voluptuous, it had been happy. It had been right. And then had come the night when, awakening from unconsciousness, she felt him washing her damaged face.

Memory, going back and back.

But she had not wanted to speak of these things to Tom, had herself been troubled because she was not sure what they really meant, and because, after all, they were useless.

The car came to a stop on a pleasant street bordered with prosperous shops and trees that would in a few months give summer shade. Between a florist's and a bookstore hung a bright blue sign on which in fine old-fashioned script was written DELICIOUS DINNERS. Beneath the sign, in a bow window, stood a table, beautifully set with a spring-yellow cloth, black-

and-white china, and a low bowl of the first daffodils. Customers were going in and customers were coming out at the bright blue door.

Two young girls in starched white were busy at the counter when Lynn went in. At the rear, behind swinging doors, the work was being done; a woman was cleaning vegetables, and Eudora was arranging a fish platter for a ladies' luncheon.

"Well, I finished the cake," Lynn said. She looked at her watch. "Plenty of time for me to do the salad bowl and the cornbread sticks. I told her that a French bread would be better, but she wanted the sticks. Is that my apron on the knob?"

An hour later she was taking the corn sticks out of the oven when one of the salesgirls opened the swinging door.

"There's a man here who insists on seeing you. I told him you were busy, but he—"

"Hello," Bruce said.

"Oh, my God!" Lynn cried, and dropped the pan on the table.

"Yes, it's who you think it is." And he opened his arms.

She was laughing, she was crying, as he hugged her and the astonished onlookers gaped.

"I thought you were in Russia! What are you doing here?"

"I was supposed to go to Russia, had my things ready, had my tickets, but then I changed my mind, changed the airline, and arrived at Kennedy this morning instead. Then I made this connection. I didn't have time to shave. Sorry."

"Who cares? I can't believe it. No warning, nothing." She babbled. "Emily's here on spring break. Guess what! She got into Harvard Med. She'll be so glad to see you. She'll be bowled over. And Annie keeps wondering whether you'll ever come to see how well she's taking care of Barney. Oh," she repeated, "I can't believe it." And pulling away from the hug, she cried, "And look who's here! Eudora!"

"Eudora? What are you doing here in the Midwest?"

"She's my partner," Lynn answered before Eudora could get the words out. "She has an interest in this place."

Bruce looked around. "You never told me when you wrote that it was anything like this. I had no idea."

He saw the shelves, the enormous, gleaming stove and freezer, the trays of cookies, the people at the counter waiting to be served.

"Why, it's stupendous, Lynn. I expected you would be doing, oh, I don't know. I expected—"

"That I'd be making dinners single-handedly? Well, I started that way.

There were only Eudora and I the first few months, but business grew. It just grew."

In his excitement Bruce had pushed his glasses back into his hair, and she had to laugh.

"You never keep them on your eyes."

"What? These? Oh, I don't know why I do it. Tell me, can we have lunch? Can I drag you away from here?"

Lynn appealed to Eudora. "Can you manage without me? I don't want to run out on you, but—"

"No, no, it's fine. I only need to toss the salad and make some pea soup. You go." Eudora was enjoying the surprise. "Better take off your apron before you do, though."

"I'll use my car," Bruce said. "I rented one at the airport. I've already taken my stuff to the hotel. I got a suite. I had too much stuff to fit into one room. Let's go back there for lunch, I'm starved. I only had coffee this morning."

"You brought all your things out to St. Louis? I don't understand."

"It's a long story. Well, not so long. I'll tell you when we sit down."

He was all charged up; it was entirely unlike him to talk so fast.

"Well," he began when they were seated in the dining room, quiet and hushed by carpets and curtains. "Well, here I am. It feels like a century since I was last in this place. Remember our farewell party here before we all left for New York? You look different," he said quizzically. "I don't know exactly what it is, but I like it. You look taller."

She was suddenly self-conscious. "How can I possibly look taller?"

"It's something subtle, perhaps the way you stand, the way you walked in here just now. Something spirited and confident. Not that I didn't like the way you looked and walked before. You know that, Lynn."

She did not answer. Tom, too, had given many a compliment, and she no longer took much stock in compliments.

"You look peaceful," Bruce said, studying her face. "Yes, I see that too."

"Well, I've made peace with a lot of things. I think you'll be glad about one of them. A while back I went with some of the women to a tea at that house where Caroline fell into the pond. I made myself go to look at the pond, and for the first time I was able to remember what happened without blaming myself. I accepted, and felt free." She finished quietly, "That was your doing, Bruce, that afternoon in your house." She smiled. "Now tell me about yourself, what's been happening."

He began. "I took the position, as you know, because I wanted to get away. And I threw myself into the work. It was a godsend. We worked like beavers, all of us did, and I do think we've made great strides. The company was pleased. I even got a letter from Monacco, offering me the post in Moscow. Well, I almost took it. But then I decided to go home."

"What made you do that? You were on the way to bigger things, like wearing Monacco's shoes one day," she said, thinking of how Robert had coveted those shoes.

"That's the last thing I'd want, heading an international corporation, with all its politics. It's good that some people want it, just the way some people want to be President of the United States, but I don't want either. I told them I'd like to go back to my old place here in St. Louis, only this time I'd be the boss. That much authority, I'd like."

"Why not New York, at least?"

"I never liked New York. Again, it's a fine place for some people, for the millions who live there and love it and for the millions more who would like to be there. But millions more, including me, wouldn't," he ended firmly.

Curiosity drove Lynn further. "So why did you go there in the first place? You didn't have to."

This time he replied less firmly, almost sheepishly, "I guess I wanted to show I was as good as Robert. It was pride, but I think I wanted to prove that I could do whatever he could, and do it just as well. I knew he never liked me and had a low opinion of me."

Astonished, she pursued him. "But why should you have cared about Robert's opinion?"

"I told you. Pride. Human beings are foolish creatures. So now that I've proved what I can do, I don't care anymore."

This strange confession touched her heart in an unexpected way. She felt hurt on his behalf, hurt for him.

He looked down at his plate and then, raising his eyes, said somewhat shyly, "I had a letter from Tom Lawrence after he came here to see you a couple of months ago."

"Yes, he was here."

And still shyly, Bruce said, not asking a question but making a statement, "Then you and Tom have something serious going."

"I don't know what makes you think that. He didn't come to see me. He had business in the city and looked me up, that's all. He's a fine man, and he has his charm." She smiled. "But he's not for me, and I'm not for him either."

"Really?" The brown eyes widened and glowed. "I thought he had come on purpose to see you. Not that he said anything definite, but anyway, I'd been expecting something of the sort." Bruce stumbled. "I always thought you and he—"

She said stoutly, "For a while I had some fleeting thoughts, too, but it was very halfhearted, a sort of desperation, I guess, still thinking that a woman can't survive without a man. I've got over that. God knows it took me long enough."

"You can't mean that you're writing men off because of what you've been through?"

"I didn't say that."

They were sparring. If they had been fencing, they would have just tipped their weapons and retreated, tipped again and retreated. She became aware that her heartbeat was very fast.

"I'm glad it's not Tom," Bruce said suddenly.

"Are you?"

"Is it—is there anybody else?"

"No. There could be, there could've been more than one, but I didn't, I don't, want any of them."

She looked away at the tables where people were talking in low voices about the Lord knew what, the movie they had seen last night or maybe what they were going to do with their whole lives. And as she sat with her forlorn hands resting on the table, she wished that Bruce had not returned to live here where she would be bound to encounter him, bound to treat him like a cousin or a good old friend. Until this moment, in spite of her intermittent longings, she had not realized how deep those longings were; they had always been stifled. Here she sat and there, only inches away, were his warm lips and warm arms. They would have their lunch and smile and part until the next time, and that would be all.

She wanted to get up and run out. But people don't do things like that. They conceal and suffer politely.

"A few weeks ago I went over that batch of pictures you gave me," he said. "I spread them out so I could travel through the years. I had—I guess I had—an epiphany."

Startled by the word, Lynn raised her eyes, which met a long, grave gaze.

"I saw everything, saw you and saw myself quite clearly. I shocked myself with my sudden knowledge of what I had to do." Leaning over the table, he placed his hand on hers. "You've always been very dear to me, I don't know whether you felt it or not. But don't misunderstand; I don't need to tell you how I loved Josie. So how could I admit that there was still room for you? How could I?"

Her eyes filled with tears and she did not answer.

"Tell me, am I too late? Or perhaps too early? Tell me."

Very low, she replied, "Neither. Neither too early nor too late."

A smile spread from his mouth to his eyes; they radiated an amber light. The smile was contagious; Lynn began to laugh while her tears dropped.

"How I love you, Lynn! I must have loved you for years without knowing it."

"And I—I remember the day you left. I turned the corner and you were waving—"

"Don't. Don't cry. It's all right now." He shoved the coffee cup aside. "Let's go upstairs. It's time."

And to think that only this morning on the way to work she had been thinking of him, with such desire and so wistful a sense of "never again"!

"Love in the afternoon," she whispered. This time there was no sorrow, no search for comfort, no guilt, only the most honest, trusting, naked joy. Tightly together, they lay back on the pillows.

"I'm so contented." Bruce sighed. "Let's not go back to your house this minute. We need to talk."

"All right. What shall we talk about?"

"I'm just letting my mind wander. Maybe someday when we're tired of doing what we're doing we could open a country inn. What do you think?"

"Darling, all the options are open."

"We could furnish it with antiques. I got some old things in Europe, Biedermeier, it's being shipped. You'd be surprised how well it looks with other things, I never liked it before, but—"

Suddenly he laughed his loud, infectious laugh.

"What's funny?"

"I was thinking of the times I must have been gypped. Those old pieces that I so lovingly restored . . . A fellow told me of a place in Germany where they manufacture them and send them over here, all battered and marred with five coats of peeling paint. I used to spend hours removing it to get down to the original. Remember how Annie used to help me? Oh, Lord!" He shook with laughter. "Lynn, I'm so happy. I don't know what to do with myself."

"I'll tell you what. Let's get dressed after all and go back to the house. I want you to see everybody, and I want them to see you."

"Okay." He kept talking. "You know, I think another reason why I took that post in Budapest was that I had always envied Robert for having you without deserving you. I was pleased to see him punished when he saw me take his place. Very small minded, I know."

"Very human too."

And she pondered, while combing her hair before the mirror, "I wonder, do you believe Robert became what he did because of his father?" The name "Robert" sounded strange when spoken in her own voice. She had no occasion anymore to use it. "Of course he could easily have done just the opposite to prove himself different, couldn't he?"

"He could have, but he didn't, and that's all that matters."

Bruce came behind her, and the two faces looked back out of the mirror.

"Bruce and Lynn. It's funny how there's really never any one person for any of us. In my case, if it hadn't been Josie, it could have been you."

She thought, Tom Lawrence said something like that, not quite the same, but almost.

"But Josie and I are so different," she replied.

"That's what I mean. Tell me, if it hadn't been Robert, could it have been me?"

She answered truthfully, "I don't know what I would have done then. Someone else once asked me that question, and I answered that not even the Prince of Wales could have gotten me away from him. I was bewitched—then. I wasn't the person I am now."

"But if you had been the person you are now? Or is that an impossible, a foolish, question?"

"Foolish, yes. Because, can't you see, don't you know, that if I had had my present head on my shoulders—" She turned about and took his face between her hands. "Oh, my dear, oh, my very dear, you know it would have been yes. A thousand times yes."

In the living room Annie was practicing scales. Downstairs in the makeshift playroom that would have to be made over, Bobby and two four-year-old friends were playing some raucous game.

"I hope," Lynn said, "you think you can get used to a very noisy household."

"I lived in a very quiet one for a long, long time. I will get used to it with gratitude."

They were standing in the little sun parlor overlooking the yard. She had shown him around the house, he had been welcomed by the family, who, perhaps guessing what was afoot, had left them in this room by themselves.

"Look out there," Lynn said. "What do you see?"

"Don't tell me you moved the birdbath with you."

"At the last minute I couldn't leave it."

A mound of grainy, half-melted snow lay at the marble base, while the rest of the lawn was bare, ready for spring.

"I have it heated in the winter. Birds need water in the winter too."

"It's like you to think of that. Nine out of ten people wouldn't."

"Look, look at that lovely thing! It's the first robin, first of the season. Watch it drink. It must be tired and thirsty after its long flight from the south."

The bird fluttered into the water, shook itself, and flew away into the trees.

"I wonder what it thinks. That there's a whole bright summer ahead, maybe."

"I can't imagine, but I know what I'm thinking."

She looked up into the dear face. The glasses were pushed back again into the curly brown hair, and the eyes sparkled.

"I'm thinking of our own bright summer, and all the years ahead."